The Case Against 2 Per Cent Inflation

Brendan Brown

The Case Against 2 Per Cent Inflation

From Negative Interest Rates to a 21st Century
Gold Standard

Brendan Brown
Economic Research
MUFG
London, UK

ISBN 978-3-030-07749-5   ISBN 978-3-319-89357-0 (eBook)
https://doi.org/10.1007/978-3-319-89357-0

© The Editor(s) (if applicable) and The Author(s) 2018
Softcover re-print of the Hardcover 1st edition 2018
This work is subject to copyright. All rights are solely and exclusively licensed by the Publisher, whether the whole or part of the material is concerned, specifically the rights of translation, reprinting, reuse of illustrations, recitation, broadcasting, reproduction on microfilms or in any other physical way, and transmission or information storage and retrieval, electronic adaptation, computer software, or by similar or dissimilar methodology now known or hereafter developed.
The use of general descriptive names, registered names, trademarks, service marks, etc. in this publication does not imply, even in the absence of a specific statement, that such names are exempt from the relevant protective laws and regulations and therefore free for general use.
The publisher, the authors, and the editors are safe to assume that the advice and information in this book are believed to be true and accurate at the date of publication. Neither the publisher nor the authors or the editors give a warranty, express or implied, with respect to the material contained herein or for any errors or omissions that may have been made. The publisher remains neutral with regard to jurisdictional claims in published maps and institutional affiliations.

Cover credit: KTSDESIGN/SCIENCE PHOTO LIBRARY / Getty Images
Cover design by Ran Shauli

Printed on acid-free paper

This Palgrave Macmillan imprint is published by the registered company Springer International Publishing AG part of Springer Nature.
The registered company address is: Gewerbestrasse 11, 6330 Cham, Switzerland

To my late mother, Irene Brown

ACKNOWLEDGEMENTS

Attacking a monetary regime is a lonely affair. Much support, encouragement, inspiration, and yes exhortation are essential to pursuing the task. I have been fortunate in having all this from a founding "trio" without which this book would not have taken shape from start to finish.

Alex Pollock, Robert Pringle, and Robert Aliber, each played essential roles in the emergence of *The Case Against 2 Per Cent Inflation*.

Robert Aliber provided the key insight that monetary regimes which have come in succession following the breakdown of the gold standard and with periods of fiat currency chaos in between are like French Republics. And he exhorted me to analyze and illustrate the relationship between the "twins" of monetary inflation in any cycle—asset inflation and goods inflation.

Robert Pringle, a joint author with me of articles on high-powered money and the myths about Japan's "deflation", insisted that a successful monetary regime requires as a pre-condition a re-pivoting of the monetary base. For this to happen, high-powered money must be composed of a distinct asset for which a broad and fairly stable demand exists, as was indeed the case under the pre-1914 gold standard.

Alex Pollock has a unique vision into the chaos where irrational forces empowered by monetary inflation determine financial, economic, and political outcomes. He has no truck with or tolerance of the central bankers who run the unsound money regimes which bear down ultimately on human freedom. They claim fantastic expertise and understanding, whilst all the evidence points otherwise; but the political systems to which they are ultimately responsible do not rein them in. This and much else I have learnt from Alex, who has stimulated my thinking and provided indispensable encouragement.

I acknowledge the vital contribution to completing this project of the Hudson Institute and the Mises Institute—both of which made it possible for my ideas along the way to reach new and wide audiences whether as readers, discussants, or listeners. At a critical juncture, my editor at Palgrave, Tula Weiss, drove and navigated this project forward.

Contents

1	Next: The Fifth Stabilization Experiment Under Fiat Money	1
2	Origins of the Global 2% Inflation Standard	11
3	Diagnosis of Monetary Inflation in Asset Markets	27
4	Manipulation of Long-Term Interest Rates	43
5	A Failure of US Checks and Balances	55
6	Digitalization, Camouflage, and Monetary Inflation	75
7	Much Ruin in Japan's Journey to 2%	95
8	Germany Abdicates Hard Money Power	115
9	Unaffordable Housing and Poor-Quality Money	131
10	Negative Interest Rates and the War Against Cash	149
11	Experiments in Crash Postponement: 1927/29 Versus 2016/18	165

12 Wealth Creation and Destruction Under the 2% Regime   185

13 From the Fifth Monetary Chaos to Twenty-First-Century Gold   207

Index   227

CHAPTER 1

Next: The Fifth Stabilization Experiment Under Fiat Money

Since the fall of the full international gold standard in 1914, the fiat money "system" has wandered through four successive stages of disorder. In each of these, we can identify the eventual emergence of a "stabilization experiment". The first three all ended in dismal failures, sometimes catastrophic. Either the experiment was deeply flawed or halted prematurely or both. The present—the fourth—is headed in the same direction, driven by essential flaws in concept and implementation. We call this last the "global 2% inflation standard". It could not have been introduced at a worst time. The main uncertainty is whether it will come to an end in an asset price deflation shock, or a goods inflation shock, or both. Then there will be the fifth stage of disorder. Question: could the fifth stabilization experiment, if and when it emerges, be more successful than the previous four? That is running ahead of our story. Let's go back to the beginning.

First Stage of Fiat System Disorder: 1914–31

Under the gold standard, currencies were fully convertible into gold or gold coin on demand. The base of the gold money system was essentially above-ground gold supplies. That system came to an end with the outbreak of World War I.

In the aftermath of that war, starting in the early to mid-1920s, there was the construction of a so-called gold exchange standard. Governments and their central bankers sought to restore stability after many years of violent fluctuations in internal and external values of the major currencies. The US dollar remained fully convertible into gold coin; amongst other main monies; some "returned" to a "gold bullion standard" (meaning that currency was convertible only for large amounts with the minimum being the 400 oz. bar, e.g. in the case of the UK); some adopted a "dollar standard" (in effect a fixed exchange rate of the national currency to the dollar but underpinned crucially in the case of Germany by a treaty commitment as drafted according to the Dawes Plan of 1924). The countries outside the US in general (sometimes with a French exception) accumulated reserves in dollars (and to a lesser extent sterling) rather than metallic gold, and this was in accordance with the recommendations of the League of Nations (in particular as set by the Genoa Conference 1922). There a "deflation-phobic" committee of experts from the British establishment (including UK Treasury officials and Professor Ralph Hawtrey (a close friend of John Maynard Keynes)) who were adamant about the importance of "stable prices" determined the agenda (see Rothbard 2005).

The Federal Reserve had large scope to determine the path for the US monetary base; it eschewed automatic rules and effected large and volatile shifts in pursuing its discretionary policy objectives including sometimes economic stimulus (efforts to stimulate the recovery from steep recession as in late 1921 and 1922) or other times international currency diplomacy as conducted by New York Fed Chief Benjamin Strong with a particular focus on supporting sterling—unnecessary if Great Britain had allowed monetary conditions to tighten under the influence of gold loss. The giant asset and credit market inflation which emerged in the US and Germany (then the second largest economy in the world at the time) revealed that Federal Reserve policy focused on whatever passing objective (e.g. cyclical fine-tuning, Strong helping out Norman) had been gravely inconsistent with sound money.

The question has to be asked: how could the Federal Reserve (founded in 1913) possibly judge the demand for high-powered money (monetary base) under the new banking regime in the US? In particular, there was considerable optimism amongst bankers and their clients that the creation of a lender of last resort (the Federal Reserve) mandated to provide emergency liquidity would mean that the repeated bank crises of previous decades were now impossible. Hence there should be less demand for cash as safety margin than pre-1914; and the shrunken proportion of gold in the monetary base—matched by an increased proportion of Federal Reserve notes and deposits at that institution—would surely mean a diminished overall demand for monetary base, everything else remaining the same.

The long-term interest rate market, transformed and considerably deepened by war financing, now took cues from the rate setting operations of the Federal Reserve. Previously money rates had been highly volatile and largely ignored there. The fact that short-term rates remained so low despite economic boom through the roaring 1920s as the Federal Reserve followed the aim of stable prices (thereby resisting the fall of prices that would have been in line with the era's rapid technological change) had a magnified and distortionary influence (downwards) on the long-term rates market (see Brown 2016).

This first stage of fiat monetary disorder including eventually its stabilization experiment—the gold exchange standard—came to an end with the bust of the global credit bubble (mainly US and German) as delineated by the declared bankruptcy of Germany in July 1931.

SECOND STAGE, 1931–68

The **second stage** of fiat money disorder followed. It featured at first the huge exchange rate fluctuations of 1931–36. As early as the tripartite agreement of 1936, there was a short-lived attempt to restore stability internationally based on a truncated gold-dollar pivot. Later the Bretton Woods Agreements set the scene for a full global experiment in stabilization. This did not get under way in fact until the end of the 1950s (given widespread persistence of exchange restrictions in Europe especially until then). The US dollar was no longer on an internal gold standard (in fact US citizens had been outlawed from holding gold since 1934). The dollar was effectively convertible into gold for non-US residents though the universe able to take advantage of that was highly restricted.

The Fed had virtually total discretion in the setting of the path for monetary base subject only to there being no run on the "gold window". By the mid-1960s, the Kennedy/Johnson Administration had installed Keynesian economists in positions of power who pursued their mythical trade-off between higher employment and inflation. Fed Chief Martin was no Keynesian but in the FOMC their influence was increasing. Martin saw the central bank's mission as managing the public debt market which in the context of the Vietnam War had inflationary consequences (see Meltzer 2009a). The end of the stabilization experiment (Bretton Woods) came in a series of developments—the floating of the gold price for non-official purposes in 1968, the transitory floating of the Deutsche mark (DM) and then its revaluation of 1969, the re-floating of the DM and the Swiss franc in May 1971, and finally the slamming shut of the gold window by the Nixon Administration in summer 1971 (see Brown 1988). In effect, ultimately the Bretton Woods architecture proved unable to prevent the US from lurching into a high inflation inconsistent with the system's continued existence.

THIRD STAGE: 1969–85

Then there was the **third** stage—the one featuring eventually the monetarist experiment. The collapse of the Bretton Woods system had brought about a generalized floating of exchange rates between the major currencies (interspersed with attempts to fix intra-European exchange rates). With any gold link to the dollar now absent, Germany and Switzerland took the lead in developing an ersatz gold monetary standard. The guiding principle: the respective central banks should expand the monetary base at a low near-constant rate, superficially resembling in concept the low rate of increase in above-ground gold supplies in the pre-1914 gold world. This was the central experiment now in monetary stabilization, and its designers rejected discretionary policy-making otherwise described as fine-tuning. Monetarism could gain credibility as an ersatz gold standard only if it became global with all the major economies including most of all the US joining the experiment. That occurred briefly in the late 1970s and early 1980s (President Carter appointed Paul Volcker to the head of the Fed in autumn 1978).

Even at that high point of the experiment, any resemblance between ersatz gold and the real gold standard was superficial. There was no built-in suppleness (e.g. under gold, a fall in prices of goods and services would lead to some increase in gold supplies as profits in the mining industry rose). There were no automatic mechanisms and unshakable beliefs in the standard—instead this featured money supply targets which could be overruled, adjusted, or ignored, and political pressures could sweep monetarism aside. Moreover there was no large and stable demand for the fiat money base in these countries (where monetarism reigned)—except in so far as high reserve requirements provided artificial backing. Such requirements, however, were intrinsically fragile (not least because they remained subject to special pleading and arbitrage operations by the banking industry).

The end of the monetarist experiment did not come because of revealed fundamental flaws, such as volatility in demand for or inflexibility in supply of monetary base, emerging in a menacing way though this might well have occurred if it had endured. Rather already in 1985, then Fed Chief Paul Volcker yielded to huge political pressure to tackle the large US trade deficit (and more specifically the emergence of a "rust belt") which was widely blamed on a super-strong dollar.

In any case, the degree of overshoot (upwards) in the dollar at that time was dubious. After all, the fact that the Federal Reserve appeared to have abandoned its inflationary policies of the previous decades could surely unleash global demand on a permanent basis for the dollar as the obvious preferred international money; a cheap dollar would not reincarnate traditional manufacturing in an age of rapid globalization. Be that as it may, Volcker (who as under-secretary of the Treasury had been in charge of negotiating the dollar devaluations of 1972–73) harnessed the Federal Reserve to the Reagan Administration's efforts (as led by then Treasury Secretary James Baker) to devalue the dollar and specifically joined in the Plaza Accord (see Brown 2013).

The Volcker Fed's abandonment of "hard money" policies and the monetarist experiment led directly to the global monetary inflation of the late 1980s featuring virulent asset inflation, most spectacularly the bubble and bust in Japan. Germany was the last to abandon monetarism formally with the launch of the euro (see Brown 2014; Schwartz 2005).

FOURTH STAGE: MID-1980S TO PRESENT DAY (2018–?)

Out of the monetarist retreat (widely regarded as defeat and failure) was born the **fourth stage** of fiat money disorder. Within a few years there was the start of a new stabilization experiment—the targeting of perpetual inflation at 2% p.a. A key milestone was the FOMC meeting of July 1996 which considered the issue of whether with inflation now down to below 3% the Fed should go easy on its drive to ever-lower inflation and accept a continuing stable low inflation around 2%. Janet Yellen presented the paper in favour. There followed no firm resolution. Nevertheless then Chief Greenspan agreed to a pause. A stronger commitment to a target of perpetual "low inflation" emerged in subsequent years, both under the late Greenspan years and more especially under Chief Bernanke.

The intellectual rationale for inflation targeting was rooted in neo-Keynesianism. A leading pioneer in the late 1970s was Stanley Fischer whose student-disciples included Ben Bernanke and Mario Draghi amongst others (see Fischer 1979). He argued that the tenets of monetarism—targeting of money supply growth at a low level and the abandonment of fine-tuning the economy—were mistaken. Demand for money—and particularly monetary base—was just too unstable now for an ersatz gold system to work well. And in any case, the monetarists' foreswearing of fine-tuning (a rejection which was consistent with the teaching of the contemporary classical economists such as Robert Barro (1976) who claimed that monetary policy could not stimulate the real economy if prevailing expectations were rational) was based on fiction. In the practical world where long-term wage contracting was common, monetary policy could stimulate the real economy. But to prevent such repeated stimulation bringing about ever-higher inflation, a target should be set for this (inflation).

The new experiment—inflation targeting—was grounded on serious misconceptions and it could not have come at a worse time. Even under the gold standard or under monetarism, there existed no firm basis for any reliable prediction linking the path of money to near or medium-term price outcomes. In so far as monetary base was indeed a highly distinct asset for which a broad and stable demand existed, there could be reasonable confidence that a monetary control regime limiting strictly the growth of this aggregate would bound the extent of cumulative price fluctuations in both directions (a topic we will revisit in future chapters of this book). Yes, in the long run under a gold standard, there was a tendency for prices to revert to the mean. Even so, such an outcome was not guaranteed. Moreover, in the short and medium term, there was every reason to think that sound money would go along with fluctuating prices both upwards and downwards (down during recession or periods of rapid globalization or productivity growth). And so it was with monetarism.

Milton Friedman had emphasized that the monetary authority should not set a price target because in fact prices were not strictly under its control. Rather, the commitment should be to a low rate of monetary base expansion (or perhaps of alternative money aggregate). As the monetary base is indeed fully controllable under a fiat money regime, the monetary authority could rightfully be blamed for any slippage from target (Friedman 1953). Yet here were the advocates of a 2% inflation standard saying that the central bank should be accountable for the inflation outcome over say two-year periods and that this was indeed under its control. They seemed to have in mind econometric models which could be well tested and applied to forecasting accurately the path of inflation and in which the key variable of short-term interest rates was fixed by the central bank. We could describe this as an "econometric standard".

Of course, inertia in expectation formation and constant propaganda (including regular press conferences by the central bank chief and extensive written briefings or statements) might help the central bank meet its target for some time. But it would be a latest version of the emperor's new clothes fable to assume that the monetary bureaucrats had indeed found new sources of power to determine price outcomes. Yes, the advocates (of 2% inflation standard could tout the competence of their increasing complex econometric tools based around the Phillips curve and the Taylor rule, but this was unconvincing at best. The theoretical rationale behind the econometrics was missing.

In fact, just when the 2% inflation standard emerged (two years on from the FOMC meeting above the European Central Bank (ECB) opened its doors and in effect adopted a 2% inflation target), the world was entering a period of rapid globalization and technological change (entry of China into the WTO, Eastern Europe integrating with the West, the internet and telecommunications revolution) for which the closest parallel might well be the 1870s and 1880s (intercontinental telegraphy, Suez Canal, Bessemer steel, railroads, and ocean liners). Back then the US and Europe were on the gold standard, prices fell persistently by 1–2% per annum, and the US recorded the fastest ever growth of income per capital—and the mid-term financial crisis and economic downturn in the early to mid-1880s were only mild. By contrast the attempt of the major central banks now to target 2% inflation at such a time produced very inferior results.

Trying to push up prices when the natural rhythm was downwards meant that the central banks drove rates to levels far below those consistent with sound money. Taken in the context of rapid globalization and technological change so conducive to speculative narratives, these low levels fuelled irrational forces in financial markets—the essence of asset price inflation (see Brown 2017)—as previously in the Mexican bubble and bust (1992–94), then the Asian and wider emerging market episode (1993–97), then the telecommunications and Nasdaq bubble and crash of the late 1990s, and then the giant global bubble of 2003–07 (including US housing, European weak sovereign debt, yen carry trade, Spanish and UK real estate, European financial institutions, and much else) culminating in the Panic and Great Recession of 2007–08/09. These bubbles and busts seriously handicapped the train of economic prosperity. And the subsequent adoption of non-conventional monetary policies aimed at pumping up asset prices impaired further the shrunken appetite for long-gestation investment. People asked: why deploy capital in that way when everyone and their dog realized there was a serious long-run danger of another asset market crash and great recession when the chickens came home to roost? Under the 2% inflation standard, the slowest economic expansion ever following Great Recession took place.

The over-riding likelihood is now that the fiat money experiment which we call "the global 2% inflation standard" characterizing this fourth stage of fiat money disorder will go the same way as the previous three experiments above—into the dustbin of monetary history. The end will come with an asset price deflation crisis, a goods and services inflation shock, or some combination of the two (staged over time). It will not be pretty.

How Would an Asset Price Deflation Crisis Emerge?

There are many possible routes to that destination, but most probably it will come through a stalling of momentum in highly speculative markets.

Vulnerable to a stalling of momentum: the numerous booming carry trades—whether from low interest rate into higher rate currencies (collecting the exchange risk premium and hoped for continuing exchange rate gains) or from low-risk credits into high-risk credits (earning the credit risk premium and perhaps continuing capital gain from rising price of high-risk credits), from short-maturity government bonds into long maturity (earning the term risk premium and perhaps capital gains) and from liquid into illiquid asset (collecting the risk premium and also hoped for further price gains on illiquid assets). If capital gains persistently stall, then the more impatient speculators will try to bail out—but who will be on the other side of the transaction? The looming menace of illiquidity becomes real. The collapse of asset prices in the newly illiquid conditions would feed back to the real economy whose descent would reinforce these negative trends.

More specifically a sudden large default or persistent string of bad news stories about long-popular speculative destinations (including Big Tech) could be the trigger. And we certainly should not ignore the potential role of bubble and bust in real estate markets—whether US commercial real estate (including apartments to rent), Canadian and Australian bubble housing markets, or the China residential real estate (where prices in the big cities prices are now even higher relative to fundamentals than at the peak of the Japan bubble in 1990).

How Could a Goods and Services Inflation Shock Erupt?

Quite simply recorded inflation suddenly spikes. Inflation expectation inertia fades. Given ever-less grounds for confidence in econometric-based predictions of inflation, why would this not happen?

Other factors: huge budget deficits (perhaps 5% of GDP in the US at an advanced stage of the business cycle expansion), the Federal Reserve harnessed (by appointments) to a 3% economic growth target under a chair chosen in particular for his good relationship with the Treasury secretary, a long-term interest rate market at least partially dysfunctional in no longer signalling inflation fears but dominated by speculation on near-term short-term rate setting by the central bank, the authorities painfully reluctant to normalize monetary policy for fear of disturbing asset markets, and an Administration favouring a competitive dollar, all these make fertile soil for a new episode of high inflation. But that could be long delayed if the asset price deflation shock came first.

Vigilantes who were famous in the long-term interest rate markets several decades ago have no modern counterpart. Who in their right mind, even a Don Quixote, would stand in the possible track of an express train if the asset price deflation shock is to come before the inflation shock?

The Looming Fifth Stage of Monetary Disorder

Whatever way the 2% inflation standard ends, it will most likely be unannounced. There is no new monetary experiment ready and backed by a crowd of revolutionaries to take over and accompany fiat monies into a fifth stage of disorder.

It is possible to imagine an eventual return of the monetarist experiment in much improved form—featuring measures to substantially boost (and stabilize) the demand for high-powered money. These would include the curtailment of deposit insurance and of too big to fail banks. There would be an attack on credit card oligopoly power alongside steps to raise the qualities of cash (including the provision of larger denomination notes). And any re-run of a monetarist experiment would certainly require the scrapping of interest payments on bank reserves at the central bank.

It is also possible to imagine that the next phase of fiat money evolution will be the return of gold to a monetary role—a scenario which reappears in the final chapter of this book. (Another possibility is a totally new monetary commodity; see Pringle (2012).)

Neither form of evolution can occur without sound money forces gathering power within first and foremost US democracy—a far cry from the present situation but one which could start to change in the aftermath of the looming asset deflation or inflation shock.

BIBLIOGRAPHY

Barro, R. (1976). Rational Expectations and the Role of Monetary Policy. *Journal of Monetary Economics, Elsevier,* 2(1), 1–32.

Brown, B. (1988/2017). *The Flight of International Capital* (Routledge Library Editions, 2017). London: Routledge.

Brown, B. (2013). *The Global Curse of the Federal Reserve*. Basingstoke: Palgrave.

Brown, B. (2014). *Euro Crash*. Basingstoke: Palgrave.

Brown, B. (2016). *A Global Monetary Plague*. Palgrave.

Brown, B. (2017). A Modern Concept of Asset Price Inflation in Boom and Depression. *Quarterly Journal of Austrian Economics,* 20(1).

Fischer, S. (1979). *On Activist Monetary Policy with Rational Expectations*. Cambridge, MA: NBER.

Friedman, M. (1953). *Essays in Positive Economics*. Chicago: University of Chicago Press.

Meltzer, A. (2009). *A History of the Federal Reserve, Vol. 2 Book 1 1951–1969*. Chicago: University of Chicago Press.

Pringle, R. (2012). *The Money Trap*. Basingstoke: Palgrave.

Rothbard, M. (2005). *A History of Money and Banking in the US*. Auburn: Mises Institute.

Schwartz, A. (2005, March/April). *Aftermath of the Monetary Clash with the Federal Reserve Before and During the Volcker Era*. Federal Reserve Bank of St. Louis.

CHAPTER 2

Origins of the Global 2% Inflation Standard

All the episodes of experiment with fiat money stabilization—the gold exchange standard of the 1920s, the Bretton Woods system, monetarism, and now the 2% inflation standard—come about in a process determined by a mixture of intellectual fashion, intellectual intrigue, political opportunism, self-interest of financial elites (especially the big banks), the interplay of idealism and realism in the political arena (including central bank institutions), and last but not least chance and circumstance.

INFLATION SHOCK OF THE LATE 1980S

Just where and when did the 2% inflation standard start?

The "point of creation" is clear and evident in retrospect: the inflation shock of the late 1980s. Inflation in the US was back to 6% by 1990, a significant reversal after the disinflationary monetary medicine administered by the Volcker Fed in the early 1980s. But that Fed had wandered off its pathway to sound money. In 1985 it succumbed crucially to pressure from the Reagan Administration (as directed by the new Treasury secretary from Texas James Baker) to change course and devalue, given the large trade deficit which had emerged alongside an apparently super-strong greenback.

Ultimately leopards do not change their spots, and Volcker could not shed his Nixon role as devaluationist-in-chief (under then Treasury Secretary John Connolly, a Texan Democrat) and his ultimate fundamental lack of faith in free-market solutions. He could have viewed the super-strong dollar as an inevitable phenomenon given the end of the Arthur Burns inflationary policies and the return of the US currency to the pinnacle of the global financial system as the hardest most desirable currency. Yet he did not make that intellectual leap.

And so Volcker was a co-signatory of the Plaza Accord (summer 1985), and the last remnants of the monetarist experiment (already faded almost beyond recognition) were jettisoned. Asset price inflation led goods and services inflation. In early 1987 Volcker seemed to be having second thoughts, helping to negotiate (with Germany and Japan) the Louvre Accord designed to stabilize the dollar (meaning no further fall) and appearing to signal monetary tightening ahead. The 30-year bond yield jumped by two percentage points between March and October 1987.

The possibility of Volcker returning to a harder monetary policy did not amuse the devaluationists and inflationists now the key power players in the White House (including crucially James Baker). Hence when it came to the end of Volcker's term in summer 1987, the Reagan Administration appointed Alan Greenspan in his place. Yes the new chief's credentials included being an Ayn Rand disciple and the author of an article praising the gold standard. One thing was for sure—he was no fan of monetarism and he claimed no knowledge of Austrian School economics! And it emerged that he resented the Louvre Accord when early in his term the dollar resumed its devaluation course without the Fed seeking to halt it immediately by taking monetary action.

The inflation shock of the late 1980s (CPI year on year peaked in May 1989 at 5.4%) though did bring a discretionary response by the Greenspan Fed in the form of big rises in money market interest rates (after having cut these earlier on in responses to the October 1987 stock market crash). Foreshadowing the inflation-targeting era, Greenspan in the course of congressional testimony (February 1989) defined the "desirable rate of inflation as one in which the expected rate of change of the general level of prices ceases to be a factor in individual and business decision-making". That nebulous formulation could have fitted experience under the pre-1914 gold standard where there had been stretches of both falling and rising prices, yet Greenspan had no intention of returning to such an environment despite his early paper in favour of gold (see Greenspan 1966) and all subsequent evidence signalling his approval for low positive inflation.

Summing up the situation at the start of the 1990s: together with other central banks, the Fed had eventually tightened monetary policy sharply in response to an inflation shock and also in some cases (particularly Japan) responding to concerns about "excess speculation" in asset markets, especially real estate. The result was a global business cycle downturn, not closely synchronized due to the German economic boom unleashed by unification. Monetarism had largely been abandoned (the Bundesbank continued to set targets, now for broad money rather than monetary base as in the heyday of the hard Deutsche mark). And there came to be a growing practice of setting inflation targets—evidently driven by the priority of bringing inflation back down from the surprise re-bound of the late 1980s and by the hope of keeping inflation down thereafter.

New Zealand Leads the Way

A tiny country on the southern edge of the earth, New Zealand, led the way into formal inflation targeting, followed soon by Canada and the UK. Additionally New Zealand had a connection to a central part of the neo-Keynesian doctrine that featured backstage to inflation targeting—the so-called Phillips curve (an empirical relationship between inflation and unemployment which had its origin in the work of a once New Zealand war hero, later a professor at the London School of Economics). The inflation targets as determined by these countries were very much improvised and set by governments seeking to keep their central banks on course to lowering inflation rather than growing out of a considered economic blueprint for a new experiment in fiat money stabilization. Work on that had been going on for many years within the economics profession as we shall see—but the implementation of an inflation-targeting regime in a large economy was still some time away.

Specifically, in the New Zealand launch (see Wheeler 2014), the impetus came from a finance minister keen to make the central bank accountable in a transparent way for its actions—with the action plan to bring inflation down from a then high level (around 5%). In 1989 the Reserve Bank of New Zealand Act came into force. The Act established the operational independence of the Reserve Bank in respect of monetary policy and specified price stability as the single monetary policy objective. Simultaneously the Minister of finance and the governor signed the first Policy Targets Agreement which specified an annual inflation target of 0–2%. (3–5% target for 1990, with a gradual reduction into the 0–2% range by 1992 (changed to 1993).

Canada followed New Zealand (see Mishkin 2000). In February 1991 a joint announcement by the minister of finance and the governor of the Bank of Canada established formal inflation targets. The target ranges were 2–4% by the end of 1992 and 1.5–3.5% by December 1995. Subsequently the range was lowered to 1–3%. The Bank of Canada is not directly accountable to the government via formal sanctions if it misses its targets as in New Zealand but rather like the Reserve Bank of Australia is accountable to the public in general.

The UK was the next country to adopt formal inflation targeting, following that country's exit from ERM in October 1992. The government set the target (initially 1–4%) and invited the governor of the Bank of England to begin producing an Inflation Report on a regular quarterly basis which would report on the progress being made in achieving the target. At the time of adoption, inflation was at 4%. The British inflation-targeting regime was similar in flexibility to the Canadian framework (and Australian which started around this same time).

Before proceeding to examine how inflation targeting spread to Europe and the US, let's tread backwards to examine the wider forces—intellectual and political—influential in advancing the new standard.

Stanley Fischer and the Neo-Keynesian Reach for Power

A key starting point was the 1977 paper by Stanley Fischer "On Activist Monetary Policy with Rational Expectations" (see Fischer 1977). The paper purports to demonstrate that "systematic countercyclical monetary policy can affect the behaviour of output and that activist monetary policy should be used for that purpose". That statement throws down the gauntlet at the prevailing monetarist wisdom of the time that fine-tuning policy is worse than useless and that monetary policy should stick to settle a stable long-run environment. That view had earned reinforcement from the economists of the "rational expectations school" such as Barro (1976) who sought to demonstrate that if no one were fooled (or taken by surprise) then fine-tuning in any case was impossible. Only unanticipated changes in the money stock could affect output.

Stanley Fischer takes issue with the rational expectations theorists who argue that anticipated changes in monetary policy cannot have real effect. First, he makes a point with which indeed many advocates of "sound money" (including the Austrian School) would agree. Money is not neutral. It enters the economy in a way that influences real economic variables. Indeed some monetarists would concur with this—and would see themselves as echoing J.S. Mill's famous line quoted and re-quoted by Friedman (see Friedman 2006): "most of the time the machinery of money does not matter, but when it gets out of control it becomes the monkey wrench in all the other machinery of the economy". These economists (monetarists and Austrian School) would say, yes, money can affect real variables, but we know so little about the interactions, and there is so much scope for bad outcomes that it is best to play safe and not engage in discretionary monetary policy-making.

Stanley Fischer disputes that version. More broadly he rejects the view that activist monetary policy works mainly through deception. In particular, the widespread use of long-term wage contracts which are not highly flexible (to take account of unanticipated monetary or other changes) means that the central bank and private sectors have much to gain in responding cooperatively to economic disturbance. Activist monetary policy can improve outcomes taking account of such frictions (see Fischer 1977). In particular, economic agents contract in nominal terms for periods longer than the time it takes the monetary authority to react to changing economic circumstances—in this chapter the relevant contracts are labour contracts. That is the kernel of neo-Keynesianism, of which Stanley Fischer was a leading pioneer.

How would these modern advocates of activist monetary policy prevent a steady upward spiralling through time of inflation—a danger apparent from any reading of the 1960s and the origins of the "Greatest Peacetime Inflation"? Fischer recognized the inflationary bias resulting from his assumed short-run trade-off between inflation and output. A government that would prefer output to be above the natural rate is tempted to exploit the trade-off by running an expansionary monetary policy. He rejects the view that such behaviour can be constrained by money supply rule (see Fischer 1977):

> At a general level, we can agree that if the government is to control the money supply, it should provide a stable monetary background against which the economy can proceed with its real business of producing and consuming goods. If there were no disturbances to money demand a stable monetary background would be a stable money supply. A constant growth rate rule would serve well.

But there are of course, disturbances to money demand. In the long run these take the form of changes in the assets that constitute money. And short-run disturbances to money demand arise both from goods market disturbances that affect the level of income and the interest rate and from random shifts in money demand.

Stanley Fischer possessed no immediate remedy on offer for this problem—other than passive policy with intermittent discretion which required continued explanation to Congress. By the mid-1990s though, Stanley Fischer is on record supporting inflation targets as the solution (see Fischer 1996); these would constrain central banks rightfully using intermittently and forcefully sometimes their discretionary power to influence the real economy. According to Fischer, there are three reasons for not aiming for long-run price level stability (as against permanent inflation at low level):

> The question then is how low to aim, and particularly why not to aim for the best, zero inflation – or even better price stability or perhaps better yet, deflation? Several factors argue for a target measured inflation rate above zero.
> The **first** is the revenue motive (trivial).
> The **second** is the long-run Phillips curve is not vertical at low inflation rates. The experiment of pushing to very low rates hardly seems worth trying.
> **Third**, and most important, is the difficulty for monetary policy at the lower bound of zero on the nominal interest rate (Summers 1991). – The argument here is that inflation greases the wheels of monetary policy.
> The **fourth** reason is that the true rate of inflation is below the measured rate. If the bias is understood in the capital markets then the need to keep open the possibility of negative real interest rates would argue for a higher target measured rate of inflation.

Of course by the 1990s Stanley Fischer was far from alone in advocating the inflation-targeting doctrine and advancing a rationale as described. But he was a professor with significant political clout. He, his disciples, and fellow thinkers in key academic positions were close and influential in power centres that determine these things. Larry Summers (an early supporter of inflation targeting) had been recruited as deputy Treasury secretary under Robert Rubin in the Clinton Administration. Summers chose Fischer as the US nominated deputy chief at the IMF. There he had been in charge of the Asian debt and Russian debt bailout negotiations in 1997–98, critical for global (including the US) bank creditors amongst others, and subsequently he accepted Rubin's invitation (Rubin had joined the Board of Citibank, replaced as Treasury secretary by Summers) to join Citibank's top management.

Why did Bill Clinton appoint so many neo-Keynesians to position of power within his Administration, whether in the Treasury, in the Council of Economic Advisers, or at the Federal Reserve? Most plausibly their activist philosophy appealed to a president who had run on the "it's the economy stupid".

Fischer's students and disciples included amongst others Ben Bernanke and Mario Draghi. The neo-Keynesians and their inflation-targeting doctrine had an evil genius for entering the corridors of power—not dissimilar to that of Maynard Keynes in the earlier two monetary experiments (gold exchange standard and Bretton Woods). And they were on both sides of the aisle. The Bush Administration could call on the same school and did so, including John Taylor, Ben Bernanke, Glen Hubbard, and Greg Mankiw. George W. Bush had evidently no inclination to walk back from activism in economic policy and especially monetary policy, and so neo-Keynesianism appealed to him for similar reasons as for Bill Clinton. Fortunately for him (though not for economic prosperity), practitioners came in Republican clothing as well as Democrat (or as the cynic would say: "the chosen economists were willing to dress the part as required").

The Glacial "Ascent" of the US to Joining the 2% Inflation Standard

We have seen that already by the end of the 1980s, Alan Greenspan was leaning towards stabilizing inflation at a low level—where sufficiently low was defined by it not affecting decision-making. But he had no inclination to adopt a formal 2% inflation target—seeing this as potentially irritating relations with Congress (where he feared that some members might question why inflation rather than price stability) and also tying down the Fed too tightly to the disadvantage of economic performance. Credibility could also be on the line given the lack of precision and stability of any empirical relationship between money aggregates and interest rates under the control of the Fed and inflation outcomes.

By 1993 Greenspan took the significant step of telling Congress (in testimony) that the Fed would no longer use any monetary targets, including M2, as a guide for the conduct of monetary policy. In July 1996 he set aside one full day of the FOMC meeting to discuss the question of whether, now that inflation had come down below 3%, the journey of disinflation should be continued all the way to price stability or halted at some point soon.

He introduced the session like this:

> The next item on our agenda – the issue of long-term inflation goals – is something that we have been discussing on and off for a long while, and I think we will continue to do so. It is important that we move forward on this issue and more specifically that we agree on what the goals mean before we can find some consensus within the Committee regarding their implementation. – We have two discussants requesting to be recognized, and we will go first to Dr Yellen and then to Dr Broaddus.

Janet Yellen gave the standard well-rehearsed case for halting disinflation at 2% p.a.:

> I think we should move to lower inflation but gingerly, because we really do not know how large the permanents costs might be in the form of higher unemployment. (She quotes the contemporary example of Canada which she believed had sought to bring inflation down too quickly and suffered poor real economic performance relative to the US in consequence).
>
> The only identifiable benefit of low inflation which could be big enough to create the needed payoff (for risks of getting there) is connected with the tax system and its interaction with inflation. But these issues are best fixed by legislation (promoting more indexation of taxation) rather than monetary policy.
>
> There are likely to be significant, permanent costs of very low inflation. First, a little inflation permits real interest rates to become negative on the rare occasions when required to counter recession. Second, and to my mind the most important argument for some low inflation rate, is the *greasing-the-wheels argument* on the grounds that a little inflation lowers unemployment by facilitating adjustments in relative pay in a world where individuals deeply dislike nominal pay cuts.
>
> As I total things up, it appears to me that a reduction of inflation from 3 per cent, which I take as roughly our current level, to 2 per cent, very likely, but not surely, yields net benefits. To my mind, to go below 2 per cent measured inflation as currently calculated requires highly optimist assumptions about tax benefits and the sacrifice ratio.

After some discussion, in which Governor Larry Lindsey was Yellen's strongest opponent on his concerns about the distortionary effect of inflation on the tax system, Greenspan summed up how to proceed:

Now that inflation is low the question is basically whether we are willing to move on to price stability. The question really is whether we as an institution can make the unilateral decision to do that. I think that this is a very fundamental question for this society. We can go up to the Hill and testify in favour of it; we can make speeches and proselytize as much as we want, but we as unelected officials do not have the right to make that decision.

In further comments, Greenspan seemed to express some preference for ultimately getting inflation down to zero on the basis that this would boost productivity performance. Businesses when they found that they could not boost prices would seek to improve productivity rather than cut wages. All a little hazy, but in line with Greenspan's view that this possible battle ahead (to get inflation down to 1% p.a. from 2% p.a.) was not for now.

Greenspan and Bernanke Complete the Journey to 2% Inflation Standard

The next important date in the passage of the US to a 2% inflation standard was 2002, when President Bush appointed Ben Bernanke, a leading economist-advocate of inflation targeting (and at 2%), to the Federal Reserve Board (see Bernanke and Mishkin 1997). Greenspan's authority was waning. The boom and eventually bubble over which he had presided in the second half of the 1990s had turned to bust. The new president was somewhat ill-disposed to Chief Greenspan given his reputation with the older Bush and James Baker for having lost the 1990 election due to excessive tightening in 1989/90. The Republican base was also uneasy about Greenspan's long cosying up to the Clinton Administration.

George W. Bush was determined to promote a strong recovery from the 2001/02 downturn by every means—fiscal and monetary—and Greenspan fell in with that. Bernanke gave his notorious speeches about helicopter money and the need to fight a looming deflation threat (which his one-time chess partner Professor Rogoff was also warning about in his present position as IMF chief economist). With inflation in 2003 on some measures down to near 1%, Greenspan presided over a novel policy to "breathe inflation back into the US economy" albeit rejecting proposals from Bernanke that the Fed embark on a programme of fixing long-term interest rates. At the same time (spring 2003), the ECB moved to target more precisely inflation at 2%, stressing that below-target results were just as much a miss as above target (more on the European and Japanese adoption of 2% inflation targets in subsequent chapters).

When Bernanke took over from Greenspan as chair in 2006, he wasted no time to complete the journey of the US on to a formal 2% inflation standard—albeit that most of this journey was against the background first of the Great Panic and Great Recession. The formal adoption of the standard occurred only in January 2012 when the Fed, in its first-ever "longer-run goals and policy strategy" statement, said an inflation rate of 2% "best aligned with its congressionally mandated goals of price stability and full employment". The trappings of transparency—important in the inflation-targeting advocacy literature—were added along the journey, meaning increasingly verbose minutes, press conferences (inaugurated April 2011), and other regular progress reports. Transparency is important for the purpose of creating inertia of expectations around 2% inflation and also for manipulating interest rates—all in the context of continuous appliance of anaesthetics to the economy and markets against abrupt monetary policy change; wherever possible, these changes in the interest rate path would be highlighted for the future rather than any immediate change in rate plans (see Chap. 4). The non-conventional tool box in defence of the 2% inflation target (from below) was unveiled and deployed.

The January 2012 statement formally adopting the 2% standard set out the basis for this:

> The inflation rate over the longer run is primarily determined by monetary policy, and hence the Committee has the ability to specify a longer-run goal for inflation. The Committee judges that inflation at the rate of 2%, as measured by the annual change in the price index for personal consumption expenditures, is most consistent over the longer run with the Federal Reserve's statutory mandate. Communicating this inflation goal clearly to the public helps keep longer term inflation expectations firmly anchored, thereby fostering price stability and moderate long-term interest rates and enhancing he Committee's ability to promote maximum employment in the face of significant economic disturbances.

Summary: The Present Case Against 2% Inflation

The journey to 2% inflation targeting in the US (and globally) occurred with remarkably little opposition, if any—whether from within the central bank (here the Federal Reserve) or from the political arena. If there had ever been a full enlightened discussion within the Fed (including an invitation to outside experts to contribute opposing views, avoiding thereby "group think") or a responsible critical attempt to defend against the standard's adoption in Congress, what are the powerful arguments which could have been assembled?

Here is a list of suggestions, to be considered more fully in the rest of this book.

First, in a well-functioning capitalist economy, "sound money" goes along with prices on average for goods and services which fluctuate both upwards and downwards over considerable periods, with some tendency to revert to a mean over the long run—but this tendency is not guaranteed. Periods of rising prices would be driven by falls in productivity, resource shortage, or cyclical boom, and periods of falling prices by recession, rapid globalization, spurts in productivity growth, resource abundance, or perhaps a change in product and labour market structure which bears down on nominal prices (as for digitalization, see subsequent chapter). Attempts of central banks to drive up prices when the natural rhythm is downwards end up with likely virulent asset price inflation (and eventual bust). These boom-and-bust sequences weigh down on economic prosperity in the long run and sometimes even in the short run (especially under so-called depression-type asset price inflations to be discussed in Chap. 3). The Greenspan Fed deliberations on inflation targeting were taking place precisely at a time of natural rhythm downwards (rapid globalization and productivity growth), and yet there was absolutely no mention of this issue. More generally suppression of natural rhythm lames the principal channel by which capitalist economies under a sound money regime revive themselves from recession—prices falling to a level below that expected in the subsequent expansion, meaning that consumers and businesses begin to bring forward spending.

Second, there is absolutely no basis for thinking that central banks can target with success a given inflation rate, except in so far as they promote extraordinary inertia in inflation expectations formation which can hold for some considerable period of time. Even then a snap will likely come as monetary forces eventually break the tranquillity. The advocates of inflation targeting are critical of the monetarists largely because rules for fixed rates of monetary expansion could be consistent with a wide range of price outcomes given potential volatility in demand for money. Given the uncertainties and lack of precise knowledge about how the actual path of money supply will determine prices now and in the future, the advocates of inflation targeting turn to econometrics instead, focusing on the "control variable" of short-term interest rates (fixed by the central bank). They wax lyrical about econometric tools based on such details as Taylor rule or Phillips curve. These econometric tools might apparently yield special insights into where lies the neutral rate of interest or natural rate of unemployment—a subject about which monetarists would have been too modest to claim knowledge. But why should we in fact believe these super claims about central bank wisdom and insight when the record suggests otherwise?

Third, as a historical matter, under the sound money regime of the international gold standard before 1914, no one claimed to know the path of near or far inflation. Yes, there was a likely tendency of prices to revert towards a mean. There could be extended periods of monetary inflation (likely only mild) due to an increase in gold supplies (new discovery, improved mining technology) or from banking industry evolution which increased the range of substitute for gold money (in particular fractional reserve banking). Overall though, the freedom which this system gave to interest rate determination and to price fluctuations, and essentially to a process of discovery in markets, was so valuable that such troubles were worth the candle. Now in their attempt to gain greater control over the price path in the short and long run, central banks have suppressed these market mechanisms and increased the dangers of asset price inflations. The boom-and-bust cycles and ultimately the revealed mal-investment and diminished risk appetites (in consequence of repeated bad experiences) weigh on economic prosperity. The self-recuperation mechanisms of the capitalist economy are weakened (in that prices of goods and services do not fall promptly in recession, accompanied by expectations of subsequent re-bound). And in itself the constant propaganda related to the 2% inflation target means that across much of the economy in their long-term contracting (whether for labour or product supply), the parties agree prices based on the target rather than on their assessments of supply and demand over time. In consequence the capacity of the capitalist economy to digest huge information known only in an individual and decentralized way and reflect this in relative prices has become curtailed.

Fourth, an inflation-targeting regime promotes fiscal irresponsibility and currency warfare and ultimately threatens political and economic liberty. These dangers are particularly acute in the situation where the central bank is defying a natural rhythm of prices downwards and thereby keeping interest rates at zero or below (deploying a variety of non-conventional tools for this purpose). It seems under such circumstances that there is no cost to tax cutting, expenditure increases, or many forms of bailout. The central bank in effect becomes a collector for a new form of inflation tax—the downward manipulation of interest rates on government debt—whilst inflation remains camouflaged in goods and services markets. Non-accountability of government flourishes. In turn political conservatism based around smaller government and constitutional limits suffers both at the ballot box and in practice. The process of asset price inflation in itself is politically destabilizing, encouraging populism and fanning in unforeseen ways (often speculative narratives which stimulate cheap equity financing) new monopoly power (in this cycle notably in Big Tech) which combines with Big Finance and Big Government to endanger individual liberty (see Chap. 6). And in an international context, there is considerable discretion as to how hard the given central bank is trying to reach its 2% target. This discretion can be used to wage currency war. The central bank which has been ambivalent or lax in achieving the 2% inflation in target suddenly comes under political direction (sometimes accompanied by change at the top) to reinforce its efforts, where the clear unspoken motive is to depreciate the national currency.

A Look-Back to Contemporary Arguments Against 2%

During the years in which the US was making its way on to a 2% inflation standard, there were some vocal opponents of the process. A good summary of these is found, for example, in Rudebusch and Walsh (1998).

Concentrating on numerical inflation objectives reduces the flexibility of monetary policy, especially with respect to other policy goals. Inflation targets place some constraints on the discretionary actions of central banks. Such constraints can be quite appropriate in countries where monetary policy has performed poorly; however, this is not the case in the US! Why change a system that is working?

Monetary policy requires the careful balancing of competing goals—financial stability, low inflation, and full employment—in an uncertain world. There is uncertainty about the contemporaneous state of the economy, the impact policy actions will have on future economic activity and inflation, and the evolving priority to be given to different policy objectives. Given the uncertainties the Fed faces, an inflexible and undue reliance on inflation forecasts can create policy problems.

A notable critic of monetary policy-making during this period, William White (Bank for International Settlements), wrote a joint paper with Claudio Borio (2004) which raised several red flags about how the new inflation-targeting regime might bring financial instability (BIS February 2004) though it could not be expected that a paper published by the central bank of the central bankers could deliver rude punches. In particular, this dissident view at the Bank for International Settlements never evolved into a public and explicit critique of the 2% inflation standard; though doubtless in private, the authors would have been sympathetic to that.

The concern of these authors was that central banks at certain times should respond to the danger that an asset bubble might be forming. Inflation-targeting regimes could prove rigid in this connection:

> At least for communication purposes, in strict inflation targeting regimes with up to two-year horizons the justification of policy actions in response to imbalances may not be straightforward. To be sure, it should be well understood by now that inflation targeting is by no means oblivious to output fluctuations. But it may be hard to rationalise a tightening in the absence of obvious inflation pressures, especially if the outcome is likely to be inflation below target over the usual horizon, even if the risk is in fact a larger shortfall down the road.

The authors recommend two modifications to the inflation-targeting regime:

> **First**, policy decisions should be articulated on the basis of longer horizons.
> **Second**, greater weight should be assigned to the balance of risks in the outlook, as opposed to central scenarios or most likely outcomes.

These early critics of the 2% inflation standard gained considerable credibility from the events of 2007–08/09 (the Crash and Great Recession). Yet the standard survived and indeed became reinforced. And the same critics sometimes subsequently encountered spells of bad publicity when they under-forecast the length of the next asset price inflation or over-estimated the strength of the goods inflation twin which accompanied this.

BIBLIOGRAPHY

Barro, R. (1976). Rational Expectations and the Role of Monetary Policy. *Journal of Monetary Economy, Elsevier,* 2(1), 1–32.

Bernanke, B. S., & Mishkin, F. S. (1997). Inflation Targeting: A New Framework for Monetary Policy. *Journal of Economic Perspectives,* 11(Spring), 97–116.

Borio, C., & White, W. (2004). *Whither Monetary and Financial Stability? The Implications of Evolving Policy Regimes* (BIS Working Papers No. 147).

Fischer, S. (1977). *On Activist Monetary Policy with Rational Expectations.* NBER.

Friedman, M. (2006). *The Optimum Quantity of Money.* New Brunswick: Aldine Transaction Publishers.

Greenspan, A. (1966). *Gold and Economic Freedom.* The Objectivist (Reprinted in Ayn Rand's *Capitalist: The Unknown Ideal*). Massmarket Paperback, 1994.

Mishkin, F. S. (2000, January). *From Monetary Targeting to Inflation Targeting; Lessons from the Industrialized Countries.* NBER.

Wheeler, G. (2014, December 1). *Reflections on 25 Years of Inflation Targeting.* Speech to the International Journal of Central Banking Conference, Wellington.

CHAPTER 3

Diagnosis of Monetary Inflation in Asset Markets

You will not find in the advocacy literature for monetarism or the 2% inflation standard—the present and previous experiment at fiat money stabilization—any mention of asset price inflation. Likewise asset price inflation did not surface as a danger in the earlier advocacy of the gold exchange standard of the 1920s or the Bretton Woods system of the 1960s. And yet asset price inflation appeared in virulent form in three of the four stabilization experiments; the exception was the monetarist experiment, but as we have seen, that lasted less than a half-decade in the US before its final shutdown there with the Plaza Accord.

There are many possible reasons for the omission—ranging from the blindness of the doctrinaire to conceptual failure. The advocates of inflation targeting have written about the problem of asset price bubbles and even conceded that in special circumstances the central bankers should use discretionary powers—regulations in particular—available under their standard to respond to their potential formation. But that is a far cry from recognizing that monetary inflation can become virulent even if the aim of 2% inflation is achieved thanks to effective camouflage in goods and services markets. Diagnosis of inflation symptoms is often complex and judgemental most of all in asset markets. The best defence against financial instability is sound money which the 2% inflation standard does not provide.

Asset Price Inflation Defined

There has been no constant concept of asset price inflation through the modern age of fiat money even amongst those who recognize the condition. The term has become most popular in the present period of inflation targeting coupled with the use of radical monetary tools. The historian of economic thought could doubtless find some common threads through the evolving concept going back into the nineteenth century or earlier (indeed the first big example is the Dutch monetary inflation of the 1630s featuring tulip mania, the bubble in stock of the Dutch East India Company and Amsterdam real estate—see p. 86). Even so he or she would have to confront much perplexity.

How could Milton Friedman and Anna Schwarz have described the years 1922–28 as the heyday of the Federal Reserve—doing everything right apparently—whilst von Hayek (2008), Rothbard (2002), Robbins (2002), and many others viewed the same Federal Reserve during the same years as responsible for a huge credit boom and asset price inflation culminating in bust and great depression? Milton Friedman and Hayek walked the same campus (University of Chicago) for many years, yet the term does not even enter *A Monetary History of the United States*. The omission is a puzzle most likely explained by an aversion to economic theory which could not be verified empirically—and there is much in asset price inflation theory which is difficult to capture in econometrics.

So let's start in this chapter with a modern definition (see Brown 2017).

Asset price inflation describes the empowerment by monetary disorder of irrational forces in asset markets. This empowerment is characterized by an unusual prominence of certain flaws in mental processes as identified by psychologists (see especially Kahneman 2012).

Examples include irrational behaviour driven by "mental pain of realizing loss" (experiments illustrate that people become risk-seeking when all their options are bad), feedback loops from price action to assessment of related speculative hypotheses (as Shiller (2000) puts it "news of price increases spurs investor enthusiasm, which spreads by psychological contagion from person to person in the process amplifying speculative stories that might justify the price increases"), anchoring effects (these result from a cognitive bias that describes the common human tendency to rely too heavily on the first piece of information offered), several others including magical thinking (the attribution of causal relationships between actions and events which cannot be justified by reason and observation), and mental compartmentalization (an unconscious psychological defence mechanism used to avoid mental discomfort and anxiety caused by a person having conflicted emotions and beliefs within themselves).

In pursuing the relationship between monetary disorder and asset price inflation (including an examination of the mental flaws described), it becomes apparent that there are two types of asset price inflations. The first is the boom type which emerges under conditions of flourishing investment opportunity and the second, a depression type, which forms when the overall economic situation is quite weak (albeit not so weak as to preclude the birth and growth of speculative narratives about investment opportunity which in turn excite highly leveraged activity across a limited range of economic activity).

These mental flaws are identifiable in various types of market conditions found under asset price inflation, whether characterized by "the hunt for yield" (characteristic of depression-type asset price inflation) or "irrational exuberance" (characteristic of boom type). There is much speculative storytelling, and many investors become abnormally ready to embrace these tales, discarding their normal scepticism. During the course of the asset price inflation, the stories come and go, as speculative excess produces outcomes (excess supplies and falling profits) which discredit them; new information also provides contradictory evidence. The amount of distortion across asset markets is not general or equal but depends on the evolving speculative narratives and the catalysts which drive these. The most powerful narrative of all may be new "magical" instruments designed by the central bank and more generally the success of the monetary experiment. There are also narratives about the wonders of financial innovations (whether new products or new forms of asset management) buttressed by the wonders of leverage and momentum.

STAGES OF ASSET PRICE INFLATION

The asset price inflation goes through different stages from start to finish. Early on, currency devaluation may play a lead role in generating speculative stories, and in practice the Federal Reserve as the dominant central bank is in front here. Even though other central banks at this early stage may not have launched their own contribution to global monetary disorder, asset markets in their country or currency (even if floating freely) can become subject to the forces of irrationality stemming from the US.

In a mid-phase, forces of irrationality have strengthened, and these spread over a wider span of asset markets giving rise to what market analysts describe as "speculative froth". Yet in some markets, the froth is already receding amidst the din of apparently isolated crashes. The central bank may respond to these, out of concern that a sudden drain of speculative froth across all markets could occur, by undertaking further monetary reflation. If successful, this might even induce some bottom-fishing in the crashed markets whilst adding to heat elsewhere. In a final phase, there is an almost general plunge in speculative temperatures, sometimes financial crisis and recession. The full extent of mal-investment at last becomes apparent.

The waxing and waning of speculative stories are central to the process of asset price inflation through time. The revelation of mal-investment (most likely via plunging profits or rents) and growing expectations of a tightening in monetary conditions (coupled perhaps with actual tightening) are catalysts to the waning. In particular, as the appearance of speculative froth grows in intensity and alongside forecasts of rising goods and service inflation gain prominence, speculation grows on "normalization" or "tightening" of monetary policy. The central bankers go on the speech-making circuit to wonder aloud when they will start the process. The president and finance minister might voice similar thoughts. Long-term interest rates begin to reflect that.

In principle we could imagine an asset price inflation coming to an end through a process of speculative stories waning (amidst accumulating disappointment) including the identification of mal-investment without any normalization of monetary policy. In the small sample size of history, though, there is no unambiguous practical example of this. The asset price inflation of 1934–37 in some respects is the closest, though there is a popular historical folklore which blames the Crash and recession of 1937–38 squarely on the Fed's error of trying to normalize monetary conditions too soon even though short-term interest rates hardly increased (see Brown 2016). It is also possible in principle for an asset price inflation to come to an end (without the arrival of a deadly late phase of asset crash and recession) with the emergence of an economic miracle which justifies values previously based on much speculative froth.

THE TWINS OF ASSET PRICE INFLATION AND GOODS INFLATION

The monetary disorder which spawns asset price inflation also gives rise to goods and services inflation. We would be surely unlikely to observe one twin without the other being present somewhere, though care might well be required in ferreting it. The vitality of each twin, both in absolute terms and relative to one another, varies through any given episode of monetary inflation. And the absolute and relative paths differ between episodes.

In looking for the twins, we should realize that the presence of asset price inflation does not mean that asset prices should be rising in any given period—rather identification depends on "markers" such as prices relative to fundamental value and prevalence of carry trades. These are described in greater detail below and involve the irrational pursuit of exchange risk premiums, credit risk premiums, term risk premiums, and liquidity premiums, in particular based often on speculative storytelling and slanted vision about the future.

Moreover, goods and services inflation may exist even where official statistics say otherwise, when account is taken of the "natural rhythm of prices". It has been an insight of Austrian School economics that prices of goods and services on average should fluctuate through time (with a long-run tendency to revert to the mean, though this is not assured) under a regime of sound money (see Salerno 2010). (Other aspects of sound money include interest rates determined freely in markets—both short term and long term—without any type of manipulation by the authorities and automatic mechanisms for guiding the growth of monetary base which is well pivoted, meaning highly distinct for which a broad and stable demand exists.) For example, during spurts of technological change, business recessions, periods of rapid globalization, the pressure on many prices would be downwards. The attempt of the central bank to stabilize prices during such episodes or even to generate a target low inflation rate induces monetary inflation. Stable official price indices, when the natural rhythm of prices is downwards, would be symptomatic of inflation.

Prices falling during a recession could in principle impede recovery if expectations were to develop of further near-term falls, encouraging some delay in purchases even though eventually higher prices are expected when the next strong economic expansion emerges. In principle and practice, this possibility of deflationary expectations should not be overstated. Yes, in hindsight we might see business cycle recessions where prices seemed to be on a falling trend. But in real time, no one would know for sure that increased economic weakness lay ahead—ex post price declines as measured by statistics do not correspond to ex ante magnitudes. Moreover recorded prices do not capture various types of unofficial discounts which may have been front-loaded in the economic downturn.

Characteristics of Boom-Type Asset Price Inflation

Boom-type asset price inflations occur in the context of persistent good economic news—likely including rapid productivity growth and ultimately living standards generally. The predominant mental flaw is the positive feedback loop—price gains across a wide spread of asset markets (as magnified by monetary conditions which are weighing down on interest rates and preventing them from rising to the higher unknown neutral level) reinforcing the credibility of the particular speculative narratives present there, including the macro-story of economic miracle or near miracle. Good performance from essentially risky investments in the context of general prosperity and of interest rates below neutral level may cause investors to slant the probabilities of good scenarios in the future above those consistent with sober-rational evaluation, and they may come to irrationally attribute skill to their own investment choices.

(Empirical estimates of the neutral interest rate as published by the central banks in particular are based on observations of whether inflation is on a sustained path below or above the target inflation rate. But this takes no account of the natural rhythm of prices. In aiming at an unchanged target during periods when the natural rhythm is downwards, the central bank in fact induces monetary disequilibrium which may well show up most visibly in "financial instability" otherwise described as asset price inflation. Inflation below target does not mean that market rates are above the neutral level.)

Under the described glow of irrational exuberance, there is likely to be mal-investment and in general over-investment. Whilst this is taking place, growth of incomes and well-being is likely to be faster than what it would have been without the unsound money. Payback starts when the asset price inflation moves into its final stage. Even so there is some cushion from the earlier period against later adversity.

Boom-type asset price inflation is likely to go along with prices of goods and services rising faster than consistent with the natural rhythm which would accompany sound money. Evidence of unsound money policies could include prices moving sideways or slightly upwards when the natural rhythm would be downwards.

The monetary unsoundness which accompanies boom-type asset price inflation may well not be deliberate but due to a flaw in the monetary framework. And this flaw or the unsoundness is not perceived generally (except by a few experts who might also be investors). Nonetheless, it has the result of steering rates falling below neutral, which contributes to the pattern of abnormally large and frequent capital gains.

The carry trades which flourish under boom-type asset price inflation include three in common with the depression type. A fourth (the term maturity carry trade—from short-maturity safe government bonds into long maturity) is found only under the depression type. The three are first currency carry trades (low interest monies into high interest rate monies); second, credit carry trades (from low-risk credits into high-risk credits); and third liquidity carry trades (from liquid assets into illiquid). In all three cases, the carry trader pursues extra income (the currency risk premium, the credit risk premium, or the liquidity risk premium, respectively) in the knowledge that there is some risk attached—whether adverse exchange rate movement, default, or market seize-up (inability to transact). Even under sound money regimes, such carry trades take place and are consistent with rational pursuit of extra yield. But under boom-type asset price inflation (as under depression type, though the mind-set is different as we shall see), the trader is sucked by speculative narratives (about which he or she is unusually accepting, influenced perhaps by positive feedback from so much investment success so far in general) into exaggerating the premium return and downplaying the risks.

For example, in the pursuit of currency risk premium, the trader may become over-confident in expectations that the high-coupon currency will continue rising or not to fall (such as to wipe out the interest rate advantage). That over-confidence may twin with a good news economic story, such that the issuing economy of the high interest rate money is undergoing a profound economic change (for the better)—becoming, for example, much more "dynamic" than previously. (One such narrative has been the great convergence story regarding the catch-up of the emerging market economies—see Baldwin 2016.) General good news and positive investment results elsewhere might contribute to false confidence about the future.

Alternatively, in the pursuit of the credit risk premium, a string of low actual defaults consistent with good economic times (and below-neutral rates) might encourage the belief that defaults will remain low, when in fact the rational investor should be giving significant weight to the possibility of bad economic or political scenarios in the future. Higher actual risk-free interest rates in line with the abnormally high neutral level might have concentrated the minds of traders on those scenarios. And as regards the liquidity premium, the high turnover which typically accompanies bull markets in assets and the exaggerated optimism that good times will continue might falsely encourage unrealistic expectations that this state of affairs will long persist.

In the liquidity carry trade, the investor, for example, may be unusually credulous about a narrative that the managers of the illiquid assets have particular skill and that in any case they have found ways to reduce illiquidity on a permanent basis. One might think of private equity here or more generally fund management products.

A final point, boom-type asset price inflations do not emerge early on in a cyclical expansion. They arrive typically after several years of good economic outcomes and of course depend essentially on monetary disequilibrium.

Characteristics of Depression-Type Asset Price Inflations

Depression-type asset price inflation emerges usually early in a cyclical expansion and is triggered by radical monetary experimentation which has the effect of causing a famine of interest income. The radicalism fuels anxiety about a break-out of high inflation at some uncertain point in the more distant future. The consequence is a desperate hunt for yield characterized by a flaw in mental processes which Daniel Kahneman (2012) describes under the heading of "loss aversion" or more generally "prospect theory". He notes from experiments that if individuals are faced with certain loss, they become risk lovers, willing to take on gambles which offer a possibility of gain (compared to the starting level of wealth) but whose expected outcome is substantially negative. The combination of risk-loving behaviour to avoid loss but risk aversion otherwise is contrary to normally assumed rational behaviour in economics (as usually expressed in the context of declining marginal utility of wealth). In particular, the individuals concerned are giving under-importance to the starting point (against which losses and gains are measured).

Under conditions of interest income famine as induced by radical monetary experimentation, many investors, especially those whose savings are normally—or wholly—concentrated in safe bonds and money, find themselves facing certain loss. They exhibit the loss aversion as described in joining the hunt for yield. In this hunt they do not become economic optimists, though they may become susceptible to speculative storytellers. The narrative may span particular industrial sectors (e.g. energy or Silicon Valley) or more generally countries (Brazil or China), but there is no master narrative about prosperity. Positive feedback loops may form where price gains stoke belief in the story, but this is not equivalent to the general optimism of boom-type asset price inflation. Hunters for yield do not like to admit to themselves that they are following high-risk strategies with actuarially negative prospects; by convincing themselves of the truth of speculative narratives (rather than assessing these with rational scepticism), they may feel better about their strategy.

It is possible that under the façade of a depression-type asset price inflation, there is a boom-type asset price inflation struggling to get out. That may have been the situation of the first two decades of the twenty-first century. Rapid globalization and technological change have been the source of many speculative narratives and much enthusiasm about these good investment stories. And so, depression-type asset price inflation typified by much yield-seeking behaviour has also been accompanied by a continued flow of investment into lead sector opportunities (for example shale oil, big tech). Yet, there is no mistaking the overall nature of this depression-type asset price inflation, of which a key element is that "everyone and their dog" know that asset price inflation is present. The wild monetary experimentation producing two great speculative pull-backs (2000 and 2007) coupled with fears of another asset market crash and recession has put the dampener on long-gestation investment—with companies rewarded for paying out cash instead and bolstering their leverage ratios. And one of the circulating speculative narratives (highly relevant to equity market valuation) focuses on the rising monopoly power across the US economy in each industrial sector (a power which may go along with limited investment), even though on closer examination what is described as monopoly rent may in fact turn out to be the fruits of leverage and more generally financial engineering.

In particular, the Federal Reserve is constantly in the news. The media is abuzz with warnings of financial market froth. The great monetary experiment is apparent to all. Everyone except perhaps the architects of the experiment put a high probability on it failing—meaning an eventual crash and recession. Many owners of small- and medium-sized businesses plan to sell these at some distant point, and under an environment of asset price inflation of the depression type, they are concerned that by then it may have reached its end stage. So they also become reluctant to enter into long-gestation investments. Similar considerations apply to executives in large companies whose compensation includes long-dated share options. Financial engineering strategies—often including increased leverage—are attractive, especially where prices of credit products are inflated in an environment of hunt for yield, as they bring cash into the early years.

And from the viewpoint of the equity owners, increasing the proportion of debt in the capital structure means benefiting from the downward manipulation of interest rates and the compression of credit spreads; in effect the equity shareholder collects this form of inflation tax from the debt holders (see Chap. 13). The equity owner via the financial engineering of the underlying companies in effect finds himself as the issuer of debt paper to the income-famished investors pouring finds into the credit carry trades (some may be both at the same time!). Why undertake dangerous long-gestation investment in the search for profit when profit margins can be widened by milking a larger proportion of debt owners (in the capital structure)? Such engineering shrinks in aggregate the supply of equity—in contrast to real capital stock expansion which adds to this—and so overall prosperity does not gain. But even without an underlying acceleration of growth in the capital stock, the big rises in equity market valuation satisfy meanwhile (during the asset price inflation) the increased demand for equity exposures.

In fundamental terms, equity outstanding is becoming more highly leveraged and thereby more risky. But this risk is camouflaged by burgeoning profit rates and interest expenses which are low relative to overall corporate incomes; and of course at frothy equity market levels, leverage calculated on the basis of current equity prices may be falling despite all the equity buy-backs. Yet once the froth disperses and the underlying rise in leverage is revealed, a continued fall in overall business values would weigh especially heavily on the equity component (of total outstanding securities of the given corporation).

Hence depression-type asset price inflation goes along with low investment and low productivity growth in general. There are no seven years of fat (as occurs under boom-type asset price inflation) to compensate for the seven years of famine to follow. And yet there can be much mal-investment, meaning that overall prosperity suffers considerably, taking the lean and the fat years together. Much of this mal-investment is concentrated around particular speculative stories which get an abnormally strong following. And usually, but not always, this mal-investment is accompanied by high leverage.

The boom of the carry trade into long-maturity fixed-rate bonds in search of a term premium (the fourth form of carry trade unique to depression-type asset price inflation as explained below) and into credits (amidst unrealistic low expectations of default) favours a build-up of speculative temperatures in residential real estate markets especially where leverage is typically high and the term of fixed-rate borrowing long. More generally in the hunt for yield which typifies depression-type asset price inflation, residential real estate with its apparent steady income stream (whether actual or imputed rents) can become attractive to income-famine victims. Owner-occupiers, however, especially where intended holding periods (of the present or future homes) are long, should not in principle feel better off to the extent that home price gains might superficially suggest. They are both the payer and recipient of the imputed rent flow through many years to come, which are discounted in the calculation of present value.

Depression-type asset price inflation is likely to be accompanied by its monetary twin—inflation in the goods and service markets, yet as for boom type, this may not be easy to find in the official price indices. Again, we should measure such inflation in the goods and services markets by comparison with the natural rhythm of prices under sound money. For example, in a cyclical period of economic weakness, prices should fall to a lower level than during a period of strong economic activity. Low and below-target inflation measured over several years of cyclical weakness may be symptomatic of camouflaged monetary inflation in goods and services markets, especially if there is rapid globalization tending to push down the prices of traded goods or technological change which is generally bearing down on wages and prices (as may be the case with digitalization—see Chap. 6) even without spurring productivity growth.

The lack of general economic optimism or accompanying irrational exuberance under depression-type asset price inflation could mean that stock markets, for example, appear less expensive using the traditional metric of price-earnings ratios. At the top of the market in a depression-type asset price inflation, the P/E ratio is likely to be well below the peak reached in boom type. Consistently, though, the stock market might be even more elevated under type B relative to "fundamentals". Within the stock market under depression type as under boom type, there may be a sector where P/E ratios are in the stratosphere, reflecting economic optimism on a particular innovation. And under depression type, this optimism is likely to combine with a flawed mental process already described above—the willingness to take on poor gambles to avoid the certainty of loss elsewhere in the portfolio (especially on monetary assets).

The recession and crash which feature in the end stage of depression-type asset price inflation can be as bad as for the boom type even though the preceding economic landscape was so much poorer (under depression type). Yes, there is no huge investment boom to turn to bust at a macro level under the depression type, but nonetheless investment could collapse by as much. All those speculative stories and the associated leverage did produce areas of sometimes spectacular mal-investment within the weak aggregates (for investment) areas. As the stories fade or become discredited, the slump of capital spending in those areas depresses substantially the investment aggregates. Moreover, the weakening of consumer spending at this point could be as much or more under the depression type (than boom type) as households realize that their future income expectations were wildly exaggerated in a context of vast financial froth.

The timing of the onset of final stage for depression-type or boom-type asset price inflation might well be influenced by central bank actions. Under the boom type, these may be prompted by concerns about rising prices of goods and services but also by much talk of excess speculation. Under the depression type, the central bank could herald a "policy normalization" prompted by much discussion of potential "financial instability". Depression-type asset price inflations, though, are more likely than the boom type to end without any effective monetary tightening or normalization at all. This is because the depression type occurs in weak economic conditions, where the emergence of excess capacity and declining profits in key sectors previously leading the upturn could emit signals sufficiently strong to cause a shift of asset price inflation into its final stage without any contribution from central bank action.

In depression-type asset price inflations, there is much commentary about whether monetary tightening or normalization could make matters worse by causing a sudden plunge in asset prices. This theme can also emerge in boom-type asset price inflations, albeit that the general optimism and less widespread wariness of over-priced asset markets mean that the sense of danger is likely to be less. This is the "point of no return" issues raised, for example, by Friedman and Schwartz (1963) in their analysis of the asset market booms in the mid- and late 1920s (they conclude that the Fed's belated actions to "cool the speculative temperature" made the inevitable downturn worse than if this had been left to occur "naturally"). After the asset price inflation has been in process long enough and there is so much froth around, the danger is that central bank signalling or action could bring a more sudden and violent downturn than allowing the asset price inflation to burn out from within. Again, the prominence of this debate could be greater under depression type than boom type given the widespread realization that a monetary experiment is in progress and that froth has been deliberately created.

Carry Trades Under Depression-Type Asset Price Inflation

As regards the carry trades under depression-type asset price inflation, much of this (as under boom-type asset price inflation) is driven by momentum-type considerations—the trend is your friend. But under both conditions, there may be speculative stories which also appear to justify the trades and which get exaggerated in importance.

For example, a carry trade into an emerging market currency might be driven in part by highly optimistic storytelling about the future of that emerging market economy. Carry trades into high-risk credits feature similarly a combined drive of income famine and storytelling (in this case about the ultimate corporate or sovereign borrower) though the latter may be less prominent in general.

The liquidity carry trade could include several elements of distortion. For example, the switch of liquid funds into private equity includes much storytelling about the efficiency which private equity managers unconstrained by quarterly earning calendars and public market filing requirements will bring to business operations. There are also the tales of how the private equity "barons" have fostered crony capitalist connections which open up paths through the regulatory maze surrounding some of their businesses.

The category of carry trade which features largely under depression-type asset price inflation and not at all under boom type is the term maturity trade—the switching of funds from short-maturity top government debt into long maturity in expectation of earning a "term premium". The idea that there is a normal expectation of extra income from lending for a long time at a fixed rather than at a floating rate is dubious at any time. Higher long-term rates than spot short term rates are likely to reflect expectations of less capital abundance in the future (e.g. if investment opportunities improve or savings become scarcer of if government spending increases) or concerns about higher inflation both of which would be matched broadly by a rise in nominal spot interest rates. The claim that there is in fact a margin in fixed rates over and above expected future spot rates cumulated over the given term (the so-called term premium) and that indeed normal equilibrium conditions call for this would normally be greeted with scepticism.

But in the hunt for yield and weak economic conditions which are intrinsic to asset price inflations of the depression type, investors are more than usually willing to chase the hypothesis that the "yield curve" is on its way to becoming abnormally flat (meaning more capital gains ahead with respect to long-maturity debt); then even small premiums on long-term rates (over short) could be an attractive trading proposition (from the long side). A big story in the present business cycle (from 2009 trough) is secular stagnation. (In the past cycle, the big story was the "Asian savings surplus".) The persistent economic weakness marked by low productivity and low investment spending is fertile ground for Keynesian economists to paint their picture of long-term depression marked by a natural rate of interest which is sub-zero or barely positive. And indeed, actual market rates get caught in a warp of self-fulfilling expectations. The low investment generated by the monetary experiment and related uncertainty in turn becomes empirical justification for the secular stagnation story.

In rational mode, investors would question whether anyone can foretell with such precision the long run and would insist on putting significant probabilities on a return of robust economic conditions several years from now. But even some of those investors who cling to such rationality may become subject (under conditions of interest income gamine) to another mental flaw which sustains the term carry trade. This is the magical thinking about the power of the central bank to determine long-term interest rates.

The story is that the central bank's "new" monetary tools enable it to fix long-term rates also. Many investors might doubt this, realizing that the stock of long-term fixed-rate paper outside the central bank is still huge and shifts in expectations amongst the holders of this (and the potential short sellers) could surely overpower the would-be rate fixers in the central banks. But for now they realize that many market participants are ready to believe in the new powers of the central bankers, and thus they convince themselves that "it is never wise to fight the Fed". Yes, at some point someone will call out that the emperor has no new clothes, but that could be a long time from now, and meanwhile the "let's get in on the ride" philosophy prevails.

2018: Depression-Type Asset Price Inflation Update

The subject of dysfunctionality of the long-term interest rate markets under the global 2% inflation standard is the subject of our next chapter.

In early 2018, there were signs that depression-type asset price inflation was "mutating" (in an extended mid-late phase with some possible near-term speculative, temperature falls as the other twin of monetary inflation—goods and services inflation—became more troublesome: the danger of a sudden transition to the end phase of asset price inflation was present). The term risk carry trade was under some threat of boom turning to bust. Coincidentally the currency carry trade from yen and euros (negative interest monies) into US dollars was exhibiting some indigestion as the narrative of US monetary normalization far ahead of other countries was encountering some rational scepticism. (The narrative regained traction in Spring 2018 when it seemed like the ECB was set to delay a start to normalization amidst a stalling of the economic upturn during the first quarter). The exploding US budget deficit under the impact of big tax cuts (at end-2017) and the collapse of monetary conservatism inside the Republican Party (meaning only four senators voting against President Trump's nomination of a Yellen loyalist to the head of the Fed) added to the risks. And the credit carry trades looked suddenly risky in view of a blow-out of the "volatility bubble" in early February.

One symptom of the build-up of asset price inflation since 2011/12 and especially since the Yellen Fed's new monetary stimulus of 2016/17 (first the Yellen Put, then "go slow" on raising rates due to "Amazon effect"—see Chap. 11) had been the fashionable risk parity style of asset management. Managers identified groups of low-volatility assets and leveraged these up so as to achieve higher targeted volatility and expected returns. Believing that volatility (the so-called VIX) was over-priced in the markets in that not enough account was taken of the new calm conditions under the 2% inflation target and related measures, the managers engaged in "arbitrage" operations, taking short positions in volatility in the market so as to match part of their overall long position in this. All worked well when markets remained calm and asset prices were rising.

But then the mini-crash on Wall Street of early February 2018 provoked by sudden (and perhaps still fleeting) perceptions of inflation danger led to a gapping down of stock prices and a fantastic jump in the price of volatility. As investors along for the speculative ride sought the exits, they found there a stampede of like-minded people. The price of volatility (so-called VIX) surged as did perceptions of this. Given that credit products are price off volatility measures—in particular the price of corporate bonds is directly related to volatility of the underlying equity and the price of calls on this equity—these could be expected to now fall in price. (Students of finance 101 know that a risky bond in company A is equivalent to a holding of equity in hypothetically unleveraged company A with a well-in the money call option written against this, the corporate bond investor essentially looking forward to collecting a big premium on expiry (maturity) provided that there has been no big fall in equity value since issue (of the option). So when the price of the call option rises, the investor should expect a higher return on new issues of corporate bonds.) Evidently the credit carry trade was now at risk of some implosion as the irrational forces present in the volatility and option markets (and stemming from the monetary inflation) lost power.

These asset management practices based on flawed mental processes do not fit directly under the subtitle of carry trades. But they give these trades a boost. The nearest historical comparison could be the portfolio insurance strategies popular in the mid-1980s which blew up in the October 1987 crash or the new cash management strategies of the 2000s ending up in the 2008 panic.

Bibliography

Baldwin, R. (2016). *The Great Convergence*. Cambridge, MA: Harvard University Press.
Brown, B. (2016). *A Global Monetary Plague*. London: Palgrave.
Brown, B. (2017). A Modern Concept of Asset Price Inflation in Boom and Depression. *Quarterly Journal of Austrian Economics, 20*(2), 29–60.
Friedman, M., & Schwartz, A. (1963). *A Monetary History of the United States*. Princeton: Princeton University Press.
Kahneman, D. (2012). *Thinking Fast and Slow*. New York: Farrar, Straus and Giroux, 2011.
Rothbard, M. (2002). *A History of Money and Banking in the United States*. Auburn: Mises Institute.
Robbins, L. (2002). *The Great Depression*. Auburn: Mises Institute.
Salerno, J. T. (2010). *Money, Sound and Unsound*. Auburn: Mises Institute.
Shiller, R. (2000). *Irrational Exuberance*. Princeton: Princeton University Press.
von Hayek, F. (2008). *Prices and Production*. Auburn: Mises Institute.

CHAPTER 4

Manipulation of Long-Term Interest Rates

In pursuing their target under the 2% inflation standard, central bankers and their political masters have experienced much frustration. The natural rhythm of prices has been downwards—reflecting rapid globalization and digitalization. Central bankers have sought to suppress this (natural rhythm) and drive prices higher on a sustained basis. They have encountered pushback from a combination of circumstances—some of their own making. They have doubled up, developing non-conventional monetary tools designed to increase the effectiveness of their policies aimed at "breathing in inflation". These tools have carried serious side-effect. In particular, they destroyed the signalling mechanisms in the long-term interest rate market essential to the well-functioning of a capitalist economy. While too early to know what the eventual cost of this dysfunction will be, there are already indications that the consequences are serious.

THE JOURNEY TO LONG-TERM RATE DYSFUNCTION

Let's start at the beginning. As we saw in Chap. 2, the Greenspan Fed responded to downward pressure on recorded inflation during the early years of rapid globalization and the digital revolution (1995–99) by countering the upward influences on interest rates which would have matched a rising neutral level. The result: the powerful boom-type asset price inflation which developed in the US and globally in the mid- to late 1990s.

This featured the boom and bust in Asian debt, Russian debt, and finally Nasdaq (and more broadly telecommunications).

The subsequent recession of 2000–02 triggered the Fed's experiment of breathing inflation back into the US economy (2003–05)—it set the stage for a depression-type asset price inflation of this period. The symptoms included giant carry trades into long-maturity government bonds and into credit paper (a key element straddling both was innovatively packaged mortgage paper, whether US subprime or Spanish mortgages) and tremendous speculation in the equities of financial intermediary firms both in the US and Europe. Overall though, the growth of productivity and investment remained sub-par through this business cycle upturn (2002–07).

Ben Bernanke succeeded Alan Greenspan as Fed chief in early 2006. This Princeton professor had written and spoken extensively on his advocacy of inflation targeting (see Bernanke and Mishkin 1997; Bernanke 2003). When the first quakes occurred in credit markets (and in the international banking system) in summer 2007, Bernanke was in no mood to aggressively ease monetary policy. His concern was that this would push inflation above target. And so the Bernanke Fed responded not by putting its foot on the monetary base accelerator and alongside having short-term money rates collapse (this would have been a version of the so-called Greenspan put). Instead the Bernanke Fed entered into vast sterilized intervention to boost liquidity without increasing the monetary base; the official peg for short-term rates was reduced only marginally. (Counterfactual historians could consider whether a Greenspan put would have worked in autumn 2007 and, if so, whether the eventual crash and downturn would have been even greater albeit from a higher level.)

As financial panic and a deep recession set in the following autumn (2008), the Bernanke Fed eventually moved to aggressive monetary base expansion—but with a sting in the tail (for any possible future of sound money). It obtained Congressional legislative authority to start paying interest on reserves at a market rate rather than fixed at zero as previously. (This authority was already contained in the Financial Services Regulatory Relief Act of 2006 but was not due to go into effect until late 2011. Under the Emergency Economic Stabilization Act of 2008, that authority was brought forward to the present.)

Why the hurry on this point, when surely market rates of interest would be at zero for some time? (Incidentally, since it started operations at end-1998, the ECB had paid interest at market rates on reserves—a stark difference from the Bundesbank regime under which reserves were non-interest bearing; Japan also started to pay interest on reserves in 2008.)

Once reserves at the central bank become interest bearing (at the market rate), then monetary base is in effect definitively removed from the pivot of the monetary system. No longer can there be the pretence that the authority is setting the path for the growth in monetary base by mimicking in some fashion the rules of operation under a gold money system whilst allowing interest rates to float freely. The transition away from monetarism is definitive. Instead, short-term rates are where they are because that is where in their wisdom (based in considerable part on econometrics) the central bankers put them. And long-term rates respond to perceptions of rate decisions guided accordingly over time.

For Chair Bernanke it was not enough to kill the remnants of monetarism by depivoting monetary base in small order. The new interest-paying regime was joined with a programme of massive expansion of the monetary base which included plans for the Federal Reserve to hold for many years (some would say an eternity) a vast long-maturity portfolio made up of Treasuries and securities issued by the housing government-sponsored entities (GSEs) (see Selgin 2018). The intention was surely to add to the apparatus of manipulation with respect to long-term rates (and incidentally to add to the bulwarks against any monetarist counterrevolution that would seek to put monetary base back at the pivot).

The Bernanke Fed's agenda was very different from an emergency increase in monetary base designed to pre-empt a contraction of the money supply which could intensify the economic downturn. Rather it was a deliberate experiment to gain new control over short- and long-term interest rates, subjecting these to incessant manipulation, and alongside the giant expansion of the Fed's balance sheet served key non-monetary purposes—including the subsidization of mortgages (see, e.g. Pollock 2017).

Let's elaborate. Milton Friedman, of whom Ben Bernanke claimed to be a disciple (see Bernanke 2002), maintained in his *A Monetary History of the United States* (1960) that if the Fed had taken aggressive action to prevent the money supply from shrinking through 1930–32/33, the US would have been spared a Great Depression. What action did Friedman have in mind? Well he approved of the "belated" open market operations of spring 1932 to swell the monetary base. So presumably he would have approved of this magnified many times. For Friedman, there was an unspecified black-box mechanism which would translate radical and forceful monetary base expansion into a powerful anti-contractionary influence on the wider money supply. Once economic expansion arrived and upward pressure developed on the money supply, then the presumption was that the emergency monetary base expansion could be reversed promptly and with no big side-effects as regards financial or economic stability.

Such presumptions are inherently dubious. And in any case, they were not put to the test in the years 1930–33. Yes it is possible that the Fed could have super-charged the monetary base and that this would have offset the decline in other bank assets (e.g. loans). Would that in itself have forestalled economic depression in the context of the German crisis of 1931 and subsequent collapse of that country into economic autarky with knock-on effects to the global credit markets (Germany the second largest economy in the world had been the focus of credit inflows during the boom of 1924–28)?

The answer is we don't know, though there are big grounds for concern that the giant asset price inflation which had stemmed from the Benjamin Strong Fed (see Brown 2013) would still end very badly. Rothbard (2005) makes the case that the failure of self-sustaining economic recovery to take place had much to do with Hoover Administration which induced rigidities in labour market functioning and restricted price competition. And even if an aggressive monetary base expansion would have produced some immediate results, there was the exit problem further down the road—how to reverse the expansion without creating a second crisis especially if asset inflation had spread (as was to be the case in 1935–37 when quantitative easing (QE), not called such, did occur under the Roosevelt Administration). And more generally, once there has been a huge discretionary change in the monetary base for a sustained period, something which never occurred under the gold standard, any path back to normal could not be sudden. It would involve continued discretion with all its pitfalls for quite some time.

BERNANKE DISLOCATES THE MONETARY BASE

Nevertheless, even if Chief Bernanke were determined (2008 onwards) to pursue the monetary base expansion policy which the Fed (according to Milton Friedman) had failed to do in 1930–32, there was no occasion to pay interest on excess reserves. The fact that the Fed set a minimum rate on excess reserves of 0.25% through the phase of rapid monetary base expansion showed there was a distinct agenda (from that hypothesized by Milton Friedman). Even in the subsequent economic expansion, the Fed according to the Bernanke agenda would continue with its hyper-inflated balance sheet rather than seeking to normalize this promptly (as implicitly would have occurred under Friedman's proposals); under Bernanke's plan, the Fed would gradually raise the interest rate paid on excess reserves as its means of steering short-term rates. By holding on to a huge portfolio of long-term bonds and by the glacial staged adjustment of short-term rates, the Fed could hope to influence the level of long-term rates for a prolonged period of time (more so than under an alternative of no interest on reserves and prompt shrinkage of monetary base once the economic and credit upturn got under way).

Under a gold standard regime, or under the ersatz gold arrangements of monetarism, the supply of high-powered money, which pays no interest, is determined either by mining constraints or fiat, whilst the demand for this fluctuates and causes short-term rates to shift both upwards and downwards, sometimes in highly volatile fashion. For a Fed chief determined to manipulate interest rates both in the short and long run, the attractions are huge of a regime where he or she decides on a short-term official rate and publicly plots its likely path over several years, with any change likely to be focused on the far-off dates rather than the present.

Long-term rates ignore the wild fluctuations of short-term rates under a full gold standard (where monetary base is determined by above-ground gold supplies) or an ersatz gold (strict monetarist) system. But under alternative monetary regimes, they definitely take note of short-term rate fixing decisions and more generally the level of official short-term rates where the central bank has in fact filtered out such volatility, even if it is "flexibly" following some target for monetary base growth over time. Some of this "noting" might be irrational in nature—a version of what psychologists describe as "anchoring" (an example where a "quoted asking price" may influence the assessment of value; see Kahneman (2012)).

Some advocates of quantitative easing and non-conventional monetary tools as implemented denied that the intention was to manipulate short- and long-term rates. Their argument ran something like this. Even at its maximum, the Federal Reserve only held around 20% of the total stock (as viewed from the long side) of long-term US rate exposure (Treasury and non-Treasury combined). The holders of the huge stock of paper outside the Fed would adjust this in line with their expectations of future inflation, growth, and so on. Yes, perhaps the large Fed holdings meant some downward adjustment of the term risk premium, but surely this would still be positive. And as regards the pegging of short-term rates, this had long occurred in practice even when the Fed was ostensibly operating monetary policy by piloting the supply of non-interest-bearing reserves.

Yes, the advocates had a semi-plausible tale but with many holes in it. The inflation targeting along with deployment of non-conventional tools had strengthened irrational forces as earlier described in this book. One manifestation of the "hunt for yield" is giant carry trades, including that into the term risk premium (investors pursuing higher yields in long maturities and showing high credulity for any hypothesis which fitted that trade—whether secular stagnation, an emperor's new clothes fable about the power of the new monetary instruments, or an insatiable term carry trade demand from negative interest rate deserts in Europe and Japan).

And ultimately, the vigilantes of old who might have sought profit from the eventual unwind—including potential outbreak of high goods and services inflation—entertain second thoughts given the potential stampede which could hit them in the opposite direction when the flight to the exits by present holders of now high-temperature risk assets occurs in the final stage of asset price inflation. Moreover, the severe asset price inflation induced by this policy regime—together with the general awareness of that condition—holds back propensity to invest, especially in long-gestation projects, and so the low long-term rates became symptomatic of a highly distorted and warped economy lacking the normal vigour.

More generally, unconventional tools, especially QE, which came to accompany inflation targeting, themselves become the subject of fantastic speculative narrative. Even though in principle there are grounds for doubting whether the central bank acquiring x% of the stock of long-term bonds could have a big sustained influence on their price, or on asset prices related to this (including the exchange rate), many income-desperate investors may come to believe so and base their strategies on this. As playwright Arthur Miller quipped, in the markets if it is Wednesday but enough people say it is Thursday, then it is Thursday (at least for a considerable time—which can be very long). The storytelling extends to the currency impact of non-conventional tool use. If a wielding of the QE tool is widely seen as having serious impact for the given currency, then this can react far, even though theorists may argue convincingly that the impact should be much smaller from any long-run perspective. Indeed the welders of the tools may well see the currency impact, for whatever reason—well founded or not—as one good reason for its use.

Once a central bank has gone down the path of massively expanding its balance sheet, there is much reason to fear that it will be ultra-cautious about restoring monetary normality in the future—in part due to concerns about a sudden fall of asset prices. Under the long period of abnormality, there will be much corruption of market signalling. Every additional dose of balance sheet expansion adds grounds for gloom on this score. Hence the sharp decline in the national currency which normally accompanies the launch of quantitative easing appears wholly understandable—except to the degree that all central banks are on the same train.

In general we can say that the use of the QE tool and other non-conventional tools (including negative interest rates) adds much scope for bad and destabilizing monetary policy discretion in the future which would not be present if these tools had not been used.

THE COST OF LONG-TERM RATE MARKET DYSFUNCTION

What are the economic consequences of long-term rate market dysfunction?

To assess these, we need to look at what we are missing under these circumstances.

Take the example of a sound money regime (no manipulation of long-term rates and where these and short-term rates are, in effect, freely floating). In this regime, short-term rates could be quite volatile, fluctuating day to day so as to balance demand and supply for high-powered money. Shifts in the short-term rate would induce adjustment of net demand. For example, a rise in short-term rates would mean both banks and non-banks would economize to a greater degree on their holdings of high-powered money, in particular holding less currency, and banks would operate tighter cash flow controls so as to reduce need their need for reserves (non-interest bearing) at the central bank or equivalent.

Long-term rates in this environment would be determined in aggregate by the mass of individual borrowing and lending decisions, project by project, firm by firm, household by household, and so draw together a huge range of decentralized information. For example, a business taking today's long-term interest rate would decide whether a particular project had positive net present value. In effect that decision is taken on the basis of equity capital market pricing for many firms, but often there is no direct quote on this—as would be the case if each project is to be considered one by one (and publicly available equity price is based on all projects present and potential bundled together). Instead the decision-maker proceeds (in capital budgeting) by taking the quoted long-term rate and adding an assumed equity risk premium. And there are areas of the economy in which there are no relevant equity capital costs to determine decision-making—for example, housing and consumer spending—though there are a range of possible "wealth effects" related to equity market performance. Yes, there would be speculative position-taking by those judging long-term rate trends based on macro-economic assessments including the path of the business cycle, but these would not take their cue from the volatile path of short-term interest rates.

By construction, the long-term rates determined as above would be closer on average to hypothetical neutral level (meaning consistent with sound money) than those dominated by the monetary acrobatics of the central bank. Also those transacting in the long-term rate markets would have greater confidence that the price there is indeed anchored in reality rather than just the result of frenzied speculation or desperation. The chances of the economy going a long way into serious disequilibrium accompanied by delirious asset prices and huge mal-investment are surely less under a monetary regime where the long-term rate markets are signalling appropriately a mass of decentralized information about micro-economic conditions than the opinions of the leading monetary bureaucrat and his or her political master. And of course equity markets, in taking their cue from mispriced bond markets, especially in an environment of income famine and "nowhere else to go", can become a driver of long-run economic misfortune.

The corruption of signalling in the long-term bond market may indeed have its most serious harmful influence via capital market mispricing generally (including equity, credit, real estate). And related to this mispricing is the promotion of speculative stories in individual sectors which assume large irrational proportions.

THE RE-ENTRY PROBLEM: HOW BOND MARKETS RETURN TO NORMAL SIGNALLING

By late in the second decade of the twenty-first century, we could say that the long-term US interest rate market had been dysfunctional for a long time. We could identify the starting point as being the immediate aftermath of the Nasdaq bust and recession of 2000/01. In signalling that the rise in the Fed funds rate would be slow and gradual over a prolonged period (described by central bank watchers as a pre-commitment to a given rate path), the Greenspan Fed put an unusual dampener on long-term interest rates at the time—in hindsight the start of manipulation under the 2% inflation standard and a powerful impetus to the asset price inflation which started to form during that period. Many contemporary market critics, including senior monetary officials, attributed the "artificially low" long-term rates not to their own manipulations in the short-term rate markets but to such factors as the "Asian savings surplus". Indeed, Federal Reserve speakers stimulated that particular speculative narrative followed widely by carry traders (including prominently the "Asian savings surplus"!) in search of term risk premium to bolster the meagre returns available in the money markets. (It is also possible that the only contained rise of long-term rates at this time reflected widespread concern that present asset inflation would end with a bust and that indeed the long series of Fed rate rises could end in speculative over-kill).

Even so the corruption of signalling in the long-maturity interest rate markets in the early 2000s paled in comparison to what was to occur under the use of the non-conventional tool box in the second decade. And the central bankers added to the corruption by citing the low long-maturity interest rates as evidence that the so-called neutral level of interest rates had indeed fallen. Yes it was a puzzle why ostensibly low long-term rates were not sparking strong growth of capital spending. Central bankers, however, were not ready to embrace the obvious explanation that their monetary manipulations had created such huge uncertainty which discouraged long-run investment spending. In particular, if almost everyone and their dog realized that a wide range of asset prices—including, crucially, equities—had become hot due to the monetary manipulations and that they were likely to crash within a few years, this would surely restrain capital spending especially for long-gestation projects to well below levels which would pertain if the hot prices were for real.

And so the prevailing central bank doctrine became long-term rates were not very different if at all from neutral. Yes, it made sense for central banks to gradually shed their huge portfolios of long-maturity debt built up during the active years of QE, but they should be ultra-cautious not to set off a snowball process of rising long-term rates and falling asset prices. Gradual should be the order of the day—or, better yet, glacial. And to match, the rise in short-term rates strictly under the control of the authorities should proceed very cautiously.

There was an alternative to the phoney normalization programme, which in any case could readily implode along the way. This would have been to turn the clock back on interest payments on reserves (permanently zero again as before 2008) accompanied by immediate action to restore the monetary base to a normal proportion of the broader money supply. Yes, long-term rates could well jump under this programme, and there could be some decline in asset prices (from the sugar highs of peak asset price inflation). But the return of reliable signalling could also have gone along with a new robustness in spending, especially capital spending, given no longer the malaise of "artificial" capital prices which could break at any point.

Policy normalization—defined as closing down the non-conventional tool box and restoring a well-functioning price signalling mechanism to the bond market—is in fact multi-dimensional. At the most fundamental level, it requires abandoning the 2% inflation standard—in particular its ignoring of the natural rhythm of prices over time. The second dimension is to get the monetary base back to the pivot of the monetary system. This means no payment of interest on reserves and the supply of monetary base in line with demand as consistent with a non-inflationary path forward. The third dimension is getting the share of long-maturity government debt in the total liabilities of the government sector (including the central bank) back to normal proportion. That can be accomplished over a period of many years.

Action in the second dimension can take place very quickly. The central bankers take their portfolio of long-maturity bonds to the Treasury and exchange them for short-maturity Treasury bills (T-bills). The central bank conducts open market operations in Treasury bills (short maturity) to shrink the monetary base to "normal". Of course there is much ambiguity about where is normal, and so the process of normalization on this dimension could go along with some considerable monetary turbulence for some time. That is an inevitable consequence of the huge experiment.

The normalization in the third dimension starts from the situation where the Treasury department, looking at the consolidated balance sheet of the Treasury and central bank, admits that years of QE mean in effect that an abnormally large share of government bonds outstanding are in the form of floating rate short maturities. Traditionally such a high proportion of floating rate is seen as exposing the central bank to large political pressure not to raise the short-term rates under their control (because of direct funding cost implications in terms of budget deficit)—even when it suspects that monetary inflation has got under way. If the central bank buckles under such pressure, then it becomes indeed an important source of tax collections for the government—in the form of inflation tax. One form is the suppression of interest rate income (to below what would be the case under sound money) on Treasury paper—the other is the capital tax (in real terms) on government bonds and monetary base enacted by inflation erosion.

Monetary Policy Anaesthesia Under 2% Inflation

There is a huge contrast between the way monetary conditions shift under the 2% inflation regime where monetary base is now totally dislocated from the pivot of the monetary system and what occurred in the past, especially under the gold standard or under monetarism. Today central bankers led by the Federal Reserve seek to anaesthetize the system (economy and financial markets) from any pain related to monetary policy shift; they do this by trying desperately to avoid any abrupt change in monetary conditions. Instead, they "get markets ready" for a shift some considerable time in the future, whilst continuing meanwhile on automatic pilot (as regards their fixing of the short-term official interest rate). Their main means of achieving this is "text editing"; there is a huge concentration of central banker intellectual power on carefully selecting each and every word in the regular messages, whether the end-of-meeting summary or the minutes of the meeting which come out some time later. The anaesthetizers meet failure if they have to suddenly make large changes to present official rates (not already pre-signalled) or indicate that big changes in the near-term future (relative to previous time profile) are on their way. Possible triggers are sudden bad news whether in the direction of high inflation or recession.

Contrast this with what happens under a gold standard or monetarist order. Here the stance of monetary policy depends on the behaviour of the monetary base. If a change in stance is to come about, this requires an immediate shift of demand-supply conditions in the market for monetary base. This can occur either due to the operation of automatic mechanisms (affecting supply or demand) or to central bank over-ride (regarding supply). The change is likely to bring an immediate abrupt change in short-term interest rates. And incidentally this has a prompt effect on commodity prices (down in the case of tightening) and likewise the currency (possibly within limits as set by gold points or exchange rate parities). Long-term rates by contrast may not move much at all.

The key point: a monetary correction under sound money regimes occurs in the immediate and with visible wide effect on a range of spot market including short-term rates. By contrast under the 2% inflation regime, the central banks follow an exactly opposite course. Monetary course correction is first telegraphed by Fed speak (or its equivalent) with the emphasis on the dot plots several quarters from now, whilst the short-term official rate fixing remains impervious. Could it be that this difference from what occurs under sound money regimes is indeed a point of weakness—likely to mean that monetary disequilibrium can become much larger before corrective action applies? That is the suspicion here.

The administrators and architects of the 2% inflation standard today of course have no idea of whether monetary base may need a path correction as this aggregate has become totally dislocated from the pivot of the monetary system. Even so, we could imagine that a monetary adjustment should surely show itself up in the same type of sharp response of spot prices (including money rates) and that the attempt of these officials to operate an Alice in Wonderland (medicine yesterday and medicine tomorrow but never medicine today) is an emperor's new clothes experiment.

The designer of an ersatz gold monetary system would try to replicate how short-term rates respond to a course correction in monetary conditions as these were brought about by the automatic rules under the gold standard. The designers of the present and the next fiat money stabilization experiment may not decide to opt for an ersatz gold-type system. Even so, where changes in monetary stance are to occur via adjusting the path of short-term rates rather than monetary base (not possible for now as the latter is dislocated), then the standard from past eras of sound money is that these rate movements would be snap and big rather than infinitesimal each time (25 bp) and delayed.

There is little evidence, however, that modern monetary officials believe there is wisdom to be gained by studying how rate adjustments occurred under sound money regimes of the past. Some of these officials may believe that rate manipulation, especially in the strong form practiced under the 2% inflation standard, can abolish the business cycle. How could a downturn start when interest rates in nominal terms are fixed near zero, even below in some cases? Yes, such manipulations mean that pro-cyclical fluctuations in interest rates will play no part in business cycle dynamics. But correspondingly other variables including asset prices and liquidity have a larger role.

BIBLIOGRAPHY

Bernanke, B. S. (2003, March 25). *A Perspective on Inflation Targeting* (A Federal Reserve Board Speech).

Bernanke, B. S., & Mishkin, F. S. (1997). Inflation Targeting: A New Fraemwork for Monetary Policy. *Journal of Economic Perspectives, 11*(Spring), 97–117.

Brown, B. (2013). *The Global Curse of the Federal Reserve*. Basingstoke: Palgrave.

Friedman, M., & Schwartz, A. (1963). *A Monetary History of the United States*. Princeton: Princeton University Press.

Kahneman, D. (2012). *Thinking Fast and Slow*. New York: Farrar, Straus & Giroux.

Pollock, A. J. (2017, June 28). Testimony to the Subcommittee on Monetary Policy and Trade of the Committee on Financial Services, House of Representatives. *The Fed Should Be Required to Provide Congress a Regular Savers Impact Analysis*.

Rothbard, M. (2005). *A History of Money and Banking in the United States*. Auburn: Mises Institute.

Selgin, G. (2018, March 1). *FLOORED! How a Misguided Fed Experiment Deepened and Prolonged the Great Recession* (Cato Institute Working Paper No. 50).

CHAPTER 5

A Failure of US Checks and Balances

At that fateful FOMC meeting (July 1996) where Alan Greenspan deliberated whether to accept inflation at 2% p.a. or apply policy to bearing down further, he justifiably aired the thought that this was a decision on which Congress should express its opinion. Would Congress accept perpetual inflation at 2% p.a. even though in apparent contradiction of its mandate (to the Fed) under the Federal Reserve Act as amended in 1977 "to maintain the growth of monetary and credit aggregates commensurate with the economy's long-run potential to increase production, so as to promote effectively the goals of maximum employment, stable prices, and moderate long-term interest rates"? Alternatively would Congress go along with the potential short-run economic costs incurred should the Greenspan Fed resolve to journey to a promised land of stable prices?

In fact through the near quarter century of a 2% inflation standard which has followed, Congress has not expressed a dissenting view on these matters. Of course there has been much criticism of the Federal Reserve through the years especially related to its role in causing the great bust of 2008–09, its participation in bailing out large financial institutions directly or indirectly, and subsequently its pursuit of policies which crush small savers and favour privileged borrowers (including the Federal government). But precisely targeted criticism of the aim of 2% inflation has not popped up in the volumes of congressional debate and testimony.

The Acquiescence of Congress in the 2% Inflation Target

How can we explain Congressional passivity about 2% inflation?

Alan Greenspan's comment is particularly apt: "we will be at price stability when households and businesses need not factor expectations of changes in the average level of prices into their decisions". Implicitly the Congressional overseers of the Fed have considered 2% seems to be just low enough for price stability in those terms.

Yes, 2% p.a. inflation means that around 20% of purchasing power of the paper dollar is lost every decade. But mostly people are not holding large amounts of wealth as dollar bills in the vault or under the mattress, and they would assume that even safe investments in general should generate a nominal return above that inflation rate. And any reader of Fed and Congressional history knows that the politicians embrace the concept of "price stability" (its practical definition changing through time—e.g. meaning "flat" in the 1920s as against 2% p.a. inflation now) as a measurable guide to monetary performance, notwithstanding the warnings from sound money purists and others about the inherent dangers of such simplicity.

For the practical-minded congresswoman or congressman, it is not plausible that many votes would be lost on account of price stability turning out to mean 2% inflation on average rather than zero. So, if that is where the experts at the Fed would aim (given all the mumbo-jumbo about zero-rate boundaries and incorrect price measurement), why object?

Well yes, there is much in the conduct of monetary policy to object about, but how do the critics make their weight felt in Congress? One only has to look at the Finance Crisis Inquiry Commission report on the causes of the financial crisis of 2007–10 to realize that the monetary critics failed to even make a mark on Congress. The Speaker of the House and the Senate Majority Leader, both Democrats at the time, made three appointments each to the commission, and their Republican counterparts made two each. The Report to Congress, released January 2011, did not even mention flawed monetary policy as one of the causes, let alone getting into the details of the 2% inflation standard.

Rather, the list of complaints in the majority report included failed financial regulation, failed corporate governance, lack of transparency, inconsistent government response, systemic breakdown in accountability, collapsing mortgage lending standards, over-the-counter derivatives, and failures of credit rating agencies. Even the dissident reports did not home in on monetary policy failure. The plausible view that it had been the breathing in inflation (anti-deflation) policies pioneered by the Greenspan-Bernanke Fed during 2001–05 and more fundamentally the 2% inflation targeting dating back to the 1996 FOMC meeting that lay behind the crisis did not even make its way into the dissident report, let alone the main findings.

1920s Precedent for Congress Ignoring Fed Policy as Cause of Crisis

This ignoring of flawed monetary policy as the explanation for bust and great recession or depression had an antecedent in the so-called Pecora Commission report (published in 1934, the commission was set up by a still Republican-controlled Senate in 1932) into the causes of the financial crash and depression of 1929–32. Nowhere is the view found there that the Federal Reserve in its flawed pursuance of the gold exchange standard—especially its support for the Sterling-dollar parity and its focus on stable prices (at a time when the natural rhythm of prices was strongly downwards)—was responsible for the tremendous asset price inflation and its violent end. Yet such views were out there, and indeed in many respects, the economists who stressed that narrative were in the ascendant (Hayek, Robbins, Roberts). The New York Federal Reserve governor, Benjamin Strong, had resisted all along in the 1920s (with one notable exception) attempts of some academic economists and their allies in Congress to impose a price stabilization rule even though in practice monetary policy was unofficially leaning in that direction. Meltzer (2003) writes:

> *Congress held hearings on legislation setting price stability as the goal in 1922–3, 1926–7, and 1928. With the important exception of Benjamin Strong in 1928, all Federal Reserve officials and staff opposed the legislation, and it never became law (p. 182). Advocates of a stable price mandate included Irving Fisher (who testified at length to the 1922–3 committee).*

Again in 1926–27 and 1928, Congress called for hearings on stabilization policy to discuss an amendment to the Federal Reserve Act making price stability an explicit policy goal. The legislation was the work of Congressman James Strong, a Kansas Republican, who was influenced by the Great Recession and Deflation of 1920–21 and also by Fisher's work. The bill generated unanimity within the Federal Reserve on the need to avoid any "mechanical formula" for setting policy. But beyond that there was not much agreement about how policy should be conducted.

Governor Strong gave three main reasons for opposing the Strong Bill. First the mandate would be difficult to carry out precisely because monetary velocity was unstable. Second changes in money or credit were one of many factors affecting price level. Third he feared that price stability would be interpreted as the stability of individual prices particularly agricultural prices. Yet also in his testimony, he indicated that he could work with Congress to improve a proposed guideline.

As a practical matter and under the influence of a chorus of opinion about stabilizing prices, Governor Strong steered monetary policy in the direction of resisting price falls which would have been occurring widely at such a time of booming productivity growth (mass electrification, the mass assembly line in particular). He was aware from his encounters in Congress about the hostility to price declines generally albeit those had been in the context of the great recession of 1920–21 rather than of economic boom.

Governor Strong's overall inclination though remained against price stabilization rules or any other mandated standards for monetary policy. Instead he told Congress that restoring the international gold standard was a better solution to the problem that concerned them. "I earnestly believe that the greatest service that the Federal Reserve System is capable of performing today in this matter is to hasten monetary reform in the countries that have suffered from the war. We cannot do it until the time and the conditions are favourable in each country."

In effect Governor Strong's commitment was to the experiment of stabilization described as the gold exchange standard. He did not realize that this experiment was a far cry from the international gold standard of pre-1914 and as such created huge opportunity for monetary instability. In effect the new monetary hegemon, the US, had tremendous scope under the gold exchange standard to exercise discretionary control over the growth of its own monetary base. If the guiding monetary principles in the hegemon (the US) became stable prices (at a time of productivity growth boom), shoring up a weak pound whose authorities were unready to allow automatic monetary mechanisms to work which would have brought prices down and providing contra-cyclical stimulus, there was huge potential for economic and financial instability.

Congress Adopts a Price Stabilization Mandate First in Mid-1970s

The arguments advanced by Governor Strong against a price stabilization rule were powerful—and it took the Greatest Peacetime Inflation (1965–75) to put Congress in a position where it could assemble a majority together with a willing president (Jimmy Carter) for legislation on this issue.

Lack of stable monetary velocity meant that the Fed, by steering its chosen monetary aggregate (most plausible, as under its control, monetary base), could not predict with any precision in the short or medium term how this would pan out in prices. Hence the setting of targets for prices would create many potential problems. The view that changes in prices were determined by other factors than just money could be interpreted as an acknowledgement that there is a natural rhythm to prices— and so under sound money conditions, prices would fall during periods of rapid productivity growth, resource abundance, globalization, and so on. The attempt to steer money supply to accomplish a rigid price target could end up being repeatedly frustrated. Tellingly, though, there was nothing in Strong's presentations to suggest that he had grasped the key fact that frustration could include vast cycles of asset price inflation and deflation. Indeed, the whole subject of asset price inflation is saliently absent from these early testimonies and debates on the subject of monetary policy—as unfortunately remained true many decades later.

If Congress were minded to take legislative action such as to hold the Federal Reserve to a sound money path, the better way than price (or inflation) targets would be indeed a binding resolution that this institution should pursue the principles of sound money. That done, there would be a whole body of clauses defining what sound money means (such as a tendency for prices to revert to mean over the very long run but fluctuate both upwards and downwards over the short or medium term, following operating procedures which do not interfere with the free-market determination of short- and long-term interest rates, keeping the growth of the monetary base to low levels such as should be compatible with absence of monetary inflation, fortifying the pivotal position of monetary base in the monetary system, etc.) But such legislation would lack political bite such as would earn its promotors in Congress elections—unless it was backed by a powerful system of "auditing" Federal Reserve policy and holding officials to account, all buttressed by a Congressional panel of investigators (with access to all Fed papers and meeting transcripts) wholly committed to and knowledgeable about sound money principle!

Back in the real world, Congress did move forward in the mid-1970s to pass Congressional Resolution 133 (March 1975) over the strong opposition of then Fed Chief Arthur Burns requiring that the Federal Reserve report quarterly to the House and Senate Banking Committees on its planned rate of money growth. In itself that was not objectionable and included no specific targets for prices or inflation. The assumption underneath was that monetary control meant piloting the growth of money; yet lawmakers did not specify monetary base for this purpose or any means of strengthening its pivotal role (so as to dampen potential volatility of its velocity), and they did not include in the resolution any citation of sound money principle. Two years later the resolution morphed into a new Federal Reserve Act or, more precisely, the "Federal Reserve Reform Act of 1977". This was signed into law by President Jimmy Carter who during the elections of 1976 had attacked "Republican monetary policies" as responsible for the great inflation and the great recession of 1974–75.

The Reform Act made explicit objectives for the Federal Reserve, whilst increasing its transparency and accountability to Congress. When the Federal Reserve was first established in 1913, Congress directed it only to "furnish an elastic currency, to afford means of rediscounting commercial paper" and "to establish a more effective supervision of banking in the US". The original act had assumed continued adherence to the gold standard regime. After the Great Depression and World War II, Congress passed the Employment Act of 1946 which declared that federal government policy was to "promote maximum employment, production and purchasing power". The Federal Reserve for the purpose of this legislation could be considered as part of the government, but the act was not in effect specifically tilted towards monetary policy and the Federal Reserve. The collapse of the Bretton Woods system (under which the dollar had been convertible into gold at a fixed rate for non-US citizens) and the Greatest Peacetime Inflation represented the antecedents of the new Congressional push aimed at the Fed.

Under the Reform Act, the Federal Reserve was directed to "maintain long run growth of the monetary and credit aggregates commensurate with the economy's long run potential to increase production, so as to promote the goals of maximum employment, stable prices and moderate long-term interest rates". This became known as the "dual mandate" (see Steelman 2012).

The sound money advocate could argue that the pursuance of sound money subsumes all these goals; under such a regime prosperity would be greater than under any alternative and long-term interest rates would be lower on average; moreover, prices would have a long-run tendency to revert to the mean. But the legislation offered no pointers to such a reading, and the contemporary congressional discussion and debate around it did not highlight that potential interpretation. The good news in the legislation for sound money advocacy was that money (steering a money aggregate) was the central function of the Federal Reserve (not pegging interest rates), whilst the aim of stable prices could be interpreted in ways which would be consistent with sound money principle, although many other interpretations were also possible.

The progressive sidelining, relegation, and eventual dropping of money supply targets, which occurred from 1985 through until the early 1990s, were in effect inconsistent with the legislation, though there was never any serious challenge from Congress on this. On July 22, 1993, Chair Alan Greenspan told the Senate Banking Committee that the Federal Reserve would stop relying on growth in the money supply as its policy target and switch instead to interest rate control (in effect meaning its pegging of short-term rates). The chair justified this by saying the relationship between money supply and economic growth (and inflation) has "completely broken down" due to financial innovation and deregulation. "Millions of Americans now move their money from savings accounts into mutual funds and particularly money market funds that many people use like savings and checking accounts."

Under the so-called Humphrey-Hawkins Act of 1978, the Federal Reserve still had to present money supply target ranges to Congress, but henceforth these would be essentially dead letters (this Act amended the Employment Act of 1946 and legislated that "unemployment should not exceed 3% for people 20 years or older, inflation should be reduced to 3% or less, provided that its reduction would not interfere with the employment goal; and by 1988 the inflation rate should be zero, again provided that pursuing this goal should not interfere with the employment goal". By the time Greenspan came into the chair (1987), no one remembered the zero inflation goal; later and in any case, the Yellen paper advanced reasons why going to zero could endanger employment, meaning that consistent with the Act, inflation should remain at a low positive level. And the eventual discarding of money supply targets even from reports to

Congress was consistent with the general over-riding statement that the Federal Reserve deliver a "Monetary Policy Report to the Congress twice a year" outlining its monetary policy).

No Murmur from Congress When Fed Abandons Money Supply Targets

In sum the journey from monetarism to inflation targeting started by Paul Volcker in the mid-1980s and consummated by Greenspan and Bernanke occurred without any pushback from Congress, notwithstanding some legislative blocks which in principle could have arrested the voyage. Some might conclude that checks should be in the constitution rather than legislation, but that is dubious. A general observation: Congress pushes for oversight after monetary calamities. Indeed, Paul Volcker had a rare opportunity to establish a sound money regime after the Greatest Peacetime Inflation, but he squandered it returning to the dollar devaluation policy out of concern (shared with the Administration and its new Treasury Secretary James Baker) about the large US trade deficit.

Why did Congress fail to intervene when Chief Greenspan gave up on monetary control as foreseen in the legislation of 1975–78, abandoning completely money supply targets and moving towards inflation targeting? The simple answer is because at first all seemed to be going well. Even the Nasdaq crash and IT recession of 2001–02 did not provoke much backlash in Congress given the overall shallowness of the 2000–02 recession and the initial apparent successes of the "breathing in inflation policy" of 2003–04.

Yes, Greenspan had his congressional critics by then—whether Ron Paul in the House of Representatives or former baseball pitcher Jim Bunning in the Senate. Both disliked the "maestro" image of monetary conjurer which Greenspan had won for himself and its implicit defiance of rules. Paul was a long-run enthusiast about a return to gold and opponent of the Fed; Senator Bunning had a more intuitive distrust without ideological underpinning. Certainly when he refused to vote for Bernanke's nomination as Fed chief in 2005, it was because he had failed to act as any check on Greenspan since his appointment as governor in 2002; but his main criticism was his failure to vote against any of the rate increases from 2004 to 2005, not that he had promoted a new rigorous inflation-targeting regime (and "breathing in inflation"); and indeed

Greenspan's re-nomination for two years by George W. Bush in 2003 may well have been conditional on his expressing willingness to take inspiration from the Princeton professor.

Senator Bunning had been the only senator to vote against Greenspan's re-appointment as chair in 2003. In his comments in late 2005 to the Senate Banking Committee, he explained his opposition to Bernanke's appointment:

> *Though I believe Dr. Bernanke has the qualifications to be Chairman of the Federal Reserve, I must oppose this nomination. When I met with Dr. Bernanke when he was a nominee to the board of governors of the Federal Reserve, he promised me that he would not be a rubber stamp for Chairman Greenspan but an independent voice who would stand up to the chairman when he believed he was wrong. Sadly, Dr. Bernanke never once cast a dissenting vote.*

Senator Bunning had been a critic of the Fed course of "measured" hikes in short-term interest rates through 2004 and 2005 in order to fight inflation, saying that there was not sufficient inflationary pressure to justify the 11 quarter percentage point hikes since 2003. The basis of criticism was not that policy had been inflationary through 2003–04, igniting in particular virulent asset price inflation. Earlier, Bunning had made frequent critical comments about Greenspan, often speaking out on a wide variety of economic issues beyond monetary policy. Bunning did not specify who he would like to see nominated as Fed chair instead of Bernanke, but he told CNBC "I know there are 20 economists out there who could do the job".

In Congress, criticism of the Bernanke Fed and subsequently the Yellen Fed multiplied and deepened after the 2007–08 panic and into the great recession which followed. The critics on the left of the Democratic Party resented the extent to which the Fed's favouring of deregulation in the previous decade (say from the mid-1990s to the mid-2000s) had contributed to the bubble. Senator Elizabeth Warren, for example, led a revolt from within the party against President Obama's looming nomination of Larry Summers as Fed chair in 2013 largely related to the role he had played as Treasury secretary (and earlier as under-secretary) in financial deregulation. On the right and left, there was much unhappiness with the bailouts of too-big-to-fail banks and other financial institutions. The Republicans widely voted against President Obama's re-nomination of Bernanke in 2009 as Fed chief (objecting in particular to his bailouts of the banks but also to his closeness to the Obama Administration including its economics team); but he won Democratic support in part due to his endorsement of severe new financial regulation (the Dodd-Frank Act).

The expansion of the Fed's balance sheet and its related amassing of mortgage-backed securities and long-maturity Treasuries did stoke resentment within the Republican ranks. But the gathering opposition did not solidify around a fundamental rejection of the 2% inflation standard and all its recent trappings in favour of a new monetary regime. Indeed, the academic experts to which the Republicans turned were for the most part purveyors of the 2% inflation regime albeit opposed to some if not all of the non-conventional tool box which Bernanke and Yellen had imported to the job.

Republicans Fail in Their Opposition to "Obama Fed"

Professor John Taylor, the one-time Treasury under-secretary (for international affairs) in the first George W. Bush Administration, was particularly popular, his advice widely sought by the formulators of monetary reform suggestions or of critiques for present Fed policies. But he was hardly a revolutionary. His neo-Keynesian pedigree was impeccable; he advocated that the Fed strictly plot the path of short-term interest rates through time (no reversion to monetary base control here), albeit that the piloting should be dictated by a set of econometric equations rather than wholly personal judgement. But why would anyone in their right mind trust the predictions of these equations, especially as they were founded on such questionable assumption as "expectation Phillips curve analysis"? And to implement the renowned Taylor rule, the Federal Reserve had to have an inflation target in place and know the so-called natural rate of unemployment, the neutral level of interest rates, and the underlying growth of productive potential.

In the House, Texan Kevin Brady advanced legislation of monetary reform which did not specifically endorse the Taylor rule. But it stuck to endorsing inflation targeting implicitly or explicitly. For example, the draft Sound Dollar Act blueprint, initially published in 2012 (R1174) and re-slated in 2015, proposed replacing the Fed's dual mandate with a single mandate for achieving "price stability" and required the Fed to use inflation targeting to achieve stable prices. The Act also required the Fed to "monitor a broad range of assets – beyond goods and services – including gold and the foreign exchange value of the dollar in order to avoid future asset bubbles".

The idea that the Fed could spot bubbles in advance, or that indeed bubbles should be the focus of Fed attention, was way off the beaten track for those (outside Congress) concerned that the inflation-targeting regime promoted asset price inflations. Asset price inflations do not usually develop into generalized bubbles though there may be one small area of the global asset markets which become manic in each cycle (think of Florida real estate in the mid-1920s, Japan golf clubs in the late 1980s, Iceland in the mid-2000s, and some would say Bitcoin in the late 2010s). And central bankers are certainly not in the lead of those able to recognize areas of mal-investment or over-investment ahead of the crowd, with most realization coming in the late stage of asset price inflation.

Rather than putting forward central bankers as advance spotters of potential mal-investment and bubbles, surely it would be better to keep them to a monetary path under which the build-up of asset price inflation or inflation generally (including goods and services markets) was much less likely or pervasive than under the 2% inflation-targeting regime. But that was not the thought behind the Republican Congress folks and their favoured academic advisors.

Congressman Brady did back a bill (HR 2912) to establish a commission to examine US monetary policy, evaluate alternative monetary regimes, and recommend a course for monetary policy going forward. The tasks of the commission would be, first, to examine how US monetary policy since the creation of the Federal Reserve in 1913 has affected the performance of the US economy and, second, evaluate various operational regimes under which the Federal Reserve may conduct monetary policy in terms of achieving maximum output employment and price stability over the long term including (a) total discretion without an operating regime, (b) price level targeting, (c) inflation rate targeting, (d) nominal GDP targeting. But the Commission could come up with no greater wisdom than its contributors, and it did not seem that the sponsors of the bill had special lines into radical thinkers about sound money.

Audit the Fed

The final strand of Republican action on monetary reform during the post-crisis years was under the umbrella of proposed so-called "audit the Fed" legislation. The idea was that the Fed under Greenspan and particularly Bernanke and subsequently Yellen had broken in important ways from "monetary orthodoxy", providing superficial and often arrogant justification to Congress or anyone else. It was time to make any Fed decision-making open to congressional scrutiny in detail and without restriction. A permanent audit committee should be in place that could go into appraising Fed performance including its multiple mistakes in much greater thoroughness than what was possible in semi-annual testimony of the Fed chair to Congress.

As Alex Pollock wrote (2015), the calls to "audit" the Federal Reserve are not for a narrow, bean-counting review of the institution's financial statements. The audit's goal is more fundamental: to assure that the checks and balances in a democratic government also apply to central bankers. It means figuring out how our elected representatives can effectively oversee unelected monetary "experts". History shows that these so-called experts are prone to destructive inflationary and deflationary blunders and that the Fed's actions over the last century represent the greatest systemic risk of any financial organization in the world. Since the Great Recession ended, the Fed has been in overdrive. It is running an unprecedented giant monetary experiment. This experiment includes years of negative real interest rates, the creation of huge asset price inflation, and the monetization of real estate mortgages and long-term bonds. Should the Fed, or anybody, be allowed to carry out such vast and extremely risky experiments without effective supervision? The correct answer is no.

A big problem though is that the auditors are likely to vociferously disagree with each other, unless they are handpicked all from one school of economic thought, in which case those who stand accused of incompetence or malevolence could repudiate judgement in the court of public opinion on this being a "political trial". And the passage of time does not remove disagreement. A panel made up of renowned economists past and present even today would come to very different judgements about the culpability of Benjamin Strong (and the Fed of the years 1922–28) for the global credit bubble and bust which culminated in the Great Depression. Even so the panel of auditors could agree on whether the Fed under review took careful note of and considered wisely all aspects of weighty decisions (including the launch of monetary experiments) or acted haughtily, with intellectual dishonesty and without due searching out and consideration of alternative viewpoints. The knowledge of such a review process may well make any Fed more cautious and wiser.

A congressional audit panel on the Bernanke/Yellen Fed would ideally reflect a wide spread of intellectual opinion which exists out there. Take, for example, the Atlantic editorial on Bernanke in April 2012. According to the authors, "The left hates him. The right hates him even more. But Ben Bernanke saved the economy – and has navigated masterfully through the most trying of times". A judicious audit panel could shred such a verdict to pieces regardless of differences in "economic school affiliation" between its members.

In particular, the panel would determine that Chair Bernanke made a definite promise at the time of opening his non-conventional tool box. He said that this would transform the usually slow expansion following financial crisis into something much better. But in fact what emerged was the slowest expansion ever from great recession. And the panel could take issue with his and his successors' repeated boasts that their actions had helped bring about the cumulative rise of employment. How could any such judgement be made until at least the end of the present cycle in full knowledge of the extent of financial crisis and mal-investment which emerged at its end?

The hypothetical audit committee's investigation into one main charge against the inflation targeters—the spurring of asset price inflation (and subsequent bust) by the breathing in inflation policy of 2002–05—would likely expose differences of opinion as indeed found in the outside world. For example, at a BIS seminar, Michael Dooley set out to prove that neither easy money policy in the US nor international imbalances were related to the subsequent crisis (2007–08) in any direct or important way. The thrust of the argument was that the Fed could not have kept real interest rates depressed for seven years; something else must have been going on. But the opposite view which he does not consider is that the germs of asset price inflation and their subsequent growth can occur within a very short span. And once asset price inflation disease has progressed beyond a certain point, it is hard to eradicate softly and painlessly—and so it continues on through subsequent phases. At best, within an audit panel, such differences of opinion might be resolved by discussion.

The House members and Senators who appoint the auditors need to consider weightily who they select. Labels such as "conservative economist", or "Fed critic", can be very misleading when it comes to choosing the gifted critic. For example, over the years conservative Republicans have seen the "shadow open market committee" as a good source of potential critics. But in fact this has been dominated by neo-Keynesian economists, many of whom were sympathetic to the experiment of "inflation targeting".

Take, for example, Marvin Goodfriend's paper delivered to the shadow FOMC meeting of May 5, 2017. He writes "In the decades since the Fed under Paul Volcker ended the Great Inflation in the early 1980s, central banks around the world have come to understand that sound monetary policy requires a credible commitment to price stability, which in practice has come to mean an inflation target". In January 2012 the Federal Reserve finally followed the global trend when the FOMC adopted a 2% inflation target in its "Statement of Longer-Run Goals and Monetary Policy Strategy".

Goodfriend as an appointed auditor would give a very different view on how officials had acted during the 20 years or more of the 2% inflation target than an auditor who viewed this experiment in stabilization as a great mistake on similar grounds to as described in the present volume.

A Coalition for Sound Money Reform

The Republican victories in the Congressional and presidential elections in November 2016 could have been the start of a period of monetary reform—with the aim being a journey away from the 2% inflation standard to a sound money alternative. But as we have seen, the Republicans in Congress were not budding reformers with a thoughtful programme ready-made to adopt.

Yes, there were the proposals to audit the Fed, but as we have seen, these were sketchy and likely ineffective in terms of greater purpose, though an improvement on the status quo. Yes, in principle, the Congressional Republicans could have drafted a Federal Reserve Reform Act. But they had only a narrow majority in the Senate, not filibuster proof. So progress would have required some cross-party support. And it would also have been greatly helped by a White House behind the proposals. This was just not the case. Yes, President Trump had said some things late in the campaign about Chair Yellen having created a bubble economy, and there were those campaign ads attacking a conspiracy between the Fed and the Wall Street barons. But all of this turned out to be the work of Chief Strategist Steve Bannon, with no follow-through remotely plausible from President Trump and his chosen Cabinet. And in Congress the Republican critics of the Yellen Fed turned to what they perceived as the much greater aim of tax reform.

In principle the new president could have implemented monetary reform without a new Federal Reserve Act by filling all those chairs around the policy-making table which became empty with like-minded reformers who would assemble around the sound money principle. But that was just not to be. It seems the Fed chair to succeed Janet Yellen was chosen on the strong preference of the Treasury secretary who could imagine a good working relationship between the two. That could provoke a sense of danger amongst those alert to future inflation especially at a time when the Federal budget deficit seemed headed (with tax cuts) to an unparalleled size relative to GDP during an advanced stage of the business cycle. And given that the Administration boasted that the soaring stock market was a measure of its success, it was just not credible that it would back a sound money programme and make choices of officials to ensure that would be implemented.

At the Davos World Economic Forum meeting of late January 2018, US Treasury Secretary Mnuchin indicated some fondness for a weaker dollar which would benefit exporters, albeit stating that in the long run strength of the US economy would be reflected in a stronger dollar. President Trump gave the same message, though showing greater enthusiasm for the ultimate ascent of the currency. There was a conundrum here.

If the Trump Administration policies were fostering an economic renaissance in the US which would make US assets even more attractive to global investors, then the dollar should already be strong. The counterpart to buoyant capital investment in the US and a raised share of foreign investment in the US would be large US current account deficits for many years to come along with a highly priced dollar. Ultimately there could be some fallback as inflows ebbed and payments of profits to non-US owners rose including dividends. The failure of a strong dollar to be evident at this time (in fact, dollar weakness was becoming apparent) tallied with a growing monetary inflation (glacial upward adjustment of official rates was failing to keep pace with a strengthening economy and rising inflation expectations). This inflation remained camouflaged in goods and services markets by digitalization and globalization but was consistent with evermore powerful global asset price inflation.

In the midst of that asset price inflation, any remnant of hard money scrutiny in Congress collapsed. In that same Davos week, President Trump's nominee to head the Fed, Jerome Powell, strongly favoured it seems by the Treasury secretary (who foresaw a good working relationship), an outspoken critic of auditing plans and a long-time Yellen loyalist, gained overwhelming approval in the Senate. Only four Republicans voted against him (Ted Cruz, Marco Rubio, Rand Paul, and Mike Lee). Who could oppose Powell for being a Fed loyalist when the economy was now booming and Wall Street was reaching daily new highs? Indeed some Democrats criticized Powell for being unenthusiastic (though not voting against) about Bernanke's QE policies at one stage in 2012/13. And when in the same week Marvin Goodfriend came in front of a Senate sub-committee considering his nomination as a Fed governor, he was savaged by some Democrat members for disapproving of Bernanke's aggressive monetary experimentation back at the same time (Goodfriend also came under understandable attack from Senator Paul for his recent advocacy of negative interest rates as an anti-recession tool).

There was an easy answer to such criticism of dissenters from Bernanke-ism. If it had not been for the Bernanke-ite and later Yellen monetary experimentation, the US economic re-bound in the aftermath of the great recession would have been much stronger. Prices would have fallen during the recession, and from that lower base, a strong recovery (of prices) would have been expected. And there would not have been the dampener on long-run investment plans by business of a feared eventual crash of inflated asset markets. Nor would there have been the fatal attraction of financial engineering (most of which involved increasing leverage) as a way to boost the profit for shareholders rather than the seeking out of new investment opportunity. The nominees could have pointed out how superficial and misleading it would be to judge the success of recent Fed policies on stock prices now and the latest quarterly growth number when no one could yet know the ultimate costs of the crash and recession to come. In particular, how much mal-investment would be revealed? But in the glow of asset market bubbles, who would have been listening? The 2% inflation-targeting regime sweeps aside common sense criticism whether from Congress or outside during its asset inflation boom phase—another peril.

Jerome Powell, the chief nominated by President Trump to succeed Janet Yellen, did make his way through the Senate, despite some cautious comments he had made on the Bernanke QE programme as a newly arrived governor. He had though a solid reputation as a Yellen loyalist and centrist, winning him some Democratic support; and his previous life as a private equity baron together with his credentials as a Republican card holder and enthusiast of the tax cuts won over the entire Republican caucus in the Senate except for four dissenters. When it came to his first testimony before Congress (the House Financial Services Committee on Tuesday February 27), he presented with great confidence a highly upbeat view of the US economic outlook, strongly influenced by the Republican tax cuts. He did not mention and was not asked by any congressman about the likelihood that his optimism could be misplaced and a growth cycle downturn already have started or be starting (as foreshadowed contemporaneously by some watchers of leading indicators or of monetary aggregates).

Many of the congressmen pleaded with President Trump's nominee to be cautious in taking pre-emptive action against an inflation-target overshoot further down the road as this would mean thwarting hopes that at last in red hot economy wage earners might get a real rise. The obvious response was that monetary inflation could not boost real wages; in fact in the big picture, they were likely to diminish them by exacerbating uncertainty and cramping business investment and long-run risk-taking, the engines of productivity and real wage growth. And none of his questioners held him or more broadly the Fed to account for having been responsible for real wage stagnation via their past conduct of monetary policy (which had fuelled past and present asset inflations and promoted financial leverage rather than investment). The subject of growing monopoly power as a source of poor wage outcomes remained unmentioned, whether by Chief Powell or his questioners.

All of this could understandably spread pessimism amongst those hoping that the US would ultimately make the journey to sound money. If not now, when? The conclusion might well be that the journey will only begin from a starting point of high inflation in goods and services markets, disliked by a broad section of the voting population. But that is not enough. The White House has to be engaged. The officials chosen to steer the monetary system to the new destination have to be committed and able to resist powerfully any backsliding. Unfortunately that was not the case in the last exit from high inflation under Paul Volcker as we have seen (see Chap. 1).

In practical terms the sound money reformers have to find a political party within which they can form palatable coalitions. They can never win an election on monetary reform as the one issue! It may be that the natural allies of the sound money advocates are the anti-trust fighters (against Big Tech, Big Finance). Indeed these forces may get on well together (see Chap. 5); another close fit would also exist with those who would fight for "open government" (full transparency) and libertarian principle. That is all the easy part. The more difficult issues of coalition building involve dealing with advocates of ideas which are partly inimical towards the purpose of the greater good.

The sound money advocates in forming their coalitions must surely indicate how they would prevent foreign countries from exploiting US hard money for their own nationalist purposes—specifically by manipulating their currencies to ostensibly cheap levels. The time for building sound money is too precious to squander on soft dollar devaluation episodes such as accompanied the Great Volcker Retreat of 1985–86 (see Chap. 1). Indeed the sound money advocates should consider the case for outlawing the 2% inflation standard globally once it has collapsed in the US—meaning that excuses for foreign currency devaluation (whether, e.g. Japan or Europe) based on the striving for an inflation goal are just no longer acceptable (in Washington).

The IMF has stood out as an institutional pillar of the global 2% inflation regime. A sound money coalition in Washington would surely review the conditions for funding that institution and should find many allies in Congress for that purpose given the inevitability of continuing difficult budget constraints. As example, the IMF in March 2018 was praising Switzerland for its negative interest and more broadly monetary and exchange rate policies just when that country was already on the warning list drawn up by the US Treasury of foreign currency manipulators. On recent occasions that institution had praised the rampant long- and short-term interest rate manipulation in Europe and Japan, essential conditions of currency manipulation against the dollar. In sum, checks and balances against unsound money should not stop at the US frontier if sound money in the US is to succeed.

Bibliography

Pollock, Alex, J. (2015, March 22). Pollock It's High Time to "Audit" the Federal Reserve. *Wall Street Journal.*
Centennial Monetary Commission Act of 2015 (HR2912).
Dooley, M. (2010, March). *Central Bank Responses to Financial Crises* (BIS Paper No. 51).
Federal Reserve, Transcript of Meeting of the Federal Reserve Open Market Committee. (1996, July 2–3).
Federal Reserve Reform Act 1977 et. Pub.L.95–188, 91 Stat.1387 (1977).
Goodfriend, M *The Fed Needs a Credible Commitment to Price Stability.* E21 Manhattan Institute.
Lowenstein, R. (2012, April). The Villain. *The Atlantic.*
Meltzer, A. (1970–86). *A History of the Federal Reserve, Vol. 2, Book 2.*
Meltzer, A. (2003). *A History of the Federal Reserve, Vol. 1 (1913–51).* University of Chicago.

Pecora Report: The 1934 Report on the Practices of Stock Exchanges from the Pecora Commission (The US Senate Committee on Banking and Currency).

Sound Dollar Act of 2012 (R1174).

Steelman, A. (2012, November). *"The Federal Reserve's Dual Mandate": The Evolution of an Idea* (Federal Reserve Bank of Richmond Economic Brief No. 11–12).

The Financial Crisis Inquiry Report. (2011, February 25). Final Report of the National Commission on the Causes of the Financial and Economic Crisis in the United States.

CHAPTER 6

Digitalization, Camouflage, and Monetary Inflation

The idea that monetary inflation's presence in goods and services markets can be camouflaged from view (at least through the lens of the official statistician) for some considerable time by "real disinflationary" forces is not new to readers of this book. Nor is the idea that such camouflaged monetary inflation in goods and services markets can co-exist with symptoms of already strong monetary inflation in asset markets. And readers should be familiar by now with the follow-on proposition that central bankers who respond with stimulation or accommodation to the semblance (due to camouflage) of no inflation (or "too low inflation") and perhaps deflation in goods and services markets even though the underlying condition is inflationary end up creating much havoc, especially in asset market pricing.

CAMOUFLAGED INFLATION

The notion of camouflage is already well documented in Austrian School literature (see, e.g. Bagus 2000). The real disinflationary forces which might camouflage monetary inflation in goods and services markets include spurts in overall productivity growth, a temporary abundance of some key natural resources, a sprint in globalization, pro-cyclical prices (falling in recession or early recovery stages), and so on. And of course these real disinflationary forces can be interdependent (e.g. globalization might spur productivity growth).

What the "Austrians" had in mind was either the appearance of deflation in goods markets when in fact there was no monetary deflation or the appearance of price stability when in fact monetary inflation was already under way. And in their analysis of the gold standard, Austrians were aware of a causal chain from disinflation (for example a spurt of productivity growth) to monetary inflation. Most importantly, they focused on the disinflationary forces that could mean growing present and prospective profits in the gold mining industry. This would induce a slow increase in gold money supply, and so some degree of monetary inflation could ensue, albeit camouflaged in goods and services markets.

Arguably a new type of disinflationary force to emerge in the last one or two episodes of asset price inflation (and related overall monetary inflation) has been the "price-transparency effects" of digitalization. Quantitative estimates of digitalization and its progress through this period are beset with measurement issues. An estimate in a recent working paper of the Bureau of Economic Analysis (see Barefoot et al. 2018) finds that the digital economy in the US (in terms of real value added) grew at 5.6% p.a. from 2006 to 2016, outpacing the average annual rate of growth for the overall US economy of 1.5%, and at the end, it accounted for 6.2% of current dollar gross output. But the point here is not the size of the digital economy but the impact of its expansion on the natural rhythm of prices.

The idea is that digitalization makes price comparison and discovery easier both for households and businesses. This is the basis of the concept of "star firm" now popular in the economics literature (see Autor 2017). The most efficient firm in each sector has an enhanced potential to gain market share and at a level of profit margins which is superior to that of its competitors. It is possible the star firm narrative is flawed, though it has stimulated many of the equity market bulls; the high profits of the star firm and impressive earnings per share growth could reflect in significant part the feats of financial engineering.

These feats include the huge inflation tax revenues in the form of interest rate and credit spread suppression which the equity owners collect from the debt holders; the hunt for these revenues spurs an increase in leverage, which might be disguised during the boom phase of asset inflation by the ascent of equity valuations (meaning that debt-equity ratios calculated at market value might actually fall despite vast substitution of debt for equity). There is all the hype about massive equity buy-back programs (especially relevant to large capitalization firms); yet these contain no magic to boost the overall investment opportunities (present and future) of the firm from a fundamental perspective except in so far as a shrinking of cash hoards disciplines management. Equity buy-backs do indeed boost accounting measures of the rate of return on equity capital;

but in so far as this rise reflects an increase of leverage (or a fall in negative leverage which is the case for a firm reducing huge cash holdings which dwarf any debt outstanding), that does not justify a corresponding rise in its equity price or diagnosis of star firm status.

Financial engineers are in strong demand during asset inflations, applying their art of how to camouflage leverage as the source of present and future earnings per share growth. Rational investors (less dominant at such times) would not pay anything for this boost if apparent as they could achieve the same on their own by reducing the share of safe assets in their individual portfolios or increasing the leverage of these. More generally there are the profits to consider from firms participating in the booming carry trades, whether in credit, term risk, illiquidity, or currency risk. The so-called star firms might enjoy an especially low cost of equity capital due to their inclusion in big cap stock indices (such as the S&P 500) and the fantastic "passive" demand for ETFs tracking these at a time of asset inflation (reflecting "hunt for yield" or "irrational exuberance"); in turn that low cost of capital whilst it lasts bestows quasi monopoly power. But let's leave that critique to one side at this point and continue with the star firm story.

The most efficient firms/providers scoop up more of the market than previously. Their profitability was likely at the high end of the range to start with—and so their expansion means higher profit rates across the industry sector as a whole. Increased market power for the most efficient firm also likely means that its profit margins increase. These star firms with amplified power might not come under market pressure to lift wages and salaries except for human capital which itself has star quality (or some particular attachment to the star firm); and it may be able to cut wages due to increased negotiating power vis-à-vis labour which comes from increased scope to find alternative lower cost alternatives and the attractiveness (from labour's viewpoint) of jobs at the star firm. The range of less efficient suppliers (and this may include quality and service provided) have to cut costs to remain in business, and this may involve cutting wages and other input prices.

The overall effect of all this is some downward movement of goods and services prices—and this may well occur without any visible spurt in productivity growth. The growth in profit margins is consistent with the emergence of star firms, and the winner takes all both with some degree of enhanced monopoly power. And correspondingly there is some downward pressure on wages overall. Globalization fits together with this story, as digitalization increases the transparency of prices internationally. Again, globalization might not show up as a productivity spurt, though there should be some gains from increased potential for trade based on comparative advantage.

In sum a plausible unique aspect of monetary inflation's camouflage in the most recent cycle has been the growing transparency of price comparison rather than a spurt in productivity that would go along with the general lack of evidence about booming prosperity; indeed, there is widespread disappointment at painfully small increases if any in economic welfare levels. The disappointment may have been made worse by the extent to which long-gestation capital spending has been curbed by monetary uncertainty (concerns that asset price inflation will turn to deflation before the projects reach fruition), meaning that productivity growth has been curtailed.

Under a regime of sound money, crumbling prices due to increased scope for price comparison and emergence of star firms would have been accompanied by a dip in reported prices of goods and services. It would not have been the trigger to a dose of monetary inflation which would result in the appearance of stable prices or stable low inflation in goods markets which in fact was a camouflaged monetary inflation. Real interest rates should not obviously be lower as a consequence of disinflation wrought by empowered price discovery under globalization. Perhaps at the short end of the maturity distribution, nominal interest rates would be lower than otherwise—in line with unchanged real rates. The overall fall in prices would be seen as consistent with a natural rhythm of prices under sound money. And in the future at some point, these disinflationary forces would lose momentum, and price declines would stop. After all, the scope for increased price comparison and related competition would surely have a natural exhaustion limit, though no one would know precisely when.

Digitalization Revolution Enables the Monetary Inflationist

In fact we could conjecture that the digitalization revolution has been a catalyst for money to become a monkey wrench in the present cycle, borrowing the phrase from J.S. Mill made famous by Milton Friedman (see Friedman 2005)—"most of the time the machinery of money is unimportant but when it gets out of control it becomes a monkey wrench in all the other economic machinery".

Digitalization, by setting off a wave of price transparency and globalization, has camouflaged monetary inflation in the goods and services markets. Hence central banks have been able to continue a wild experiment with their non-conventional tool box in the pursuance of their aim of 2% inflation (and perhaps also a group of other aims, not always disclosed, including "doing whatever it takes to save monetary union", "helping the leveraged home-owner especially those entering the house market for the first time", "providing cheap finance for the government so as to avoid cut-backs in costly programs"). The big visible effects remain restricted so far to asset markets and these enjoy considerable popularity.

Under a "monetarist" or "gold standard" regime, this would not have been the monetary outcome. Yes, the drift down in prices and possibly wages would have meant some downward shift in the growth of demand for monetary base in nominal terms. But nominal interest rates would also have been somewhat lower than normal (corresponding to an unchanged real interest rate) given near-term price forecasts, and demand for monetary base is higher at a lower level of rates. (In technical terms, the neutral level of rates could have fallen in nominal terms but been unchanged in real terms.) And so an unchanged pace of monetary base expansion would not have fed monetary inflation (especially evident as explained above in the asset markets). That conclusion would be reinforced if the "constitutional rules" determining monetary base growth under a monetarist regime took the natural rhythm of prices into account—not necessarily a good practice given the pitfalls of discretionary monetary management.

A conduit essential to the spread of asset price inflation—the telling of speculative narratives which pierce through investors' outer wall of rational scepticism—has gained strength from a coincidental aspect of digitalization. "Big Tech" (meaning in particular GAFA—Google, Amazon, Facebook, Apple) has had a uniquely captivating narrative matched by a tremendous power to spin the story.

Capital investment, fuelled by the narrative, has in turn pushed out further the economic potential of digitalization, extending the camouflage of monetary inflation in goods and services markets. Yet in all of this, it remains likely that the overall gains in prosperity will fall far short of those in previous "technological revolutions" (see Gordon 2016).

We won't know until the end of this cycle how much mal-investment has occurred under the great monetary inflation which started in 2010. We may already suspect, though, that some considerable part of this will be in "Big Tech" and related fields. Any final reckoning should include wider political and socio-economic damage not included in a narrow economic calculus.

Scott Galloway (2017) describes skilfully and colourfully the power of the Big Tech narrative. The general critic would take issue with his repeated use of a four-letter expletive. The monetary critic can point to a bigger problem—a lack of any analysis linking the amazing spread of the Big Tech narrative to the prevailing monetary disorder.

If central banks had not created a famine of interest income, the Big Four would surely not have enthralled investor audiences to anything like the actual extent. Hunt for yield means that investors become willing to take on bad bets (featuring an actuarial value highly negative but some possibility of a big pay-off) rather than suffer certain loss on monetary assets. This is an example of "loss aversion" as diagnosed in the pioneering work on mental flaws of investors by Daniel Kahneman and now prominent in behavioural finance theory.

Speculative Narratives Justify Bad Bets

A hypothesis not yet explored in that literature (behavioural finance), but which seems to fit the spread of asset price inflation in present and several previous episodes (in fact of depression-type asset inflation as distinguished in Chap. 3), is that investors do not like to admit to themselves that they are taking on bad bets in their desperate effort to avoid the certain negative real outcomes from "safe assets" under conditions of monetary inflation. They turn bad into good by awarding irrationally high probability of truth to speculative stories which accompany the wagers. The positive feedback loops from initial capital gains add to their complacency with the metamorphosis.

Galloway (2017) identifies the success of the Big Four in being able to attract cheap capital by articulating a bold vision that is easy to understand. This book does not include monetary analysis, but the visions can be fitted into the diagnosis of asset price inflation as described in this volume. These visions are the speculative narratives.

For Amazon, the story is earth's biggest store: the strategy—huge investment in consumer benefits that stand the test of time—lower cost, greater selection, and faster delivery. Google's vision is organizing the world's information. Based on that strategy—with its compelling reason for investors to buy its stock—Google has more money to invest in engineers than any media company in history. Facebook's vision: connecting the world. Strategy: similar to Google, it too can place more bets and offer more generous parental leave, hire buses that transport you to work, turn the roof of your office building into a park, and devote yourself to a seemingly significant contribution to the species—connecting the world.

As Galloway puts it:

The strength of visionary capital begets competitive strength. Why? Because you can more patiently nurture assets and place more bets on more pockets of innovations. Of course, you ultimately have to show shareholders tangible progress against your big vision. However, if you are able to make the jump to light speed and the market crowns you the innovator, the reward is an inflated valuation – and the self-fulfilling prophecy that comes from cheap capital. The ultimate gift in our digital age is a CEO who has the storytelling talent to capture the imagination of the markets while surrounding themselves with people who can show incremental progress against that vision each day.

Galloway hints here at the "messianic" nature of some of the storytelling in the speculative narratives. We have the CEO and founder who the markets crown as King Midas—everything he or she touches will turn to gold, or at least that is what investors seem to believe as speculative temperatures climb; and they are patient, even if no gold today, their messianic belief spells confidence in gold tomorrow.

All the storytelling cannot hide the fact that the digital revolution has not delivered the general increase in prosperity associated with some previous technological revolutions. The stories have been captivating, told by narrators who find unusually credulous audiences given that monetary disorder and hunt for yield (derived from that) have dulled normal scepticism. The contrarian spirit cannot help noticing that living standards have been stagnant or falling except at the top (including especially those working in the Big Four). The suspicion grows that the fantastic wealth generated for the shareholders of Big Tech depend on a tale of growing monopoly power alongside the visible transformational effects which are not in themselves bound to be the source of productivity miracle. And another tale sometimes lurks behind the glamour of the main speculative narrative—crony capitalism.

For obvious reasons, the Big Four themselves are not instrumental in spreading a tale of monopoly rents present or future. But one does not have to look far in the popular media to find this story line. For example, a popular equity market narrative for Facebook and Google has been the scope for huge and growing monopoly rent as domination grows over advertising. In turn businesses find themselves trapped into higher advertising outlays.

The figures are something like this. In the US economy, advertising revenues could rise from 1% of GDP in 2017 to 1.8% by the mid-2020s (since 1980 the average has been 1.3%). Tech platforms have done a brilliant job of persuading smaller companies to spend money targeting customers. Adverts could become even more effective at identifying potential customers and enticing them to spend money, using troves of data that have been gathered to anticipate their needs. To some extent, as commerce shifts online, firms will cut back on conventional marketing. Facebook and Google are able to extract monopoly rent for the adverts (and in the case of Google, we see this in the auctioning off of top spaces next to key search words).

There are grounds for scepticism about this particular narrative which are easily ignored in the glow of the fantastic valuations prevalent under asset price inflation conditions. For example, if businesses in aggregate are paying a growing monopoly rent to Facebook and Google, perhaps eventually of the order of 1% of GDP, that is likely to get passed on to consumers. And so even on the so-called consumer test, there would be ever-stronger grounds for anti-trust action. More generally, there is the likelihood that consumers would become advert resistant, growingly annoyed at the manipulations and interference with their internet and social media experiences, meaning that alternative ways to achieving these should be able to make competitive gains (using breakthrough technology in some occasions). There is the scope for ad-blocking technology to become more powerful and commercially available. Ultimately there might be such popular revulsion against the abuses of data privacy that new technology based on the block chain described as sovereign identity systems to become commercially viable and indeed successful, thereby removing the basis of monopoly power in this instance of the social media platforms.

The scope for Facebook and Google to earn their vast advertising revenues turns on there being no regulatory or legal assault on these companies as regards their use or misuse of private data. And in looking for friends in their fight against these potential or actual threats, Facebook and Google may realize that they have none. Yes, many businesses may comment publicly that they rely on these Big Tech companies' algorithms and privacy "intrusions" to reach customers for their products and services. But in aggregate, in many cases, this is a large negative sum game. The advertising companies have to penetrate these platform audiences for self-defence purposes—to prevent inroads into their market share by competitors. But as they all seek to compete in the new highlighted important psychological moments of each consumer's choice, they don't win additional business overall (aggregated across all platforms and the world outside these).

Yes the digital platforms may become very effective at mounting "shows" in which competitors present their wares (and services) in innovatory ways (using the expertise of the ad agencies), and a rising share of final purchases may derive from these shows, and the sellers cannot afford to be absent from these shows, whether arranged individually with consumers at their most vulnerable psychological moment or in aggregate, but the total business, including show and non-show derivation, does not rise. And it is dubious whether consumers themselves are better informed or able to make wiser decisions, compared to what would happen if the advertising dollars were spread more widely and less in total, and less sensitive to potentially fraudulent or misrepresented claims about viewers' attention.

A great majority of the sellers and the viewers might well sigh in relief at events which would roll back the power of Facebook and Google to collect advertising monopoly rent—and they would not join those companies at all in resisting a legislative and regulatory assault. Yes, the consumers of Facebook and Google might like their free use—but this would surely continue even under scenarios where legislative reform slashed monopoly or duopoly rents for the platform owners (by restricting abuse of private data and reinforcing the anti-trust authorities). And yes, there may be a minority of sellers in a highly heterogeneous universe, who really do gain from the advertising potential of the Big Tech platforms run by Google and Facebook in particular even when they consider their total sales including those outside the platforms (including bricks and mortar); the ads they are able to show globally at selected show times, which suit and are tailored to each category of individual, may be strikingly successful, especially if there are no close substitutes of competitors featuring (as would be the case if there are no close substitutes and competitors!) and if they were poorly placed to gain benefit from the traditional media. Their benefits are ultimately paid for by others.

The speculation on monopoly rent goes beyond Facebook and Google, even though no public face of the asset management industry would admit so much to the media! Just as many of the depositors in a Ponzi scheme may secretly suspect what is happening, so it is with giant profits from possible monopoly abuse. The astute may be calculating on monopoly rents and monopoly abuse growing but would not admit that this is the case. Stelzer (2018) writes:

> *Amazon has the means and the incentive to strangle competitors in the cradle. – One sign that we might be dealing with a firm intent on distorting competition by creating barriers to entry is the practice of pre-announcement. A newcomer appears and offers a better mousetrap. It shows signs of winning a place in the hearts and purses of consumers and being able to raise capital to enable it to become a competitor of the dominant incumbent in one of these*

markets. So the dominant firm announces that it, too, is planning to enter that market, perhaps not tomorrow, but soon enough to persuade venture capitalists and other investors that they do not want to risk money on the newcomer. Absent careful investigation of the facts (by a team from the anti-trust division of the Justice Department, perhaps), it is impossible to know whether Amazon has deployed just such a tactic on occasion.

We have re-learnt in this cycle that the speculative narratives which spread asset price inflation under conditions of overall monetary inflation do not always depend on a surge of prosperity and productivity. Instead they can thrive on a transformative re-organization of lifestyles which provokes much buss and excitement together with the hushed promise of vast monopoly profits. Alongside this may be the actual or potential riches from deals with Big Government. During the hot phases of asset price inflation, the vulnerability of future or present profits from monopoly and Big Government deals to political backlash is seriously under-weighted in valuations, typical of the irrational suppression of healthy scepticism at such times.

In the case of Amazon, a main background story of Big Government "working together" not found in the main speculative narrative but nonetheless out there was the alleged sweetheart deal with the United States Postal Service (USPS) arranged under the Obama Administration. Critics (see Sandbite 2017) argued that this "last delivery mile" was in effect a huge present for Amazon—a gift token of $1.46 per delivery. Amazon apologists argue that there was no gift—and that the company indeed made substantial contributions towards overall costs which the USPS would bear in any case towards carrying out its mandate (six days' delivery to every postal code throughout the US).

The counter to this "apology" was that without this contribution, the USPS would long have succumbed to a politically induced earthquake of reform; huge losses over a decade related in part to privileged position of the Postal Union would have left no option, even given its friends in Congress, to root-and-branch changes, including reduced mandate (perhaps only two-days-a-week delivery), a combatting of postal union power and privileges, and so on. Amazon's deal allowed a highly loss-making status quo to persist (otherwise the losses would have been much greater), and the company gained for itself a subsidy advantage compared to its rivals whether online or bricks and mortar. Critics saw Amazon pursuing a similar "free rider" strategy of gaining competitive advantage thanks to the public sector in its launching a competition for cities to bid for a package of privileges in return for its building a new giant headquarters there.

Outside its Big Government deals, another side narrative to the main glittering narrative in the equity market concerning Amazon and its founder CEO was the cooperation with Big Finance. Yes, there was much media comment (positive) about how Amazon and the biggest bank working together on health care could spark a "revolution" akin to what this company had brought in the retail sector, and equity investors seemed to believe again in the Midas touch here. But a more mundane and less glittering story was the common interest of both (Amazon and Big Bank) in disadvantaging cash payments and promoting payments by bank cards. As discussed in a subsequent chapter, a key component of online retail business success is that payment by cash (not possible in the online space) should not bring the advantage in transaction costs which underlying economics would merit. Also key is the containment of charges which the card supplier takes from the merchant (in this case Amazon), and one could imagine how Big Bank and Amazon cooperation might bring advantage here. Amazon and the Big Banks might gain in their own ways from forming a common front in the "war on cash" (see Chap. 10), but the sceptical equity investor would be justifiably cautious about extrapolating vast profits from this cooperation into the long-run future.

The monopoly theme in the Amazon story extends to other chapters, including such vexed (and disputed by legal experts) issue as to how the largest capitalization smartphone maker and the biggest internet search engine formed an alliance in which the latter pays the former a fee to be the default setting (and so huge advantage for promoting the size of its advertising audience). Yet against the background of monetary inflation, the large grounds for scepticism about the speculative narrative for Big Tech remain in a semi-state of repression. Even so, the sceptical narratives can break out unexpectedly, most likely when the course of events give them a boost.

As we have seen, the dazzle of the narratives depends in part on the extent to which the Big Four have dominated re-organization of our everyday environment—internet search rather than encyclopaedias and library visits, instant messaging rather than fax, groceries within a two-hour time slot to one's door rather than driving to the store, trading firms getting the latest information in fractions of a second rather than several seconds. The unattractive downsides of the re-organization have not yet dimmed the sparkle, at least in frothy financial markets—whether hacking, the empowerment of Big Brother, the abuse of private data (and in particular scant regard to promises that this will be "safeguarded"), the "commoditization" of broad swathes of human capital, or the aggravated ability of employers to monitor, control, and exploit employees especially in the context of enhanced monopoly power.

The long history of asset inflations, going all the way to the Great Dutch Monetary Inflation of the 1630s, includes many instances of monopoly narratives. These ignore the factor of monopoly mortality, whatever the cause. Indeed the Great Dutch Monetary Inflation of the early to mid-seventy-seventh century featured a virtually synchronous bubble in tulip bulbs and in the stock of the Dutch East India Company (the latter had monopoly rights bestowed by the Dutch state regarding trade; the expanding frontier of its operations fascinated investors who turned a blind eye to tales of abuse including slavery) both peaking and then collapsing in 1637 (see French 2006, for a history of the Great Dutch Monetary Inflation which spanned also high inflation in goods markets and was driven by the Bank of Amsterdam's innovation of in effect deposit banking and free gold coinage).

The excitement about monopoly power and the downward rhythm of goods prices in the present inflation might turn out to be much more transitory than many imagine contemporaneously in the marketplaces. A technological revolution which increases transparency and lowers information costs has a once and for all downward influence on prices and wages although spread over some years; this is consistent with increased profits in the star firms. The disinflationary forces as described are self-limiting in time and scope. As they wane, and as monetary disorder grows, the camouflage of inflation in the goods and services markets wears thin. Meanwhile the speculative narratives grow tawdry amidst tales of abusive monopoly and consumer revulsion. We could find that reported goods inflation climbs just as asset price inflation moves on to its final stage.

THE DIGITALIZATION REVOLUTION AND THE NEUTRAL RATE OF INTEREST

The apparent difficulty of central banks in meeting the 2% inflation target (from below) in recent years has made many commentators and the official themselves conclude that the neutral interest rate level in this cycle has fallen to abnormally low levels. Implicitly, according to the commentators, the neutral rate of interest is that at which inflation would stay around target level. But suppose the natural rhythm of prices is downwards for some years—whether due to a spurt of productivity, globalization, digitalization, or some combination of the three. Then keeping to a steady state, 2% inflation would be inconsistent with sound money and financial stability (the two are of course related!). No one knows the neutral level and estimation are treacherous. If in fact it were unchanged in real terms, then it is possible that for short maturities the neutral rate could dip in line with the downward rhythm of prices (and under sound money that would not be resisted by the monetary authority or monetary rules in place).

One argument was that digitalization had fuelled the growth of profits (monopoly) in the economy and so brought increased inequality in income distribution. And rich people save more than less, savings surpluses had tended to increase. Moreover, the costs of capital investment had typically been falling as the key focus had shifted to IT equipment from heavy machinery. But surely if monetary uncertainty had not been so great (including widespread unease that the end of asset price inflation would be another crash and great recession), there would have been more buoyant capital spending generally in line with investment opportunity meaning that the neutral rate might even be higher than usual.

Another argument for lower-than-usual interest rates (but not the neutral level of these) was that better measurement of inflation meant that inflation on its old definitions had been overstated. Hence if the target for inflation was 2% according to new and better measurement, there was some scope meanwhile for inflation according to its older measurement to accelerate above 2%. Suppose the overstatement of inflation according to the old definitions had been around 0.5% p.a., meaning that 2% was actually 1.5%. Then it would be appropriate for monetary policy to be easy for some time (with rates below long-run neutral), so that inflation would accelerate to a steady-state path of 2% p.a. on its new definition from say 1.5% p.a. on the old. Yes, that controlled acceleration could mean some period of asset price inflation, but so be it.

There has been a collection of papers about such measurement issues during the present cycle. (A good summary is found in Groschen et al. 2017). A related sub-theme has been that the official economic data have understated real productivity and economic growth due to measurement issues related to offshore profit shifting (see Guvenen et al. 2017); in principle these would point to a higher than normally estimated neutral level of interest rates in real terms though not in nominal terms.

There have also been opinion pieces such as Gavyn Davies (2017). This economist was referring to a run of inflation data in the US in spring 2017 which had come somewhat lower than expected, most likely due to measurement improvements by the Bureau of Labor Statistics (BLS). The argument in this opinion piece was that new technology had led to official statistics under the old definition being overstated to a greater degree than had been the case historically. The BLS had belatedly made some changes to its methods of calculation, and so the reported inflation rate was now likely somewhat lower; if it had been correctly measured all along, it would have been unchanged at that now perceived rate. Rather than accepting the new lowered reported inflation rate as the new target, Davies argued that the Fed should ease policy so that inflation on the new definition would catch up with the old. That is what happened. The fall in inflation through the middle months of 2017 triggered a pull-back in the Yellen Fed's programmed series of mini-rate rises. In itself missing one 25 bp rate hike was trivial, but it was enough to indicate policy normalization was even more bogus than previously assumed. No wonder speculative temperatures across many asset markets rose, helped by the new speculative narratives of "coordinated global economic recovery" and a "big business corporate tax cut in the US".

The strongest counterargument (not mentioned by Gavyn Davies) to the view that monetary conditions should be eased in response to the dip in reported inflation was that the Federal Reserve should not be fighting the natural downward rhythm of prices, but should accept it. Fighting would mean the inflicting of an even more serious asset price inflation disease.

Around this time, Martin Feldstein (2017) made an important intervention into the policy debate, with the publication of his article in the *Journal of Economic Perspectives*. Feldstein maintained that despite the attention to this subject over many years (including the Stigler Commission 161, the Boskin Commission 1996, and Schultze Commission 2002):

> *I have concluded that despite the various improvements to statistical methods that have been made through the years, the official data understate the changes of real output and productivity. The measurement problem has become increasingly difficult with the rising share of services that has grown from about 50% of private sector GDP in 1950 to about 70 % of private GDP now. – In considering these issues, I have been struck by the difference between the official statistics about economic growth and how people judge whether their own economic condition has improved. Whereas the real income of the median household according to the official data did not rise at all between 1995 and 2013, a Federal Reserve survey (2014) of household attitudes reported that two-thirds thought they were doing as well or better than they had been five year earlier and that they were either living comfortably or doing ok.*

The critic could make the point here that the survey of 2014 was picking up only the fact that households felt better now (2014) than during the dark days of the Great Panic and Great Recession (2008–09/10). At any rate, Feldstein makes the following conclusion relevant to monetary policy.

First, "The evidence that the true inflation rate is less than the measured inflation rate may imply that the true inflation rate is now less than zero. Moreover, the real rate of interest is higher than the conventionally measured one".

That is true, but if has always been so. Under the gold standard pre-1914, for example, official index or private index calculations made no allowance for product improvement which was very considerable (trains rather than horses, public sanitation, etc.). And so, a 2% nominal interest rate would be high in real terms if we used today's widely practiced hedonic price accounting. We cannot conclude that real rates under the gold standard were typically "too high"; after all it included two decades of rapid growth (the gilded ages of the 1870s and 1880s) when prices even according to non-adjusted data were falling—and over the very long run, prices returned to a constant mean.

Second,

uncertainty about the true rate of inflation should affect the optimal monetary policy. There seems little point in having a precise inflation target when the true rate of inflation is measured with a great deal of uncertainty. The goal of price stability also takes on a new meaning if true inflation is substantially negative while measured inflation is low but positive. Would it be better to have a target range for measured inflation as the Federal Reserve does now? Or to have a target range for measured inflation that is higher and further from the zero bound, thus leaving more room for larger changes in nominal interest rates while recognizing that the actual inflation rate is lower than the officially measured one? Or to restate the inflation goal of monetary policy as reacting when there is a rapid movement in measured inflation either up or down?

In the last few years the perception of slow real growth is often mentioned in support of a Federal Reserve policy of exceptionally low interest rates, but if real growth rates are actually higher (or if real growth rates have not dipped as much as the official statistics seem to show), then the Fed's policy of ultra-low interest rates has been providing little gain while contributing to certain risks of potential financial instability.

How to respond to this second group of points raised by Feldstein in the light of the earlier content of this chapter?

The argument against precise inflation target because no one knows the true underlying rate if "correctly" measured has been around a long time and is not the strongest argument against inflation targeting. It is nonetheless an argument which most people would not refute.

Should the inflation target be say 3% p.a., if the extent of bias is established at around 1% p.a. because that would give more scope for central banks to pursue stimulatory policies in recession? The short answer is no. Pro-cyclical price fluctuations are the way in which capitalist economies move from recession to recovery and from boom to cyclical downturn under sound money regimes. Giving even more scope to central banks to pursue wild monetary experimentation with non-conventional policy tools to meet inflation targets with all the problem of asset price inflation is surely not advisable. Moreover, it is surely questionable whether, in an economic slowdown or recession, market expectations would remain in line with the 3% p.a. target; or would there be widespread scepticism that the target would be met any time soon given a powerful natural rhythm of prices downwards?

The idea of having central banks respond to sudden spurts of inflation or sudden falls smacks of the fine-tuning which has been so harmful through the more than a century more of Federal Reserve history.

Finally, if indeed the underlying economic condition of the past decade or more has been rapid growth in productivity and prosperity (though this has been disguised by poor data), then yes market-determined interest rates in real terms under a sound money regime would have been far above those set by the inflation-targeting central banks on the basis of defective data (for real GDP, productivity, and prices). And the divergence has been the source of powerful inflation, so far apparent in asset markets rather than goods markets, where camouflage has been due not just to a natural rhythm of prices downwards but also the defective statistical reporting.

The Camouflaged Monetary Inflation Boost of 2016–17

Let's review the crucial last two years of the Yellen Federal Reserve (2016–17) in light of the analysis above.

The Federal Reserve drove monetary policy into a new stronger inflation zone during this period. But the monetary inflation was even more heavily camouflaged than before in the goods and services markets, meaning that the visible (increasing) effect of the giant monetary disorder was still largely in the asset markets; and "visible" did not mean apparent to all, as there is much disagreement between the experts about the meaning and symptoms of asset price inflation.

The 3% p.a. quarterly growth of the US economy from spring 2017 and through the rest of that year, about which the Trump Administration crowed, may in fact have had most to do with the strengthening of monetary stimulus through 2016–17.

As Milton Friedman observed long ago, rising nominal interest rates do not mean that monetary conditions are tightening. The reverse may be true. Yes, the Yellen Fed had made three tiny rate rises over two years, but if economic conditions have been strengthening and the unknown neutral level of rates rising in line, a gradual token nominal official rate rise may be increasingly "behind the curve".

In fact, there have been two stages of the Fed's journey into increasingly inflationary monetary policy during 2016–17.

The first was its reaction to the downturn in global equity markets through late 2015 and early 2016 in response to the "China shock". This was a classic Greenspan put operation (directly traceable back to the Benjamin Strong Fed in 1927) in which the Fed walked back from a planned series of official rate rises so as to provide a "coup de whiskey" to a seemingly sick stock market. On this occasion, it succeeded, not least due to the accompanying journey of the ECB and Bank of Japan (BoJ) and Chinese authorities into radical monetary-easing measures.

By early 2017 it might have been thought that the dose of whisky had been sufficient and the Yellen Fed would be pulling back from its previous year's implemented policy of monetary inflation overdrive. But that was not to be the case.

The progress of the digitalization revolution together with further changes in how the official statistics office calculates inflation (reforms which take account of product improvement in service area) meant that the official inflation data started to seriously undershoot the Fed's official target (and the same was true in some degree in Europe and Japan). And so, the Fed (and foreign central banks) shuffled and postponed their so-called normalization programmes. The result: a further coup de whiskey to asset price inflation globally.

Note that under a "sound money regime", monetary conditions would not ease in response to a digitalization revolution which puts downward pressure on prices and some wages, nor to a belated change in calculation methods by official statisticians. Instead, prices would fall without meeting brittle monetary resistance. Nominal interest rates, though weighed down by soft price expectations, would in general reflect a healthy positive real equivalent. In technical terms, the demand for monetary base may be largely unchanged; yes, falling prices and falling nominal wages may reduce demand by low-income households, but there are likely to be compensating shifts by households at the top end of the income spectrum and from the corporate sector in part explained by lower nominal (but not real) interest rates. Hence if the supply of monetary base continues on an unchanged path, there is no trigger in the process outlined to monetary inflation (which would be most visible in the asset markets).

There may be a modest fall of medium-term and short-term rates in nominal terms to reflect less likelihood of price rises for some considerable period ahead, but real rates would not be affected (note that the change in official calculating methods would have zero effect on nominal or real rates unless the changes brought new information to market participants about underlying inflation correctly measured which they did not know already—which is highly unlikely).

In the bizarre and destabilizing world of the global 2% inflation standard, the outcome has been quite different.

The assumption becomes that the central banks will ease policy—meaning lower real rates than otherwise in the short and medium term—in response to any setback on the road to getting inflation back to 2% (from territory below). The consequences may well be a further intensification of asset inflation such as we witnessed through 2017. Under these circumstances, the rise in gold prices ($1280–1350 per ounce in the first half of 2018 compared to 1040 at the start of 2016 and 1180 at the start of 2017) made sense. The rise was in line with intensified monetary inflation (even though camouflaged in goods and services markets as detailed earlier) reflecting the Yellen Put (in response to the stock market setback of late 2015 and early 2016) and the Fed's caution to move boldly beyond this. There was also the ultimate break-out danger for goods and services inflation in the long-run future.

As regards the long-maturity government bond markets under these circumstances, appraisal should take account of the strong forces of irrationality (yield-seeking behaviour) as nourished by the monetary disorder, especially negative rates in Europe and Japan.

In broad terms, the dominant expectation was that central banks would pursue their nominal interest rate repression policies for many more years as visible inflation in goods and services markets stayed "contained". Containment would come from the camouflages of digitalization and official methodology updates (statistical). Meanwhile monetary uncertainty (in particular when will all the bubbles ultimately burst) would hold back long-term capital spending, so a sustained economic boom would not emerge.

Bibliography

Autor, D. (2017, May 1). *The Fall of the Labor Share and the Rise of Superstar Firms.* NBER.
Bagus. (2000). Deflation: When Austrians Become Interventionists. *Quarterly Journal of Austrian Economics, 6*(4), 19–35.
Barefoot, K., et al. (2018, March 15). *Defining and Measuring the Digital Economy* (US Bureau of Economic Analysis Working Paper).
Davies, G. (2017, May 26). The Fed's Lowflation Dilemma. *Financial Times.*
Feldstein, M. (2017). Underestimating the Real Growth of GDP, Personal Income and Productivity. *Journal of Economic Perspectives, 31*(2), 145–164.
French, D. (2006). The Dutch Monetary Environment During Tulipmania. *Quarterly Journal of Austrian Economics, 9*(1), 3–14.
Friedman, M. (2005). *The Optimum Quantity of Money.* Piscataway: Transaction Publishers.
Galloway, S. (2017). *The Four: The Hidden DNA of Amazon, Apple, Facebook and Google.* New York: Random House.
Gordon, R. J. (2016). *The Rise and Fall of American Growth: The US Standard of Living Since the Civil War.* Princeton: Princeton University Press.
Groschen, E. L., Moyer, B. C., Aizcorbe, A. M., Bradley, R., & Friedman, D. M. (2017). How Government Statistics Adjust for Potential Biases from Quality Change in an Age of Digital Technologies; a View from the Trenches. *Journal of Economic Perspectives, 31*(2), 187–210.
Guvenen, F., Raymond, J. M., Jr., Rassler, D. G., & Ruhl, M. J. (2017). *Offshore Profit Shifting and Domestic Productivity Measurement.* Cambridge, MA: National Bureau of Economic Research.
Sandbite, J. (2017, July 13). Shy the Post Office Gives Amazon Special Delivery. *Wall Street Journal.*
Stelzer, I. M. (2018, January 26). A High-Stakes Game of Monopoly. *Weekly Standard.*

CHAPTER 7

Much Ruin in Japan's Journey to 2%

Adam Smith's famous caution against pessimism based on a perceived national setback (in this case a military defeat of Britain in the American Revolutionary War) that "there is a great deal of ruin in a nation" has much relevance to Japan. Despite all the misfortunes of the path to 2% inflation on which the Bank of Japan and its political masters set their nation, it remains wealthy and, if measured correctly (taking account of the falling population especially of aggregate hours worked), boasts an economic growth record in the past two decades which is high up the list of advanced economies. Nonetheless, ruin avoided is consistent with much opportunity lost.

Japan's monetary history of the past 40 years (and in particular the last quarter century) has drawn a huge amount of interest especially from US monetary economics professors who have played important (sometimes lead) roles in the construction of the global 2% inflation standard. Some leading ex-monetary officials in Japan resent that interest, albeit belatedly, regretting their influence on the evolution of Japanese monetary policy. They complain that these US experts did not understand the particular situation and nuances of Japan's economy—whether the extent to which monetary inflation in goods and services markets has been camouflaged by integration with East and South East Asia (cheap imports), digitalization, and labour market shifts (decline of seniority pay in big companies) or a range of demographic factors. These former officials argue that political leaders in Japan were too ready to embrace the ideas of top US academics—especially those with prestigious pedigrees—without sufficient perspicacity as to what ideology or otherwise they were pedalling and with what ulterior motive (not uppermost the interest of the Japanese themselves).

The purpose here is not to assess that blame which implies lack of critical pushback from within the Japanese economic profession, political system, and media. Such an exercise in blame—in finding fault with how the global 2% inflation standard spread and became entrenched—would have many chapters beyond the Japanese story. Rather, the intention is to explore how Japan's journey to adopting the 2% inflation standard and then its experience to date under that standard have critically increased the dangers ahead for this country. Yes, the long-running monetary inflation has been largely camouflaged from view in goods and services markets so far; but camouflage in one area does not mean danger eradicated.

And in looking further back, to before the journey started, the huge scope of the Japanese bubble and bubble economy in the late 1980s is a challenge to any serious purveyor of monetary or broader economic theory. Can this theory explain what happened and what went wrong in Japan? Our examination should also test any such theory in the story of Japanese deflation (itself largely myth rather than fact). The battle has been joined by sound money theorists drawing on Austrian School economics, who argue that Japan's and indeed the globe's economic outcome would have been much better if in fact there had been some period of declining prices.

We could describe Japan as the battleground for monetary theorists. The architects of the 2% inflation standard can view Japan as a laboratory where in recent years the most powerful non-conventional tools yet have been deployed. The Abe government was victorious in the political arena in terms of taking Japan on to the 2% inflation standard and in authorizing such tools. And at the time of writing, the world is basking in a stock market boom and global economic upturn in which Japan is fully sharing. Its apparent successes could be pyrrhic if indeed Japan adds to the evidence that the 2% global inflation standard is harmful to prosperity.

Towards organizing the material and the evidence, this chapter subdivides the evidence into sub-periods from 1965 onwards.

The Miracle Years End in Great Inflation

Japan's miracle years of near double-digit economic growth extended through the 1960s and early 1970s. In fact, the miracle was likely already over by the mid- to late 1960s, but high growth continued (see Brown 2002) until 1973 under the influence of giant monetary inflation. Through the first half of the 1960s (when the miracle was still under way), Japanese inflation was well above that in the US (by around four percentage points on average each year). That translated into a similar real exchange rate appreciation of the yen, which in turn was consistent with a miracle whose focus was the traded goods sector in Japan (productivity growth there much more rapid than in the non-traded goods sector).

When US inflation accelerated sharply in the second half of the 1960s, the Japanese monetary authorities understandably became reluctant to continue playing by a set of rules where relative productivity gains (in the traded goods sector) were offset by an inflation excess, thereby keeping export prices in line with US prices, as that would push Japanese inflation into double digits. Yet by restraining an upturn of inflation, the real exchange rate of the yen began to slip (relative to fundamental equilibrium), meaning that the real value of the yen in terms of dollar declined, and correspondingly the trade surplus of Japan started to balloon. That in turn fuelled US protectionism which triumphed in 1971 with President Nixon's closing of the gold window and imposition of an import tax.

Japan responded ultimately by floating the yen but simultaneously importing US monetary inflation policies (which in any case suited the vast economic expansionary ambitions of the then Prime Minister (PM) Tanaka—see Babb 2001). Inflation surged, surpassing that in the US by a wide margin through 1973–75. The speculative boom in the yen came to an end and indeed went into reverse gear. The real external value of the yen which had skyrocketed from summer 1971 to spring 1973 plummeted.

This was the first instance of a pattern which was to re-establish itself in Japanese monetary policy-making in the decades which followed. At first, Tokyo might try to avoid following Washington down the path of a new inflationary monetary experiment. But in consequence the export sector of Japan comes under threat in various forms, whether from US protectionism (as in the late 1960s) or from yen over-valuation (as in 1986 or 2003 or 2010–12) or both in sequence. Ultimately Tokyo decides the best course is to copy US inflationary monetary policy. The eventual result is the hit to Japanese prosperity from an inflation storm—including spectacular asset price crash in the final stage.

JAPAN ON THE EDGE OF MONETARIST EXPERIMENTS 1977–84/85

In the wake of the inflation crisis of the mid-1970s, Japan embarked on a weak form of monetarist experimentation—joining the hard money countries of Europe but without the rigour (unlike in Switzerland or Germany, there was no focus on monetary base as the pivot). The Bank of Japan followed implicitly a money supply target, but there was no setting of monetary base targets and no abandoning of policy discretion in the setting of interest rates. Under the brief monetarist experiment in the US (approximately 1980–83/84), the US dollar surged against the yen and European currencies. The global demand for a US currency now apparently hard surprised most investors (and analysts) on the upside.

The super-strong dollar and the related widening of the US trade deficit caused a surge of protectionism in the US political system to which James Baker, installed as President Reagan's new Treasury secretary in 1985, responded by organizing a devaluation of the dollar. Paul Volcker, the then Fed chief, had never changed his spots from his days as the devaluation diplomat when he served as under-secretary of the Treasury in the Nixon Administration (the then Treasury Secretary John Connelly, like Volcker, was a Democrat). Volcker had also become anxious about the giant trade deficit, viewing this as unsustainable and unacceptable rather than a benign feature of international payments, reflecting enhanced US investment opportunity and the global appeal of a newly hard dollar. He joined in the new dollar devaluation campaign, easing monetary policy ostensibly in response to the economic slowing but also in effect a key component of the Plaza Accord negotiated in late summer 1985.

JAPAN'S CAMOUFLAGED MONETARY INFLATION IN RESPONSE TO PLAZA 1985–89

Hence Volcker, despite his reputation as an inflation fighter, in effect launched the US (it could be said "unintentionally") into a new episode of monetary inflation which featured both rising goods and services inflation and powerful asset price inflation around the globe. The Japanese yen and the Deutsche mark soared in the currency markets. Both developments proved to have seriously destabilizing consequences. In Europe, the Bundesbank was even more reluctant than the Bank of Japan to ease monetary policy with a goal of braking currency strength. But the new volatility of the Deutsche mark against European neighbours provided a fillip in the German political arena to the case for forming a European Monetary Union (EMU)—an enterprise which eventually was to be so fateful (in a seriously negative way!) for Europe (see James 2012). In Japan, the monetary authorities pursued an expansionary path in response to "yen shock" and indeed could maintain that such actions were consistent with the Plaza Accord which featured calls for globally coordinated monetary easing (so as to combat a perceived weak phase in global economic activity). The easing seemed also to be justified by a simultaneous vanishing of recorded inflation in Japan, in part related to the super-strong yen but also to a spurt of productivity growth.

From a contemporary viewpoint, the 1980s (after the 1981/82 recession) were a period of economic renaissance for Japan—as it seemed to be shifting into rapid service sector growth (centred around Tokyo) and aided by an accompanying liberalization, especially in the financial sector. Productivity growth had accelerated. In broad terms sound money under these conditions would have meant prices were falling broadly. Instead, the Bank of Japan generated a powerful monetary inflation, responding at first to what it regarded as excessive yen strength from mid-1986 onwards (in the aftermath of the Plaza Accord of September 1985) albeit that this mostly showed up in asset price inflation rather than goods and services inflation. A productivity growth spurt and yen appreciation were camouflaging inflation in the goods markets. Speculative narratives in Japan had much to do with the "new economy" which was emerging—and of course there was the related compelling story of a large rise of demand for space in urban centres, especially Tokyo. This fed real estate speculation and eventually mania—perhaps most of all in golf club memberships.

The historical record shows that officials in the Bank of Japan had misgivings about their easy policies (see Itoh 2015). It was not until the spring of 1989, however, that the Bank of Japan started to change course. This occurred against the background of strong economic growth, no or little reported inflation, an evident asset market boom (many commentators described it as a bubble), and crucially a strengthening dollar as the Greenspan Federal Reserve responded to a late-cycle powerful rise in reported goods and services inflation.

A question by then (late 1988, early 1989) haunting Japanese policymakers, even if not spoken out loud, was could monetary policy normalization at such a late stage induce a dangerous asset market correction? Maybe the "point of no return" hypothesized by Milton Friedman (see Chap. 11) regarding late 1928 had already been reached—meaning that a late monetary response (including regulatory actions) to the high speculative temperatures could do more harm than good; it would likely be too weak to end the bubble but strong enough to send the economy into recession. Perhaps at this late stage, it would be best to let the bubble burst from within, whilst the central bank remained focused on fighting any potential fall in prices and avoiding discretionary actions which might trigger recession.

In the event, such qualms did not halt the Bank of Japan under its new Chief Yasushi Mieno (from December 1989) sharply tightening monetary policy especially into early 1990. He saw as his mission the bursting of the land bubble and more broadly the asset market bubble. For Mieno, who had supported his parents and ill siblings by peddling black market commodities during the immediate devastation of post-war Japan (see Peterson and Jameson 1990), bubble fighting was a moral crusade (influenced doubtless by the mafia involvement in the highly speculative markets including real estate).

The Depression and Rapid Recovery Which Did Not Occur 1990–97

High interest rates were sustained by the Bank of Japan through the next two years, with no prompt or deliberate easing of policy as recession set in through 1991–92. One factor often quoted in this reluctance to ease boldly was the backdrop of a trade confrontation with the US (first with the Bush Administration, then with the incoming Clinton Administration). Mieno saw a strong yen as essential to bringing down the trade surplus and in any case viewed a hard yen as an objective in itself. The notion that a rise in the savings and current account surpluses of Japan would be a normal accompaniment to the aftermath of a bubble economy was as strange to Mieno as to the US economic diplomats on the other side of the discussions.

Yet strangely there was no downward drift of goods and services prices. These and wages continued to rise through 1990–92/93. Indeed Ueda (2012) sees this as symptomatic of the Japanese economy mal-functioning in this period; price and wage flexibility was seriously lacking. By the time the US trade war offensive against Japan was finally called off (spring 1995), Japanese prices were no longer rising, and there had indeed been small episodes of price falls. These became significant during the 1997 economic downturn marked by the belated eruption of financial crisis; a focal poin of this was the rescue of Yamaichi securities in autumn that year which ex-BoJ Governor Shirakawa (see Shirakawa 2014) describes as the Lehman test for Japan which was avoided.

Radical Monetary Experimentation Fuels a Giant Yen Carry Trade 1998–2007

In effect through the second half of 1997 and 1998, the Bank of Japan kept rates stuck at around 0.5% as measured by the overnight call rate (at this level since 1995) despite a gathering tech boom centred in the US but in which the Japanese economy was enjoying a big role. Unlike the Federal Reserve and the ECB (which had just opened its doors), the BoJ was not operating under an unofficial or official 2% inflation-targeting regime. Even so in February 1999, the BoJ reduced its overnight call rate further to virtually zero, influenced no doubt by the eruption of the Russian and wider liquidity crisis in global markets of autumn 1998 during which the yen had shot higher as carry trade positions were suddenly liquidated (see Ueda and Nobuyuki 2005). Eventually the Bank of Japan implemented a small rate rise in autumn 2000, but of course with hindsight, the asset price inflation of the late 1990s had by then already entered its late stage of disinflation.

The BoJ responded to the subsequent economic downturn (in the US and globally including Japan) through 2001–02 by pioneering quantitative easing. The operating target of monetary policy changed from the overnight call rate to the outstanding balance of current accounts held by financial institutions at the Bank of Japan. The initial aim was for a current account balance of around 5 trillion yen, and the BoJ raised the target step by step; at its maximum the balance of current accounts reached around 30–35 trillion yen, about five times as much as the amount of required reserves and constituted about 7% of nominal GDP (compared to 25–30% for FED QE in 2014).

The launch of QE and its intensification coincided with considerable anxiety in Japan about the climb of the yen in the context of the exceptional US monetary ease; and from early 2003 the Fed put extraordinary emphasis on fighting the dangers of deflation, described by Fed Chief Greenspan as the attempt to breathe "low inflation" back into the US economy. The BoJ did not engage in a programme of massive purchases of Japanese government bonds (JGBs) in this first QE experiment, focusing instead on operations in short-maturity Treasury bills. It introduced the so-called banknote principle whereby JGB purchases conducted for facilitating money market operations were subject to the limitation that the outstanding amount of JGB holdings (on the central banks' balance sheet) should be limited within the outstanding amount of banknotes in circulation. The BoJ made clear that such purchases were for conducting monetary policy and not for financing fiscal deficits. The BoJ declared that QE would continue until the change in the CPI would register at zero or above for a few months and there would be a recognizable tendency to this effect.

In sum QE was pioneered in Japan not as a non-conventional tool of the 2% inflation-targeting regime (of which Japan was not yet a member)—but as a means of combating "deflation" and defending against a US currency war offensive. Prices of goods and services were falling—but in a regime of sound money, this would have been wholly benign during a weak phase of the business cycle (see p. 21). Hence the Bank of Japan was fully on board with the central bankers' club deflation phobia. In general wages and prices had become much more flexible downwards than in the serious recession of the early 1990s, and this could have been viewed as a welcome development likely to shorten economic downturns by strengthening self-recovery forces. A further reason for non-concern about a fall in prices at this time was the rapidly growing economic integration between Japan and China. This meant that the natural rhythm of prices in the Japanese economy was downwards (see Beacon Reports 2012). The attempt by the BoJ to resist this rhythm in the pursuit of stable prices fuelled strong asset price inflation (the empowerment of irrational forces by monetary disequilibrium—see Chap. 3), of which a key symptom was the booming carry trade out of yen into foreign currencies. But the BoJ carried on regardless, evidently recognizing the dangers in the carry trade (in particular the swing from an under-valued yen now to an expensive yen in the future when the trade bust could go along with much squandering of economic resources and ultimately prosperity most obvious via mal-investment in the export sector) but not convinced to shift monetary policy accordingly.

QE remained in operation for a remarkably long time despite strong economic recovery setting in from 2003; but prices were still falling slightly. Only in March 2006 on stronger evidence of prices rising did the BoJ resolve to end QE. The yen had fallen considerably since the highs at the time of QE's initial phase amidst a growing global carry trade in the Japanese currency and a strong momentum of capital outflow from Japan. Accordingly, the BoJ announced that it would change the operating target for monetary operations from the current account balance back to the uncollateralized overnight call rate. It also decided that initially it would guide the overnight rate towards remaining effectively at zero. The BoJ proceeded to run down the excess reserves—with the intention of regaining control over the overnight money rate, positioning to raise this from zero at a later point. Given that the main asset accumulated to offset the growth in reserves had been T-bills, this operation could occur quickly without disrupting the bond markets (other than via expectation effects).

The rise in rates from zero was painfully slow. By February 2007 the overnight rate reached 0.5% and was maintained at that level until the BoJ responded to the Lehman shock (autumn 2008). That was despite the continuing strong depreciation of the yen during 2006–07 as the speculative temperature in the yen carry trade reached new heights. The so-called yen carry trade was a spectacular feature of the global asset price inflation in these years (2002–07) stretching far and wide to spread by contagion fever from one asset class to another. For example, yen carry trades helped fuel speculation in many real estate markets in Europe and Asia and was often joined with credit and liquidity carry trades in their various forms. The Swiss franc was a smaller twin but nonetheless very significant in the currency carry trades.

The attraction of the yen (like of the Swiss franc) in the carry trade was its low or zero interest rate compared substantially higher nominal interest rates in euros, pounds, and dollars. As the game increased in scope, more downward pressure occurred on the yen, and the trend became the friend, firing up irrational expectations with respect to further profits to be made. If it had not been for the boom in the yen and Swiss franc carry trades during the great global asset price inflation of 2003–07, the yen and Swiss franc would have been at considerably higher levels on average during that period.

The carry trade boom turned to bust in the midst and aftermath of the 2008 panic. Then the governments of both Switzerland and Japan embarked on massive foreign exchange market intervention to contain the sudden appreciation of their currencies. That reaction to potentially disorderly foreign exchange market conditions was consistent with the rules of good behaviour in foreign exchange markets; but the failure to subsequently offload the massive build-up of reserves albeit slowly amounted to serous foreign exchange market manipulation (the same can be said of Switzerland's non-disposal of reserves accumulated during the EMU sovereign debt crisis several years later). Both governments could defend non-disposal as consistent with following a 2% inflation target (as currency appreciation would have meant lower inflation in the short and medium term)—an illustration of the pitfalls of that regime (including the stimulating of currency manipulation).

THE SHIRAKAWA RESISTANCE TO US-LED MONETARY INFLATION 2008–12

The counterfactual historian could consider what would have happened during the course of the great global asset inflation of the mid-2000s if the BoJ had been less focused on near-term prospects for prices (combating "deflation") and instead operated policy within a framework of sound money. Higher interest rates in Japan during these years would surely have curtailed the carry trade. Yes, they would have meant a more expensive yen but relative to a level which became fantastically cheap. In real effective exchange rate terms, the yen in 2007 reached a level some 5% or more lower than a decade earlier in the depths of the Japan banking crisis and the South East Asian debt crisis.

There is a more general point here. How can countries outside the US best persevere with sound money in the face of a US monetary inflation shock? And when is there no real alternative but to get on board and follow the US into severe monetary disequilibrium rather than suffer the pain of a huge temporary overshoot of the national currency with a related dislocating effect on the export sector? Japan could be seen as a case study in this respect, albeit a particularly large and advanced economy.

In principle, Japan could have defied the central bankers' club and the Washington consensus, allowing its prices to fall substantially through 2002–05 say and its exchange rate to become temporarily very highly valued. In Japan's export sector, wage rates would have fallen as bonus pay was cut or eliminated temporarily. Households would have had a strong incentive to economize meanwhile by switching to cheaper imported goods, and within the domestic, traded goods sector prices would have fallen in line. These falls in prices and some wages would no have been the start of a deflationary process. Quite the opposite: there would have been an expectation that in the longer term prices would rise from these depressed levels (an expectation which would be reinforced by the monetary base following a parth consistent with prices returning to the mean). That expectation would have gone along with both households and businesses bringing some spending forward from the future to take advantage of spectacularly cheap prices now.

Japanese investors would have had the "once in a lifetime opportunity" of buying up foreign assets cheaply (in yen terms). Even though some of these would be at inflated prices in dollars (corresponding to asset inflation), the potential for the yen to fall further ahead would be an important cushion against any loss (in yen terms). The yen as a lone sound money would have gained in popularity as an international investment currency, and a build-up of foreign holdings would have matched large outflows of Japanese capital even as the current account surplus in the balance of payments was tending to shrink (under the influence of the strong currency). Alongside, the Japanese government and central bank could have informed the public about the nature of the monetary crisis which stemmed from the US having embarked on a monetary experiment of unknown but likely high danger. Japan as a medium-sized economy in a global village could not avoid the consequences, but these would be milder if Japan persevered with sound money and allowed labour and product markets to function as flexibly as possible.

None of this happened and there was a special problem anyhow. The monetary base in Japan had never been strongly pivoted in the monetary system. The demand for this was not renowned to be stable and the asset (monetary base) with distinctive properties—as had been the case for the Deutsche mark under the monetarist regime (see next chapter). Yes, the Japanese authorities could have done much to create those conditions—and indeed the strong preference of Japanese households for cash as a medium of payments would have been helpful in this respect. Indeed, the Bank of Japan started to pay market interest on reserves in November 2008, at the same time as the Federal Reserve; and the payment of interest means that the monetary base in effect becomes dislodged from the pivot of the monetary system (see Bowman et al. 2010).

In sum, Japan was not well set up to withstand the next huge monetary inflation shock to come from the US—that of 2009/10 onwards when the Bernanke Fed launched a series of aggressive QE policies and opened alongside a non-conventional tool box including the deliberate manipulation of long-term interest rates. The BoJ governor at that time, Masaaki Shirakawa (a University of Chicago-trained economist who had been nominated in early 2008 following the sudden resignation of the previous governor amidst trivial impropriety allegations) was deeply sceptical of Bernanke-ism. Unusually the main opposition party, then the Democratic Party of Japan (DPJ), had decisive veto power in the Upper House regarding nominations and would have blocked a Finance Ministry loyalist. That had been Shirakawa's chance.

Governor Shirakawa was strongly disinclined to throw in the towel and import the US monetary experiment to reduce the upward pressure on the yen. And the DPJ government formed in 2009, made up of an unusual coalition of opposition parties to the Liberal Democratic Party (LDP), did not put intense pressure on the BoJ to do so. Ex-senior finance minister official Sakakibara, an economic advisor to the DPJ, was antagonistic to earlier BoJ policies of breathing in inflation as fuelled by US academic input and viewed downward movement of prices as benign, reflecting mainly integration with China. Even so the inexorable upward pressure on the yen through the early years of the new Obama Administration as the Bernanke Fed doubled up on QE and interest rate manipulation as the European debt crisis erupted (2010–11/12) brought the BoJ refusal to follow suit increasingly into the Japanese political spotlight.

The triple natural disasters of March 2011 added to the political pressure on the BoJ to change policy, not least as the shambolic response of the DPJ government led to its popularity plummeting. The LDP leader, Shinzo Abe, promised an end to deflation and the joining in effect of the 2% global inflation standard; everyone knows this was code for a yen devaluation policy; indeed on occasion, the code was dropped. In fact there had never been deflation in Japan—but overall price stability. In broad terms we could say that consumer prices had been on a flat trend from the early 1990s to 2012/13 with dips during episodes of recession or accelerated productivity growth and rises during cyclical boom periods. Yes, prices had been surprisingly inflexible on occasion (especially the early 1990s as mentioned above). The CPI in Japan at the peak of the cycle in 2007 was virtually at the same level as at the trough of the post-bubble recession in 1993 and up a few percentage points from the 1989 business cycle peak. Prices fell persistently through 2008–12 in part explained by cyclical factors and in part by the relentless climb of the yen.

As to the lost decade which featured in the Japanese (and US) QE architect narrative, and in the Shinzo Abe election propaganda, the reality was more apparent than factual when we turn to the data. The only period during which the Japanese economy under-performed other advanced economies (as measured by the growth of GDP per capita) was from 1992 to 1997. In fact, recent work from the BIS (see BIS 2015) suggests that Japan seriously outperformed the US during the first decade of the twenty-first century when proper adjustment is made for demographic influences. In particular real GDP per working-age population grew cumulatively by 20% in Japan from 2000 to 2012, compared to 11% in the US. For the period 2000–07, the comparative statistics were 15% and 8%, respectively (see Borio et al. 2015). Interestingly, BoJ Governor Shirakawa had repeatedly taken these same themes up in his resistance to growing pressure within the Japanese political system to take radical monetary measures against "deflation".

Shinzo Abe Puts Japan on the 2% Inflation Standard

Whatever the expert opinion outside Japan and outside the global central banking club consensus, and whatever the counterarguments of Masaaki Shirakawa, Shinzo Abe won a landslide victory for his LDP/Komeito coalition in late 2012 with its three-pillar economic agenda (2% inflation, budget stimulus, and economic reform). Immediately a new leadership was installed at the Bank of Japan—with Haruhiko Kuroda selected as the chief to design massive QE operations towards achieving 2% inflation and (unsaid) devaluing the yen. Alongside, the Tokyo stock market surged, and this was a key component of the success claimed from early on by the new government (see Ueda 2013).

Over the subsequent three years, the programme was expanded and radicalized, far exceeding (relative to GDP) the QE operations in Europe and the US and including a significant equity buying programme as one component. In March 2016 the BoJ cut the overnight rate to negative level responding surely to some re-bound of the yen triggered by the Federal Reserve contemporaneously abandoning all its planned rate hikes. That Fed policy shift came in response to a pull-back of global stock markets and some US growth cycle weakness (especially related to the recent slump in energy prices) and the Chinese currency devaluation along with emerging market slowdowns and commodity market downswings. The political blowback in Japan from negative rates was so unfavourable (and the immediate dip in Tokyo Big Bank equities so severe) that the BoJ did not proceed to implement European-style negative rates.

It is foolhardy to judge the success or impact of any monetary policy until at least one cycle is complete—so that one can reckon in full the severity of the recession and the amount of mal-investment revealed. Several of the leading advocates and architects of inflation targeting and radical experimentation alongside have broken that rule, claiming success at half-time. And so it has been in Japan. Certainly, the stock market boom, the Tokyo real estate boom, and accompanying profits boom (especially in exports) have made the Abe government popular with important segments of the population. The weakness and divisions of the opposition have facilitated a political path in which snap three-week election campaigns, fought under the banner of delaying fiscal normalization which had previously been promised or even legislated, have ended in landslide victory for PM Abe and his allies. The critics say this is sad for Japanese democracy. And the delays in fiscal normalization have been possible, of course, thanks to the dysfunctionality of the long-term interest rate market in Japan. If the government can borrow ten-year funds at zero cost, what is the hurry to implement budget cuts along with the painful effort to explain these to voters?

The dysfunctionality of the long-term interest rate market in Japan reached a new pitch when the Bank of Japan in autumn 2016 implemented a strategy of fixing the ten-year JGB yield at close to zero. According to the text books, such an operation would be a stage on the road to hyperinflation. As the mass of non-official holders of long-term bonds (still around 40% of the total at this time) sought to offload their paper (concerned about the inflation break-out danger), the central bank would be obliged to print even more money in its price support operations (or, alternatively, issue short-term Treasury bills, which would also be problematic for inflation). But this is not how things turned out in Japan. In fact, the many institutional holders of JGBs preferred to hold on to existing stocks of such paper and continue collecting coupons. Yes, the income would be offset by capital loss as maturity of the bonds came nearer, but these calculations would not make it into the arcane accounting presentation of profits and loss. There could have been massive short-selling of long-maturity bonds (or equivalently short positions in the long-maturity yen interest rate swap markets). But these failed to form, even though the running costs were very small.

We should not put all this inertia down to "institutional-type" explanations. Also, there have been widespread expectations in the marketplace that prices of goods and services in Japan would remain broadly stable despite all the efforts of PM Abe and his central bank chief to achieve their 2% inflation target (see Shirai 2017). The story here has been that investment opportunity in Japan continues to be constrained in large part by unfavourable demographic dynamics as well as by the huge monetary uncertainty (how will the Abe monetary inflation all end up, especially in terms of the yen, stock market, and public finances?) and households remain obstinately large savers (perhaps not so obstinate but rational given lack of confidence in the viability of pension funds—whether public or private—and the population's lengthening life expectancy). Additionally, disinflationary forces from globalization and digitalization would continue to be strong. The resilience of the yen (which at the beginning under Shinzo Abe's premiership had fallen steeply but subsequently recovered in part) and lack of any evident capital flight both testified to the strength of such disbelief that the Abe target of 2% inflation was serious.

No One Believes the Bank of Japan's 2% Inflation Megillah

Yes, the Bank of Japan recited a megillah at each policy meeting about how it would continue radical monetary policy until inflation was at a sustained rate above 2% per annum, but few if any market participants seemed to believe this was a short- or medium-term prospect. Certainly many Japanese may well have preferred to have hard money uncorrupted and unspoilt by constant threat from the national issuer that it intends as soon as possible to lift inflation, and in that journey, holders should expect real interest rates to be significantly negative for prolonged periods. But that was a plight of all the main fiat monies—whether dollars, euros, yen, or Swiss francs. For a time in the years 2014–15, it had been possible to believe that the US dollar was on the road back to normality.

President Trump's continuous celebration of monetary inflation's present "success" in the stock market made it hard for these believers. Also unsettling was the new president's appointment of a long-time Bernanke/Yellen loyalist as Fed chief. Why the appointment? Powell ostensibly gets on well with his Treasury secretary, himself a fan of a weak dollar, who is committed now to demonstrating that the Republican tax cuts would bring 3% growth. This means crucially the end of interest rate manipulation seems a long way off also in the US. And with the US fiscal deficit widely forecast to reach 5–6% of GDP within 18 months, a record for US advanced economic expansion, the Federal Reserve would surely be seeking to manage public debt costs (crucially the interest component).

If inflation in Japan did suddenly surprise and start climbing, say into a range above 1% p.a., there would surely be a wave of short-selling JGBs and investors' sales of such paper. This surprise would most likely reflect the wearing out of the camouflage to monetary inflation in goods and services markets—whether in the form of rapid integration with South and South East Asia, digitalization, or the decline of excessive renumeration particularly related to seniority bonuses in Big Company Japan. Were the Bank of Japan to respond to this by massive new issuance of T-bills or monetary base creation to finance a price support operation (for JGBs) the yen could plunge? Worse yet, the operation might fail totally (only encouraging more sales). Given the absolute importance of the strategic alliance between Japan and the US, would the Abe government really risk angering Washington with a monetary policy which smacked of currency manipulation? So yes, bond yields and interest rates would likely rise despite all the protestations to the contrary in an early phase of inflation acceleration well before the 2% target was reached. Another consideration here: if the BoJ failed to move up short-term rates as inflation rose and then lost control of prices in the JGB market, there would be widespread fear of a ballooning fiscal deficit as any new debt issuance would have to be financed at higher rates.

Overall the Japanese economy joined a strong global cyclical upturn through late 2016–17. The monetary policy of the Abe government broadly favoured exports and government spending whilst curbing private consumption (the dynamic here included a large elderly population anxious about the undesirable impact of the possibility of rising prices and continuing yen depreciation—and this more than offset any positive wealth effect from higher asset prices). How would the Japanese economy have performed under the previous monetary policy outside the 2% inflation standard and without radicalization? Perhaps consumption would have been significantly stronger, especially if prices had fallen to a perceived bargain level from which rises could be expected in the future. And Japanese investors (including businesses) would have been able to take advantage of a strong yen to buy foreign assets cheaply. There would have been stronger pressure on the government to take remedial action for the public finances.

The many downsides of the monetary path chosen by the Abe government remain to be determined and assessed over the remainder of this cycle. These include the inflammation of irrational forces in markets as yield-starved investors sought to gain income in risk-markets. Japanese investors became big participants in booming carry trades (currency, credit, illiquidity, and term premiums), and some of these (but not all) involved assuming foreign currency risk. For example, there was a boom in the sale of illiquid structured products into the Japanese investment markets with kickers on the performance of the FAANGs (Facebook, Amazon, Apple, Netflix, and Google). Surveys suggested that at least 50%of Japanese households thought that global markets were in a bubble, but they nonetheless participated. Japanese institutional investors emerged as huge buyers of long-maturity US fixed-rate paper on a hedged basis, collecting thereby a thin nominal term premium (very likely negative when account was taken of potential loss in the future under any rational assessment). Some Japanese companies succeeded in getting on the bandwagon of spinning attractive speculative narratives—some to do with prowess in selecting foreign high-tech investments on a highly leveraged basis, others on home-grown potential and with global markets (e.g. robotics). And of course, an old favourite returned to the centre of the scene—Tokyo real estate markets.

Japan Heads Towards End Phase of Asset Price Inflation

At the time of writing (winter 2017/18), it is a matter of speculation how the Japanese economy will suffer in the eventual end phase of this global asset price inflation. There are considerable grounds for concern though that it could be highly vulnerable. Japanese investors boldly participated in the many irrational strategies around the globe; and a range of Japanese companies engaged in strategies both with respect to investment in Japan and outside which may be later categorized as mal-investment, and in some cases, this has been done on a highly leveraged basis.

Yes, the counterfactual analyst would likely hypothesize that if Japan had pursued sound money in defiance of the 2% inflation standard reigning in the rest of the world and the yen had been much stronger in consequence, Japanese investors would have still participated in the asset market boom elsewhere. But the highly valued yen would have meant a cheap entry point (in terms of yen); the long-run decline of the yen from its high point when Japanese and global monetary conditions were at their maximum divergence during the boom phase of global asset price inflation would have provided a cushion against subsequent loss. Foreigners who had piled into the rising yen at that time would turn out to have been the supplier of that cushion. And overall it is surely plausible that the participation of Japanese in the global asset price inflation would have been less under this alternative monetary regime given that they would have not have become subject to intense interest income famine with its knock-on effect of strengthening flawed mental process amidst desperation for yield. A build-up of the yen as an international currency based on its new "soundness" would have been an advantage for Japan when it entered the phase of population ageing where the savings surplus would fall and even move into deficit (with the very old consuming large amounts of their capital).

This is not how ex-Fed Chief Ben Bernanke viewed the Japanese situation when he delivered the Mayekawa lecture in November 2017. He started:

> Much of my writing on Japan has been motivated by the unique – or at least, initially unique – challenges that the Bank of Japan has faced in dealing with deflation and the effective lower bound on short-term interest rates. As an academic, I found these challenges intellectually fascinating

(**Critique**: what deflation? And if prices are flexible both downwards and upwards there is no reason why is a well-functioning capitalist economy nominal interest rates would ever fall below zero under a regime of sound money).

> I certainly did not get it all right. I was too optimistic (in my earlier writings) about the ease with which a determined central bank could conquer deflation. I criticized the Bank of Japan for showing insufficient "Rooseveltian resolve".
>
> The Bank of Japan is still some distance from achieving its 2 per cent inflation target, with core inflation recently hovering close to zero. Should the BoJ just declare victory and give up? Some might argue that extraordinary efforts are no longer needed. Although Japan's economy is growing only slowly, that largely reflects longer term forces, notably a shrinking labor force and slow productivity growth. So why continue with the inflation target?

One argument which Bernanke advances for continuing is that it would wipe out a portion of the public debt (in real terms). Success in reaching the 2% target along with the corresponding rise of long-term rates (in nominal terms) would reduce the public debt by around 21% of GDP, due the levying of the so-called inflation tax "perhaps not a game-changer given that the ratio is currently about 200%" (the extent of the inflation tax would depend on much detail as to the amount of fixed-rate debt held outside the Bank of Japan and how long delayed was the rise in short-term interest rates as inflation rose).

> However, for me, the more important benefit of achieving the inflation target is that it will promote greater economic stability in the future, by restoring the ability of monetary policy to respond to recessionary shocks. Over the past two decades, that ability has been limited by the proximity of short-term rates to their effective lower bound.

Bernanke quotes projections based on the Taylor rule (estimated specifically for Japan) according to which the call rate might have fallen to as low as −4%, not only during the global Great Recession but also during the long Japanese recession (September 2000–April 2003) at the beginning of the last decade.

> Achieving the inflation target in a sustained way, which would presumably also raise nominal interest rates above 2 percentage points from current levels, would not solve these problems but would likely meaningfully reduce

them. In short, if the Bank of Japan wants to restore its ability to respond to future economic shocks, it needs to remain aggressive in pursuit of its inflation target.

There is absolutely no mention at all in Bernanke's lecture of asset price inflation! This blind spot in his vision as Fed governor and then Fed chief appears uncorrected to date. The key concern of Bernanke is to provide scope for stimulatory monetary policy when the next recession and possibly great recession arrive.

A first point here is that the likelihood of a great recession is a function of monetary disorder. If sound money were prevalent (including of course the US), then the sequence of giant monetary inflations including the element of asset price inflation and deflation would be banished. If the US is running unsound monetary policies, then Japan would be vulnerable to the periodic hard landings and great recessions which ensued. The vulnerability would be less though if Japan had not gone down the same route of unsound money but had pursued a sound money path. Yes, there may have been more dislocation from a super-strong yen during the period of US currency war offensive, but that would also have been an opportunity (as described above). There would not have been the engagement in ultimately ruinous carry trades and giant mal-investment including the export sector, and the local (Japanese) stock and real estate markets would have been insulated in some degree (not rising so much during the bubble period).

But suppose nonetheless it were possible for Japan running sound money policies to get trapped by the greater power of the US to create monetary disorder, meaning that it fell eventually into a great recession. Could it be better for Japan to get with it and run a similar monetary policy to the US throughout (meaning inflation targeting)? Bernanke argues that a 2% inflation target would allow the Bank of Japan to pursue a more powerful stimulatory policy to combat the recession whenever it came. This is dubious. For in any severe recession, what would keep inflation expectations anchored to 2% p.a.? Yes, the central bankers may continue to mouth the target, but why would anyone believe this was feasible to achieve in the short or medium term?

As we have already seen, the 2% inflation target represents an emperor's new clothes standard (see Chap. 2). And this applies to another idea (not in the lecture) which Bernanke has put forward (since leaving the Fed)—that upping the inflation target to 3% p.a. could provide even more scope for monetary stimulus in a great recession, by making the zero-rate bound more absent. But if it is hard for economic agents to give plausibility to 2% p.a.

inflation any time soon in the midst of great recession, they would surely give less to 3%. Interest rates at zero would in no way be equivalent to −3% in real terms just because the Bank of Japan and Fed are trumpeting a 3% inflation standard. The best way to get to substantially negative real rates in the severe down phase of a cycle is to let flexible prices fall sharply to a level from which a substantial rise would be expected in the subsequent global economic re-bound.

Bibliography

Babb, J. (2001). *Tanaka: The Making of Post-War Japan*. London: Routledge.
Beacon reports. (2012, August 2). *Japan's Economic Integration with China*.
Bernanke Ben, Mayekawa Lecture. (2017, November). Tokyo: Monetary and Economic Studies.
Borio, C., Erdem, M., Filardo, A., & Hofmann, B. (2015, March 18). The Costs of Deflations: A Historical Perspective. *BIS Quarterly Review*.
Bowman, D., Gagnon, E., & Leahy, M. (2010, March). *Interest on Excess Reserves as a Monetary Policy Instrument: The Experience of Foreign Central Banks*. Board of Governors of the Federal Reserve System, International Finance Discussion Papers No. 996.
Brown, B. (2002). *The Yo-Yo Yen and the Future of the Japanese Economy*. Gordonsville: Palgrave.
Itoh, M. (2015, November). Koike Ryoji and Shizumi Masato, "Bank of Japan's Monetary Policy in the 1980s: A View Perceived from Archives and Other Materials" Monetary and Economic Studies BoJ.
James, H. (2012). *Making the European Monetary Union*. Basel: Bank for International Settlements.
Peterson, J., & Jameson, S. (1990, March 16). The Banker Behind Japan's Rising Rates. *Los Angeles Times*.
Shirai, S. (2017). *Mission Incomplete: Reflating Japan's Economy*. Tokyo: ADBI Institute.
Shirakawa, M. (2014, October). *(Is Inflation (or Deflation) "Always and Everywhere" a Monetary Phenomenon?* (BIS Paper No. 77e).
Ueda, K. (2012). Deleveraging and Monetary Policy: Japan Since the 1990s and the United States Since 2007. *Journal of Economic Perspectives, 26*(3), 177–202.
Ueda, K. (2013). Response of Asset Prices to Monetary Policy Under Abenomics. *Asian Economic Policy Review, 8*(2), 252–269.
Ueda, K., & Nobuyuki, O. (2005, April). *The Effects of the Bank of Japan's Zero Interest Rate Commitment and Quantitative Monetary Easing on the Yield Curve: A Macro-Finance Approach* (Bank of Japan Working Paper Series No. 05-E-6).

CHAPTER 8

Germany Abdicates Hard Money Power

It's easy to imagine the European nations at any point in the past half century getting together to discuss how to form a sound money union. A key catalyst: the recurring episodes of huge US monetary instability and the search for a European better alternative. This might well be second best to a sound global monetary order but preferable from a European standpoint to either copying US unsound money practices (for the sake of exchange rate stability vis-à-vis the dollar) or alternatively coalescing (pegging the exchange rate) around the currency of the largest economy in Europe (Germany) which would pursue a sounder monetary route than the US.

FOUNDERS OF EMU HAD NO SOUND MONEY VISION

In the diplomacy leading up to and exploring the possibility of a sound money union in Europe, there would have been much discussion about and eventual drawing up of principles which would guarantee that second-best outcome. In a world in which the dominant central bank, the Federal Reserve, could be expected to continue pursuing unsound policies for much of the time, how could Europe best adhere to a sound route? Germany's hard money protectors apparently thought this problem had been solved when European Monetary Union was launched at end-1998.

© The Author(s) 2018
B. Brown, *The Case Against 2 Per Cent Inflation*,
https://doi.org/10.1007/978-3-319-89357-0_8

After all the principles of price stability and no monetary financing of government deficits appeared to be enshrined in a constitution (the Maastricht Treaty) untouchable by the political arena. This could well be superior to the dubious legal underpinnings—in effect subject to the whims of the German parliament—of the highly popular Deutsche mark order (see Joerges 2015). Yet there were many smoking guns to suggest trouble ahead.

If sound money had been at the core of the drive for European monetary integration in the years from 1987 to say the early 1990s, then surely there would have been much intensive negotiation about how to achieve that. And Germany, as the hard money sovereign and hegemon of Europe, would have zealously ensured that the new European monetary authority (EMA) did not become a vehicle for the automatic monetary financing of weak banks and sovereigns throughout the union.

There would not have been large grey areas about the role of the EMA as lender of last resort, no "open market operations" or other forms of collateralized lending by the EMA except strictly as necessary for piloting the growth of monetary base according to a set of rules established in constitutional law (see Chaps. 10 and 13), no overdraft facilities of national banking systems (via the intermediation of the national central bank) in the payments clearing entity (target 2) unsecured by gold or dollars, no national central banks having discretionary power to draw on unsecured credits at the EMA to make emergency loans to weak domestic financial institutions (possible in the context of capital flight) or to authorize related emergency euro banknote printing (at the national level by the respective member central bank) except as in accordance with usual strict criteria.

If European Monetary Union were not to spin into an unsound union with huge potential transfers from Germany and other financially strong Northern European nations, it would surely be best not to have a European central bank at all—just an authority which steered the growth of the monetary base. In fact under these provisions, banks would have had a large demand for reserves (cash and deposits at the central bank) even without any compulsory reserve requirements, and so monetary base would have been a strong pivot to the monetary system overall.

It may well have been the case that if Germany had insisted on all of this that most if not all of the present EMU members would have decided not to join. Implicitly they wanted a soft money union in which there would be much scope ultimately for monetary financing of governments and banks and much of this at the expense of taxpayers in other countries especially Germany. When Jacques Delors said that monetary union would force the pace on European Union, all of this is plausibly what he had in mind. An ECB operating in the chaos of fiat money and with huge discretionary power despite the Gulliver-type constraints of a loosely and imperfectly drawn constitution and despite a one-time hard money hegemon (now gone soft) would create intergovernmental issues of control that could only be resolved through greater economic and political integration.

From the viewpoint of the builders of Europe, there must never be any going back. Problem: a sound money union as described was unimaginable without the possibility of exit. A member country subject to capital flight for whatever reason and without access to monetary financing would have no alternative but to exit the union at least temporarily. But the founders of monetary union had absolutely no wish to set out clauses on how an exit would occur; no member could take a reverse voyage from monetary union. Only a soft money union could meet that requirement. Even so there is soft and soft. The ECB's renouncing of monetarism and adoption of the 2% inflation target were stepping stones to a depth of softness that few if any could imagine at the start.

As point of fact, monetarism had been the guiding principle of the Bundesbank since the early 1970s, and in principle this had meant steering the growth of monetary base according to a semi-automatic set of rules and sustaining a high and stable demand for monetary base via high reserve requirements; but from the mid-1980s and especially in the aftermath of German Monetary Union, the application of monetarist principle had become highly corrupted. As illustration, high reserve requirements which had underpinned demand for monetary base had been gradually whittled down under the pressure of the bank lobby and scope for arbitrage with reserve-free deposits in Luxembourg. (Dr Otmar Issing, later of euro-fame, had sided with the reformers on this issue (the bank lobby) rather than the Bundesbank "backwoodsmen".) In the world at large, only the Bundesbank had been left with any pretence of applying monetarism. The Federal Reserve had exited monetarism after a short trial in the mid-1980s, the Bank of Japan a few years later, the Swiss National Bank (SNB) by stages from the late 1970s (see Hildebrand 2004); and to those in the know, the inflation-targeting experiment was spreading.

In the post-DM era, there has been much reflection about whether the Bundesbank during those years was in fact applying monetarist principle. Or was this institution just mouthing respect whilst in reality steering a path for short-term nominal interest rates on similar considerations under the inflation-targeting regime? On balance the conclusion is that monetarist principle remained bedrock of practice (see, e.g. Worms et al. 2004). The conclusion is that "the Bundesbank took its monetary targets seriously, but also responded to deviations of expected inflation and output growth from target". That conclusion is for a long period, stretching from 1971 to 1998, so it is possible that during the "Emminger era" (say the mid- and late 1970s), the monetary target was even more serious. (Otmar Emminger was vice-president and later president of the Deutsche Bundesbank, during the heyday of German monetarism in practice; he was also a leading advocate.)

The founders of European Monetary Union never contemplated the possibility of a union with a central monetary authority as described but without a central bank. Indeed, quite the converse, they left all the details from start to finish up to the central bankers to decide—from the Lamfalussy Committee (of central bankers) which drew up the original blueprint (see below) to the unofficial "Issing Committee" within the ECB just prior to the launch of the union which decided on the monetary framework. The German government under Chancellor Kohl went along with all of this. By the time the ECB opened for business (end-1998), the "Issing Committee" had essentially abandoned monetarism and taken Europe on to the 2% inflation target, though it would certainly not admit that (see Brown 2015).

The committee had resolved to introduce a dual-pillar monetary framework—one pillar the 2% inflation target, the second pillar a long-term indicative range for broad money supply (M3). No one had the slightest idea what indicative range was consistent with monetary stability in the new union, and high-powered money (monetary base) had been removed from the pivot of the monetary system. That pivot position had been sustained under the hard DM regime by high reserve requirements and zero-interest payment on reserves; these conditions were summarily swept aside in the founding of monetary union. Publicly, the two pillars sounded good. In reality, however, there was only one pillar of the new regime, and this was not a pillar of sound money.

Professor Issing completed the process of putting Europe firmly on the 2% inflation standard in spring 2003 at his notorious press conference. He signalled that the ECB would be as concerned about inflation falling below 2% p.a. as rising above. This announcement was virtually simultaneous with the Federal Reserve announcing that it was breathing in inflation so that this would rise to 2% p.a., countering thereby a "deflation threat".

Some would blame the failure to construct sound money on the original "sin" of French President Mitterrand. In his drive for monetary union in Europe, the adroit politician forewarned that if you want an EU agricultural treaty, you exclude the agricultural ministers from the pre-diplomacy; and in similar vein, concluding a monetary treaty means excluding the finance ministers (see Brown 2015). Accordingly, there was agreement that the key negotiations for monetary union should be within a central bankers' committee chaired by the then chief of the Bank for International Settlements, Alexandre Lamfalussy (the renowned Belgian economist long involved in the European integration process and especially in European financial regulation but not ideologically committed to sound money principle).

The Details of German Abdication

Yes, the Kohl government secured an eminence grise role in the ECB for the then top Bundesbank economist, Otmar Issing, but he was hardly a paragon of sound money. It was possible in one's worst moment of anxieties to believe that he could just be or become another fellow member of the global central bankers' club following the doctrine which became fashionable there (and that could be inflation targeting).

Yes, there were those monetary clauses in the Maastricht constitution, apparently enshrining the principle of central bank independence from government and the guiding aim of stable prices. Yet there were enough warnings from Germany's past not to trust this. After all, the Weimar Republic had had a model constitution, with checks and balances and independent courts. The Reichsbank had been made independent of government by the Allies in their attempt to pursue reparation claims. Yet independence did not prevent a government hell-bent on defying reparations from creating hyper-inflation. The complicit Reichsbank president (Dr Rudolf von Havenstein, originally a Prussian judge and then president of the Prussian State Bank) took pride in the efficiency of the money printing presses. And which court ever stood in the way of the collapse of Weimar?

Fast forward to the present, who really believed that central banks under the 2% inflation standard were independent of politics? And how could a supranational central bank (the ECB) contain national political influence? Was it unimaginable at the beginning that an Italian national as head of the ECB might have a preference for policies that would bolster Italian solvency and prosperity even if these were ultimately underwritten by transfers from Germany? And might not a French national as head of the ECB be strongly influenced by opinion emanating from the traditional elites in the French finance ministry and Quai d'Orsay? This might all be the case though each and every senior monetary bureaucrat mouthed European supranational language and independence principles.

Yes, to be fair, the red-robed judges of the German Supreme Court did hear various complaints about how the ECB had broken the law in pursuing essentially monetary financing and back-door lending to weak governments in the union, but they always came out with the same lame solution—that the definitions under dispute should be referred first to the European Court of Justice for clarification. And who would trust the latter given its well-earned reputation of kowtowing to Brussels?

Yes, the German chancellor and the Bundesbank president could defy the ECB if it acted in contradiction of the Maastricht monetary constitution, without waiting for the matter to be tried over many years by European constitutional judges heavily biased in favour of Brussels. Both (the chancellor and the Bundesbank president) could threaten to withhold transfers of funds from the Bundesbank into the euro-clearing mechanism. Even without going that far, they could both work on German public opinion to turn it against current trends in European Monetary Union.

The question of whether the 2% inflation regime is contrary to the Maastricht constitution is not one ever likely to be considered by judges. There is much less obviously a possible breach than in the case of alleged monetization of sovereign debts. Maastricht did not set out principles of sound money to be followed, other than as regards constraints on the ECB lending to governments. Yes, there was the ultimate aim specified of stable prices, but what judges would take issue with this having been interpreted in a particular way by the founding Bundesbanker, Otmar Issing?

Even though not a matter for the courts, Germany possesses considerable power to influence the evolution of the monetary framework. A German chancellor and finance minister convinced that the 2% inflation regime represents a big mistake could quite readily let their view be known widely and loudly. In time, they could appoint a Bundesbank president who shared their views. The president could become a loud dissenter, both in speeches and writing, from the ECB consensus. The German chancellor and finance minister after their summit meetings with the ECB president could let their disagreement about 2% be known publicly and become the subject of widespread debate.

Any ECB chief with a modicum of political sense would acknowledge that without German popular backing, the European Monetary Union would flounder and ultimately disintegrate. From the viewpoint of spring 2018, the prospect of Germany leading European Monetary Union away from the 2% inflation regime may seem remote but perhaps less so than either the Republicans or Democrats putting the US on an escape path. Much could depend on the looming conflict in the euro battlefield between German and Italian nationalisms.

BUNDESBANK FAILS HARD MONEY ADVOCATES THROUGHOUT EMU JOURNEY

Even without the benefit of hindsight, there were grounds for doubting right at the beginning of monetary union that German citizens or anyone else could count on present and future Bundesbank chiefs to boldly defend German fiscal independence (not to be sucked into huge potential transfers including implicit loan guarantees) or the monetary principles which had made the DM hard and popular. The Bundesbank chief was a political appointment after all. Yes there had been Dr Otmar Emminger in the past, but there had also been Dr Hans Tietmeyer (appointed by Chancellor Kohl in the crucial years leading up to the launch of EMU and renowned for never raising interest rates once).

In fact in the history of the hard Deutsche mark, it had been finance minister Karl Shiller (the SPD economics and finance minister in the crucial years 1969–73) who had refused to go along with the Nixon-Burns monetary inflation and insisted on DM revaluation or flotation—leading rather than lagging some key Bundesbank officials on this (see Beyer et al. 2009). Dr Emminger, the famous Bundesbank chief who presided over the glory days of the hard DM, owed his appointment to the finance minister and chancellor—then in Bonn (see also Emminger 1977). Subsequently however there have been finance ministers and chancellors who put European integration or other political purposes ahead of monetary hardness.

Weak and soft-principled Bundesbank chiefs should have been well within the realm of expectations. The Bundesbank president following Hans Tietmeyer (retired August 1999) was Ernst Welteke (nominated by Chancellor Schroeder and his finance minister Hans Eichel in May 1999: Eichel had been Premier of Hesse where Welteke had been the regional Bundesbank president and prior to that the state finance minister). The successor to Welteke (the latter resigned in 2004 under a small cloud related to questions about who paid for a trip to Monaco), Axel Weber, also appointed by Hans Eichel, did make clear his unhappiness about the start of the euro bailouts and resigned (February 2011) to take a top job in the global banking industry. He is not on record as a dissident from the prevailing monetary direction taken by the ECB during the years 2003–06 including its adoption of a strict inflation target. During those years the "threat" of "deflation" seemed to be centred in Germany rather than elsewhere in the union.

Even so, how did it escape the Bundesbank's notice that the pursuance of a 2% inflation target in a situation where there existed a strong natural rhythm downwards (from globalization and technological change in this instance) would empower asset price inflation and in a way which would ultimately burden Germany? The carry trades which boomed in this episode of asset price inflation (2003–07) included the huge speculative inflows into weaker European sovereign debts, with government bonds of Greece, Spain, and Italy, selling at only tiny yield margins above German government debt at the peak. Ultimately it was German taxpayers who would backstop the rescue efforts for this. If the Bundesbank experts had thought about all of this, then we should not have seen Professor Issing leading the introduction of the 2% standard and the current Bundesbank president raising no objections. They did not serve Germany well.

Their apologists or defenders could say that although the German taxpayer might eventually have been burdened (and there could be a long interim when the burdens were contingent and hypothetical rather than actual), German export industry could do very well out of the situation, gaining an increased competitive advantage versus counterparts in Italy, Spain, or France and enjoying buoyant markets in these countries where credit growth was rapid. But overall this was surely false prosperity in aggregate—though there could of course be individual gainers and losers (and the gainers might include those with heavy bearing on government policies given the closeness of the big exporting companies to the ruling CDU party). The gains had a counterpart in eventual bad debts and in a long period of subsequent under-performance in the weak debtor economies.

Under Chancellor Merkel, Maastricht Monetary Constitution Becomes Dead Letter

Chancellor Merkel nominated her top economic adviser Jens Weidmann to succeed Axel Weber and did not oppose the appointment of Mario Draghi as ECB president in 2011 (though having previously indicated that Weber would be her preferred candidate for the job). Weidmann certainly mouthed some opposition to the continuing back-door bailouts and money printing policies of the ECB under Chief Draghi, but many critics view this as too soft. In particular in a key speech early in 2016 at a time when politicians within the Christian Democratic Union were rebelling against Draghi's negative rate and quantitative easing policies, Weidmann stood up for Draghi and expressed his loyalty to the ECB on these issues (see Brown, April 2016). The Bundesbank under his lead has not launched a serious critique of the 2% inflation standard, and indeed all the evidence suggests that this institution has been broadly behind this.

Jens Weidmann sees it differently.

In his interview with the *Financial Times* in early April 2016 (12), he said:

> *It's not unusual for politicians to have opinions on monetary policy, but we are independent. The ECB has to deliver on its price stability mandate* (Weidmann does not clarify here, but he means 2 per cent inflation) *and thus an expansion monetary policy stance is appropriate at this juncture regardless of different views about specific measures.*

In other words, according to Germany's top central banker, the most important issue currently at stake was the preservation of unquestioned independent authority for his own and other central banks. For all practical purposes, German Chancellor Angela Merkel agreed with him about this, and the two of them sided with Draghi and the ECB against the chorus of German politicians who had been savaging the ECB's further dive into negative interest rates and massive balance sheet expansion.

There's no reason to question the sincerity of Dr Weidmann's belief in the EMU-era mythology that European monetary stability depends first and foremost on the independence of the ECB and other central banks from interference by mere politicians. But even the most sincere belief in a myth cannot make it true. The old, hard DM was born and flourished during an era when the Bundesbank—closely allied with the German government—was prepared to defy conventional central bankers' club wisdom and pioneer a monetary policy regime on its own (strictly limiting monetary base growth while allowing interest rates to be freely determined by markets).

Maybe even some sceptics about monetary union were surprised by the rapidity with which Professor Issing adopted the 2% inflation standard— first in a soft form (1999–2002) and then in a rigid form from spring 2003 (an undershooting of the inflation target as serious as an overshooting). The journey had started in the run-up to EMU with the abandonment of any pivotal role for monetary base. In particular there was the decision that a market interest rate was to be paid on reserves (rather than zero interest as under the hard money regime of the DM and indeed all monetary regimes up until this point) as from when the ECB opened its doors. The high reserve requirements which helped buoy the demand for high-powered money and strengthen its position at the pivot under the hard money DM had progressively been lowered already through the 1990s (the Bundesbank responding to pressure from the bank lobby) and had been virtually scrapped as part of the pre-EMU negotiations. (Apparently the UK negotiators whilst UK membership of EMU was still a live possibility had been adamantly against substantial reserve requirements.)

The ECB presidents were all "internationalists", part of the global central banker's club consensus, with no inclination to defiantly pursue an independent path. And here was a central paradox. According to lead founders and advocates of the European Monetary Union, a fundamental purpose was to bolster monetary independence and insulate Europe from unstable US monetary policies. This aim had been prominent in their discussions during the Volcker-Greenspan monetary inflation of 1985–89 (post-Plaza) when the DM had been driven up once more against European neighbours as the German currency assumed its characteristic safe-haven role (and indeed the Bundesbank still had sufficient resolve and defiance not to stomach a Japan-style importation of US monetary policy so as to limit currency overshoot). Yet no sooner than the ECB started life did it become clear that the central bankers there would not boldly defy the next episode of US monetary inflation (which started in 2002–03 in response to the recession and sluggish economy in the wake of the IT and Nasdaq bust). Instead, as the euro started to strengthen, the ECB was quick to follow the US monetary lead, creating a scare about "deflation danger" and intensifying its targeting of 2% inflation at exactly the same time as the Federal Reserve (spring 2003).

The ECB Embraces the 2% Inflation Standard

Even at that point, the ECB still had the opportunity to distance itself from the Federal Reserve, by clarifying that the pursuance of 2% inflation should not be seen as a precise exercise and that it was more worried about overshoots than undershoots. In practice though it elaborated specific European reasons for interpreting "stable prices" as inflation at 2%, not significantly more nor less. Sticky prices and wages at the level of national economies were one important such reason advanced by the ECB for choosing a 2% inflation target say rather than 1%. The hypothesis: a big cluster of wages and prices could get out of line at a national level, and it would be easier to re-establish equilibrium relative price levels between the national members at a positive average inflation rate of 2% rather than at 1% or 0%. In fact, the need for absolute price or wage falls should be avoided (although perhaps not for small countries which had little weight in the average).

This was another version of the "sticky" or "non-flexible" price or wage behaviour used by advocates of the 2% inflation standard in the US. The additional wrinkle (or reinforcement) suggested in the case of the eurozone was that the need for price and wage falls could be general across a member country, rather than unevenly dispersed across regions (of which there would be several in at least the large members) or sub-regions, adding to potential frictional costs. Take the example of the immediate aftermath of the boom and bust in 2010. There was a widespread perception that during the boom prices and wages in Italy and Spain had risen far above their sustainable long-run level. In principle this could be rectified by a steep and quick fall in those countries with core country prices (in particular Germany remaining flat). ECB policy-makers appear to have in mind a preferable outcome—a 2% p.a. climb in German prices over say five to ten years alongside stable prices in Spain and Italy.

But this preference was problematic. To get 2% inflation in Germany would require the pumping of monetary inflation, thereby activating the twins of asset price inflation and goods inflation. The latter though might be camouflaged by spurts in productivity growth, globalization, and digitalization. And the 2% inflation standard empowers inertia regarding inflation expectations, though this might ultimately prove brittle. With downward pressure on wages and prices in Spain or Italy relieved by overall monetary inflation, it could be that overall relative price adjustment in the union would be stultified by inertia and more generally economic frictions could be stronger than in a non-inflationary environment. In particular, monetary inflation could mean a huge gravy train into Italy (as the Bundesbank provided giant credits for the ailing Italian banks and indirectly the sovereign via the ECB target-2 system), relieving the pressures thereby in the Italian economy for an adjustment down of prices and wages and for profound structural adjustment. The gravy train was a drug train.

The ECB officials arguing for 2% inflation had a second familiar string to their bow—the problem that interest rates could be blocked from reaching equilibrium negative real levels at low rates of inflation or zero rates by the zero-rate bound. ECB policy-makers no more than their Fed counterparts were willing to contemplate that negative real rates could come about via pro-cyclical moves in prices and wages.

The non-conventional tool box and more generally the pursuance of a 2% inflation standard at a time when the natural rhythm of prices was downwards globally and in Europe due to globalization and the digitalization revolution had particular appeal to an ECB chair committed to "doing whatever it takes to save the euro" and in particular to salvaging the financial situation of his home nation (Italy). Mario Draghi did not aspire to his portrait being next to Otmar Emminger in the Hall of Fame—but next to Count Cavour and Guiseppe Mazzine, that was possible! As in the previous decade, there is absolutely no evidence that either Berlin or the Bundesbank realized just how serious the dangers could ultimately be for Germany. Again, superlow or as now ever-negative interest rates would fuel desperation for yield amongst investors—meaning that Italy, for example, could re-finance its debt despite the fragile fundamentals at yields below those on US Treasuries. Weak banks could attract capital into equity-type liabilities which would have been exorbitantly expensive under sound money conditions. And now radical monetary policy options in support of the 2% inflation standard included vast expansion of the central bank balance sheet, which in the European case would be the source of huge resources for "doing whatever it takes".

Draghi-Merkel Pact on Vast Monetary Base Expansion

ECB Chief Draghi when campaigning (with the central bank and also in his discussions with Berlin) for quantitative easing in the pursuance of a 2% inflation target was actually opening the route to years of massive inflation in asset markets. This would drive up the prices of weak debts (including many Italian) allowing re-financing of these and also for a takeover of some of these debts by German taxpayers. And the whole process of monetary inflation was to bear most heavily on German households who for years would have to put up with substantially negative real rates of return on their savings (a reflection of prices rising more rapidly in Germany than elsewhere and the zero or negative rates as fixed by the ECB). Meanwhile the ECB via its quantitative easing was silently imposing huge potential liabilities on Northern European taxpayers, most importantly in Germany. The Bundesbank and Berlin could have said a strong no to the 2% regime which enabled all this. But the silence was deadening.

Plausibly German politicians (including Chancellor Merkel and those around her) counted on the general prosperity and satisfaction of the "haves" with booming real estate and equity prices to outvoice and outweigh (at the ballot box) the losers. The Big Business exporters were particularly heavy haves on the political scales. And meanwhile Chancellor Merkel would not have to face or admit the unpleasant truth that the monetary union she had played such a large part in bringing about and then defending was a fateful wrong turn for her fellow citizens in aggregate.

These may or may not have been the calculation of both sides (Draghi and Merkel) when they met in Berlin in early 2016 (just before the launch of ECB QE). And we should allow for the diplomatic skills of the ECB Chief. The Bundesbank had drawn up a neat plan which seemed to limit potential loss for German taxpayers. Each national central bank would buy only the government bonds issued by its own government—meaning that the Italian central bank would be the only member of the ECB buying Italian government bonds. That was intended to mean no assumption of new contingent liabilities due to the money creation process for German taxpayers.

However, events turned out differently.

The investors who sold Italian government debt to the Banca d'Italia for the most part did not want to continue holding the proceeds in the Italian banking system. So they transferred the deposits to Germany. The resulting large surplus of funds in the German banking system was re-lent in Italy via the central banking clearing mechanism (target 2), meaning that the Bundesbank emerged with a huge credit position in the so-called target 2 system, where the Italian central bank was a matching large debtor. In effect, the Bundesbank had monetized the Italian government debt, and the German taxpayer would end up standing behind any eventual loss (as would occur if eventually Italy broke away from the European Monetary Union).

Perhaps the realization of all this played a role in the surprisingly strong election result (September 2017) for the anti-euro anti-immigration party (the Alternativ fuer Deutschalnd (AfD)). But there was no general exposure of the dangers. The Bundesbank president, Jens Weidmann, was certainly not the man to draw his fellow citizen's attention to an "Italian" or wider plot within the ruling council of the ECB; and it remains unclear at this late point that he even fully understood the significance of the 2% inflation target in camouflaging a blatant transfer of huge resources via the ECB.

Chancellor Merkel could never bring herself to say no—even to greater and greater extravagance of ECB Chief Draghi in his efforts to do whatever it would take to save the euro. Before that, she had not said "go" to French President Sarkozy on that fateful Saturday evening in Brussels (March 2010), when the former threatened to take France out of EMU if she would not agree to the ECB funding a massive rescue operation for Greece (and other weak sovereigns). She could not say no to ECB Draghi when he pleaded with her to agree to the start of a massive QE operation in 2017.

The monetary constitution of the Maastricht Treaty could have been defended, but the German chancellor and the Bundesbank presidents of those years did not have the courage or the honour to do so. The German political or legal system did not hold them to account.

The irony is that the gravy train into Italy or elsewhere, which Germany financed, could not help build a sustainable European monetary and economic union. In fact the trains were filled with "monetary opium" which drugged the recipient nation's economy, paralysing the "invisible hands" (market forces) which could create economic and political renaissance. In the case of Italy, artificially low interest rates and QE facilitated pushing the can down the road—the government sector, banks, and zombie firms in the private sector were all able to demonstrate turnarounds without any real reforms. The big adjustment down in prices and costs and the flourishing of investment especially in new firms just did not take place. The verdict of history on Mario Draghi and his enablers in Berlin may well be that they strove, as did Chancellor Metternich, to sustain a European order—including Italy's place in that—which was already fundamentally bust.

The effective abdication of monetary power by Germany in comparison with the heyday of the 1970s when its pioneering and practising of monetarism made it the European monetary hegemon was a misfortune for world economic and financial stability, albeit that the "euro-nationalists" in Paris and elsewhere were celebrating. In the aftermath of Bretton Woods' collapse, the hard DM had set a limit eventually even to the US power to create monetary shock. The Arthur Burns Fed had found that its pursuance of "bold monetary expansion" eventually triggered a collapse of the dollar against the world's number 2 currency (the Deutsche mark); this collapse in turn translated directly into increased momentum of inflation in the US economy. In today's world with no effective monetary competitor to the dollar, the inflation-mongers at the Fed can enjoy a much longer ride before the chickens come home to roost.

COULD GERMANY YET LEAD THE WORLD BACK TO HARD MONEY?

That is a pertinent question at a time when the US has apparently abandoned any prospect of taking that path, even though the Republicans under President Obama's Administration had sponsored "sound money bills" which got nowhere. And there was the earlier abandonment to consider. Paul Volcker after attacking the high inflation of the late 1970s and endorsing a monetary experiment abandoned this in the mid-1980s in pursuing a dollar devaluation policy as orchestrated by the Treasury Secretary Baker in the second Reagan Administration. Volcker signed up to the Plaza Accord, pledging the Fed would pursue an easy money policy in accordance with its aim (of a lower dollar). That was a historic opportunity lost.

Volcker had second thoughts it seems by early 1987 as the US economy re-bounded out of growth recession and inflation dangers increased visibly. But his remorse did not make friends in the White House, where James Baker blocked his hopes of a rollover appointment as Fed chief. Alan Greenspan succeeded him in summer 1987, and the new Fed chief soon hinted that he would not be keeping to the so-called Louvre Accord of earlier that year (of which Volcker had been a keen advocate) under which the US would cooperate with its G-7 partners in bringing the dollar's slide to an end around present levels. The Bundesbank under Chief Poehl would not go along with the easier US monetary stance and proceeded with an early autumn tightening of German monetary policy. The setback for the dollar brought attention of markets to the rising US inflation danger. According to one well-known commentator (an anti-Baker conservative, Jude Wanniski), this state of inflation alert was a key factor precipitating the October 1987 equity market crash. Equity investors did not warm to the prospect of inflation danger, realizing that Uncle Sam's take was likely to increase (in various forms of inflation tax) and that episodes of inflation acceleration usually end up badly.

Some would argue this was the last day of glory for the hard Deutsche mark. The Bundesbank got the blame in the US political arena for the Crash, whilst in Europe the run-up of the Deutsche mark against other European currencies gave a fatal spring to momentum gathering towards the European Monetary Union (German export industries did not like the DM swings up against its key European neighbours, and elsewhere there was resentment at the new intra-European currency tension). There has been no hard money glory for the euro; that is sure. The path forward for sound money advocates, though, in Germany is particularly challenging. It is difficult to imagine any such path without revealing the huge costs for German citizens which have so far been camouflaged. But it is possible that these costs will become exposed anyhow by events. That would be the opportunity.

For example, the next episode of Crash and Great Recession could well bring a new sovereign debt and banking crisis within the European Monetary Union. Then the German chancellor and Bundesbank president could deliver their ultimatum of what continued German support for the European Monetary Union would require. Top of the list would be a repudiation of all the constitutional erosions that occurred in the past two decades—no more bailouts through the ECB back door and the definition of what a sound money regime means (not 2% inflation perpetually). And there would have to be an agreed provision (and possibly limited help) for member countries to exit EMU if they could no longer sustain their present situation without subsidized external help.

The chancellor and Bundesbank president would have to be of a very different ideological persuasion from the present office-holders for anything like this to happen. The political currents behind a shift that would bring such a change at the top are largely unpredictable. We could imagine the Christian Democrats moving to the right with the strategic aim of winning votes back from the AfD (the anti-euro, anti-immigration party) and forming a new government with the FDP (Free Democrats). It is also within the realm of possibility to imagine the Social Democratic Party adopting a sound money programme, portraying this successfully as a way of improving the economic conditions of the middle class many of whom resent the plundering of their savings by negative interest rates and perpetual inflation. They would point out that the gainers of inflation and euro-monetary solidarity (including huge potential tax liabilities in the future) as it was practised under Chancellor Merkel and ECB Chief Draghi were the big business exporters and the wealthy.

BIBLIOGRAPHY

Beyer, A., Gaspar, V., Gerberding, C., & Issing, O. (2009, March). *Opting Out of the Great Inflation: German Monetary Policy After the Break Down of Bretton Woods* (ECB Working Paper Series No. 1020).

Brown, B. (2015). *Euro Crash*. Basingstoke: Palgrave.

Brown, B. (2016, April 21). *Jens Weidmann's Disastrously Misplaced Loyalty to the Central Bankers Club*. Hudson Institute.

Emminger, O. (1977, June). The D-Mark in the Conflict Between Internal and External Equilibrium 1948–75: Essays in International Finance, No. 122.

Geberding, C., Seitz, F., & Worms, A. (2005, December). How the Bundesbank Really Conducted Monetary Policy. *The North American Journal of Economics and Finance., 16*(3), 277–292.

Hildebrand, P. (2004, November 23). *From Monetarism to the Inflation Forecast: 30 Years of Swiss Monetary Policy*. Public lecture, University of Berne, Berne.

Joerges, C. (2015, November 18). *What Is Left of the European Economic Constitution After the Gauweiler Litigation* (pp. 99–118). ZenTra Working Paper in Transnational Studies, no. 60.

Weidmann, J. (2016, April 12). Interview with the *Financial Times*, Bundesbank's Weidmann Rebukes Draghi Critics in Berlin.

CHAPTER 9

Unaffordable Housing and Poor-Quality Money

Modern capitalism has failed to deliver two pre-requisites for the enjoyment of economic freedom: first, cheap and ever-improving quality of shelter and, second, a currency that performs well in its three functions (medium of exchange, store of value, and measuring unit). The two failures are intimately connected.

The wild experiments that governments authorize in pursuit of their chosen monetary regime have undermined the overall quality of their currency, whether dollars, euros, or yen. At best, the monetary outlook is for perpetual goods and services inflation at 2% per annum with prolonged episodes of downward manipulated interest rates, especially at long maturities; and there is an abundance of many worse prospects than that (including yet another era of high inflation in goods and services markets). As a medium of exchange, fiat money (except for cash) leaves an extensive digital trace which many users of libertarian inclination resent. And almost without exception, government printing presses fail to provide large-denomination notes despite plentiful evidence that these would enjoy strong transactions demand from wholly legitimate sources and would help combat oligopoly power amongst the providers of credit and payment cards (see Chap. 10).

Along the way these experiments have been the source of asset price inflation disease (the monetary twin of goods and services inflation, whether camouflaged or not by such "disinflationary" factors as globalization or more broadly technological change). Long-term interest markets rendered dysfunctional by the present monetary regime have facilitated the spread of this disease into the residential real estate markets.

A Plague of High House Prices

At the time of writing (spring 2018), broad indices show house prices nationwide in the US at more than 15% above the levels of the last peak (2006/07) or in real terms less than 10% lower. How can this infernal circle of unsound money and housing price spirals be stopped?

The phenomenon is something new. As Robert Shiller has noted, "over the long-run it hasn't been so" (see Shiller 2016). He notes despite solid price increases over the last few years, land and homes have actually been disappointing investments.

Over the 100 years from 1915 to 2015, Shiller finds that real home prices (as calculated according to the S&P/Case-Shiller US National Home Price Index) grew 1.8 times, an average of only 0.6% p.a. (as against real GDP at 3.2% p.a.). A good part of the answer according to Shiller comes from rising supply (as prices rise, companies build more houses, and the supply floods the market, keeping prices down).

Of course, underneath every home is a piece of land. "Sometimes that little piece of land dominates the value of the home, particularly in dense urban areas." But as Shiller explains, people in such places aren't buying land for its own sake but for the myriad services that housing provides. These services have developed enormously. There are vastly more highways and automobiles, telephones, and various electronic connections, enabling people to leave centre cities and still obtain the housing services they want. Thus from a long-term perspective, these developments have relieved a great deal of the upward pressure on home prices in cities.

Shiller is non-fazed by the price surges of the past 20 years (even taking account of the bust in 2007). "The slow long-term pace of home price increases is not surprising. Nor would it be shocking if this trend continued for the next century. A more extreme outcome is also quite plausible. It's far from inconceivable that the real price of land could be ever lower than it is right now."

Shiller does not mention the fact that the surge in house prices in the US from the late 1990s and through to the present was coincidental with the adoption of the 2% inflation-targeting regime. Indeed he does not refer to the monetary environment at all at any point of his historical explanations (or more generally his psychological explanations). Nor does he discuss in more than passing fashion the thorny topic of zoning restrictions.

In broad terms we can think of several essential reforms which would make housing "affordable again" without waiting for largely unexplained 100-year trends to re-assert themselves.

SOUND MONEY FOSTERS AFFORDABLE HOUSING

The guiding principle of the monetary regime should be to produce sound money that the public would embrace (not one which is primarily a vehicle for neo-Keynesian policy implementation and for levying inflation tax in its various forms as discussed in Chap. 13). According to Mises, sound money principle has two aspects (see Salerno 2015). It is affirmative in approving the market's choice of a commonly used medium of exchange. It is negative in obstructing the government's propensity to meddle with the currency system.

In modern times many of us may reminisce about the hard Deutsche mark or Swiss franc and their popularity in the 1970s and 1980s. The sound money theorists would dispute their soundness in absolute terms—with the central banks administering these regimes following at best mixed principles. Indeed they would claim that for all the century since 1918, the monetary system in the US and globally has been plagued by unsoundness—whether the Irving Fisher exhorted price stabilization of the 1920s or the Keynesian and neo-Keynesian macro-management more recently.

And through this "modern era", there have been many asset price inflation episodes, some involving residential real estate (including the boom of 1925–28). Overall though, until the 2000s, the residential real estate markets in the US did not in aggregate become the star focus of the asset price inflation. That is an area where the past two decades stand out as different and where the extent and type of monetary distortion under the global 2% inflation standard likely played a dominant role.

In any case, the hard monies of the 1970s and 1980s, whether sound or not, are long gone and instead Americans, Europeans, and Japanese continue to suffer the cursed monetary climate of asset price boom and bust, long stretches of enforced negative real interest rates, and the perpetual menace of a new high inflation era at no uncertain future date. For ordinary citizens, the Yellen or Powell dollar, the Draghi euro, and the Kuroda yen are unloved and miserable enforced alternatives to the hard money which many would prefer.

The global 2% inflation standard has been with us for almost a quarter century. It set the stage for three great asset inflations (1996–2000, 2003–7 and 2011–?) as central banks led by the Federal Reserve have sought to resist the decline in prices brought by rapid globalization and technological change (especially digitalization). Wild monetary experimentation has led households to search for yield and safety against inflation storm in the long run.

EMOTIONS STOKE ASSET INFLATION IN HOUSING

And as regards safety, residential space has a special role. Individuals are anxious lest they and their families are shut out of occupying desirable residential space in the future by a surge of demand as monetary inflation fears gain pace. They get frightened by stories of the ever-larger demand from wealthy foreigners and fear that they and their children will be "priced out". And the positive feedback loop—from a long time of rising prices (even with some dips)—reinforces them in their boldness.

Altruism and sense of family preservation add to the potential feedback loops from house price boom to ever-more speculative behaviour. We talk about the "bank of the parents" supplying deposits to their children, so they can get on the housing ladder and avoid the related frictions and unpleasantness that sinks so many marriages. No one can fault the human motive of helping one's children, but translating this into big positions in an over-priced housing asset is surely questionable. Parents might do better to tie the gift to "anything other than a home".

Ultimately the gainer from soft loans to children to buy houses is not the children (in aggregate) but the present owners—landowners or homeowners—who are selling at even more inflated prices. It comes under the same heading as state help in various forms to support low-income households pay the rent; collectively this support pushes up the rents and sometimes prices of "affordable" housing—and the hand-outs would be better spent in a general income-related pay-out rather than tied to a particular commodity (in this case housing).

The whole subject of residential real estate rents—the public policy options and private household decisions regarding owning or renting—is dominated by a perception (largely correct) that the rental market is highly imperfect. Yes, rents may be less volatile and have less potential to appreciate than capital prices. But typically tenure of rented accommodation is highly uncertain, and there are high agency costs (potential disputes between tenant and landlord and difficulty in enforcing repair covenants). The tenant proverbially does not enjoy security.

Hence the apparent case for buying real estate under unsound monetary conditions especially the 2% inflation standard is strong. The danger of another high inflation era looms large on the horizon as widely perceived—even though short-run inflation prospects seem contained according to the economic forecasters. Their projections and the central bank commitments are all based on various degrees of inertia, and who would trust the econometric models which together with politics guide the central bankers?

DYSFUNCTIONAL LONG-TERM RATE MARKETS FUEL HOUSING DISTORTIONS

As we have seen (Chap. 4), long-term rates are severely depressed in a dysfunctional market that no longer provides reliable readings of high inflation danger in the long-run future. The present monetary regime distorts the thermometer's function. So individuals seeking safety in residential real estate have strong incentive to couple the ownership of such an asset with a big mortgage. There is a natural hedge here. The long-term rate market may become functional again, with rates there jumping far above present levels. Real estate prices would then fall sharply but so would the market value of the outstanding loan, so long as the interest rate on this was fixed. So the profit on re-financing (so long as institutional arrangements allow this) would offset some of the loss on the underlying real estate.

And there is much scope for irrational behaviour here under the influence of distorted long-term rates. In particular many would-be homeowners take the cost of housing as the mortgage servicing cost times the house price. In principle they should be treating the home with a large loan outstanding as a risky asset (full of specific risks which are hard to diversify as well as general market risk) on which commensurate returns should include a substantial risk premium; and the loan outstanding multiplies the inherent risk. But under the monetary regime of the 2% inflation standard amplified by the opening of the non-conventional tool box, many see the abnormally low interest rates as a boost to housing affordability (less monthly payments).

And in a climate where most assets are rising strongly, including real estate, the capital gains might seem like an almost sure thing—with speculative narratives (foreign buyers, parents' bank, mega city formation) to support this. Non-leveraged homeowners and investors can make similar calculations distorted by various forms of irrationality (versions of what in the equity markets during a long period of zero or negative interest rates is described as the "nowhere else to go story").

SUBSIDY ON LEVERAGE HITS AFFORDABILITY

Moreover in many fiscal systems, the mortgage enjoys favorable tax treatement (and the Republican tax act of December 2017 did not end the subsidy, though it was curtailed in some respects). Mortgage interest deductibility is in fact a subsidy on leverage in the housing market.

The price of homes, however, is typically pushed up by the subsidy, which fuels demand to a higher level than otherwise. The exception is where the supply of residential space is highly elastic in response to price change (as would be the case if new residential land is in virtually unlimited supply at the present fixed price, which could be near zero in the case of land "at the frontier"). But in the context of serious restrictions on supply, many in the form of state- or municipal-level zoning regulations, the subsidies in effect enrich current homeowners and penalize would-be new entrants to homeownership. Most impacted of all? Those not collecting the subsidy on leverage (i.e. cash buyers).

And some cash buyers most of all at the high end of residential real estate markets (where tax subsidies on mortgages are less of a relevant factor, given that the deductions are usually subject to a cap) in globally popular metropolitan centres may be paying some premium for tax benefits even though these are not being used by themselves. In particular, high-end residential real estate has in some centres retained its role as an asset which offshore companies with anonymous ownership can purchase without any hindrance—and so demand from this source can result in substantial price premiums (unless supply of land is highly elastic).

Other tax subsidies lower down the scale (of luxury) push up the price of homeownership. For example, the Fed's asset purchase programme, which has involved accumulating vast quantities of mortgages, has suppressed the long-term interest rates on such paper. Fannie Mae and Freddie Mac and their effective semi-official guarantees to bond holders have similar impact. And ultimately subsidies in the banking industry related to "too big to fail" encourage lending beyond what would occur in a free-market context and do the same thing: push up house prices but reduce the cost of leverage taken on to pay those high prices.

Alex J. Pollock in a recent piece (2017) makes some poignant criticisms of US subsidized mortgages. In particular:

in 1967 the US home ownership rate was 63.6%. Today, in 2017 it is 63.7%. The government mountain labored mightily (intense government mortgage credit promotion and guarantees) and brought fourth less than a mouse.

Pollock calculates that almost 60% of total mortgage loans outstanding in the US ultimately have their risk put on the taxpayer—and that is before considering the involvement of the Federal Reserve through its mortgage purchase programme.

We can see that the US now has a giant Government Housing Combine. There is a tight interlinking of three principal parts – the US Treasury, the Federal Reserve and Fannie-Freddie-Ginnie.

What has this massive government intervention in housing finance achieved? There are two very large results: inflating house prices and inducing higher debt and leverage in the system.

Confronted with these inevitable effects, one school of politics always demands still more government guarantees, more debt and more leverage. This will result in yet higher house prices and less affordability until the boom cycle ingloriously ends. A better answer is instead to reduce the government interventions and distortions and move toward a housing finance sector with a much bigger private market presence.

If the idea is to harness fiscal incentives to reduce the price of homes, then those should relate to boosting supply of residential space not demand. Consider alternatively expensing of capital expenditure against tax, where the expenditure increases the supply of effective living space (e.g. replacing warehouse or offices with residential space or building residential space higher than previously). These incentives are related to a third area of reform—deregulation.

DEREGULATION AND DEZONING

The chief regulatory restraint is land zoning. Consider Tokyo as a live example of what can happen. Certain districts within Tokyo have largely been deregulated, meaning that there is no limit to turning warehouse space into residential or on building high. And so for a similar population influx (yes, despite a steadily failing Japanese population, there has been persistent influx to Tokyo), the volume of residential construction in Tokyo has far outpaced great metropolitan areas in Europe and the US. Interestingly price rises have been slow at best in spite of the wild monetary ride under Abenomics.

Beyond land zoning, targets for reform include the dismantling of handicaps to innovation and flexibility in rental contracts whilst eliminating the perverse tax incentives that favour homeownership over renting. Ultimately the ordinary citizen would gain from greater choice in how to acquire residential space whether as owner or renter without having to navigate/encounter snakes and ladders as installed on the drawing board by the myriad regulatory and tax offices.

Real Estate Taxation: Neutrality, Burdens, and Exemptions

In general terms, though there are some notable tax breaks on residential real estate, it is a highly taxed asset in most jurisdictions. In so far as high taxes curb the supply of living space (this is the case where the supply of land is price elastic) they fan unaffordability. As an immobile asset, real estate is easy to tax—and in the front line for the take are local and state governments. The scope for avoidance or evasion of tax burdens on real estate is correspondingly less than for many other forms of investment. The central or federal government may also weigh in with inheritance taxes and capital gains taxes (though often owner-occupied primary residence is exempt from the latter at least when rolled over into a new home).

In principle in a tax-neutral regime, the consumption of real estate services (including space availability) would be taxed at a similar rate to other consumer goods and services whether in the forms of sales tax or value-added tax (if that is not the case, with the real estate consumption tax relatively low, the tax system in effect induces "over-spending" on residential space, which in the context of inelastic supply would mean a significantly higher than otherwise price; where supply is elastic though, as is the case where residential land supply is not restricted, a low rate of consumption tax should mean more availability of residential space than otherwise). In practice this consumption tax on real estate is levied on tenants and owner-occupiers by local or state governments.

Income from residential real estate whether in the form of net rent received from tenants or imputed rent from owner-occupation would be taxed (under a neutral regime) at similar rates to income from other assets, after making suitable deductions for all costs including depreciation and maintenance. Under many tax regimes around the world, imputed rents do not come directly into taxable income directly though as described below real estate turnover taxes may be applied as a very imperfect substitute for income tax. Where tax on income from residential real estate is low (relative to that of other assets) which in some jurisdictions is the case for the imputed rents from owner-occupation in particular, then there could be an inducement (from prices reflecting the income tax advantage in part) to extra construction of real estate space, so long as supply of land is elastic.

In practice, tax neutrality for residential real estate is not found either on the spending or income side, though there are big differences between states in federal unions and between sovereign states. Local annual taxes related to "rental value" are like a sales tax in principle; in the US no general statement is possible about whether these are above or below the relevant sales tax (in the particular state in question); and in some places, the taxes are regressive (not rising fully in line with rental levels, so hyper-luxury is relatively under-taxed). In Europe, and especially the UK, the tendency is for the local taxes calculated as a percentage of rent to be substantially less than the VAT rate especially at the high end, but again generalization is not possible (in the UK taxes are relatively low on rents). In some jurisdictions, local governments or the federal government levies capital or turnover taxes on residential real estate apparently as a substitute for tax on imputed rents (which is not levied), but in doing so, they induce much distortion and indeed dislocation in the marketplace.

This may be particularly the case with respect to turnover taxes. These are popular with governments given the low administration and collection costs. And they may seem from a political viewpoint as more palatable than taxes on imputed rental income to homeowners and indeed a substitute for these, but in fact they are quite distinct. They in effect levy a penalty on homeowners who intend to hold the given space only for a short time or even worse on homeowners who have a sudden change of mind or circumstance.

The new homeowners may discover, for example, that soon after moving in, they don't like the new home as much as they thought they would; or they may find that they have to move elsewhere for over-riding job or other personal reasons. How can one defend a system of taxes which may inflict spectacular large losses on individuals who change their minds or find themselves in such changed circumstances? Homeownership then becomes the preserve of those bold enough to imagine that the long run means the long run. And if they know in advance this is not the case, then they are heavily incentivized to opt for rentals, with all their inconveniences (agency costs). There are some fixes possible for the extreme side-effects of the turnover tax, such as rebates on sale of part of the previous tax paid, and these shrink with years in occupation. But they are not found in practice.

As illustration, a 5% turnover tax on residential real estate in a marketplace where rents are around 4% of capital value and where the average holding period for owner-occupiers is 10 years would translate into a 12.5% annual tax (on imputed gross rents before any deduction for maintenance and depreciation). That may seem a good guess as an equivalent to a neutral tax on net imputed rental income. But the owner-occupier who holds for just one year is clobbered—and somewhat less for two years and so on. At the other end of the scale, the generational owner-occupier, who holds for 25 years, is taxed much more lightly than any neutral equivalent (to income tax) would suggest. An approximation to tax neutrality would require the levying of supplementary turnover tax every decade even if no transaction, perhaps with payment deferred until any eventual actual sale. The real estate investor who does not occupy the home (but lets it out instead) is in any case subject to income tax on net rents so in principle should not be subject to the burden of turnover taxation (where this is levied as a proxy for income tax). In practice such investors may hold for very long periods of time, so minimizing the burden—but the implication is to reduce their buying and selling activity through time, surely bad for market efficiency, flexibility, and liquidity.

Turnover taxes as described are generally low in the US but high in many other countries, ranging up to 10% or more. Accordingly it may be the case that in the US the imputed income from homeownership is indeed somewhat "under-taxed", even when taking account of amortizing the turnover tax over time. And in the US, inheritance tax is much less burdensome than in many foreign countries (e.g. Europe or Japan). Even so, it is not obvious that residential real estate overall in the US or Europe, taking account of consumer and income taxes as analysed here but before considering the subsidization of leverage, is favoured relative to other assets, especially taking account of effectiveness of collection.

SMALL-COUNTRY DILEMMA: HOW TO PREVENT OVER-HEATING OF REAL ESTATE?

These housing market issues become of particular relevance to small- and medium-sized economies under the regime of the 2% inflation standard.

The governments/central banks here face a particular dilemma, especially if there is an attractive narrative which could buoy speculative interest (carry trades) in their national currency. For example, a range of commodity producing and/or emerging market economies have found themselves during the present asset price inflation episode encountering huge demand for their still-positive interest rate monies. That narrative is sometimes rapid growth potential. And a sequence of capital gains on the related currency carry trade imparts positive feedback loops to still more participation in that.

In principle the central bank of the small country could stick to its hard money principles, though these cannot be applied easily in the context of a small money with likely unstable demand and no well-established pivot in the form of high-powered money. If, accordingly, the central bank rejects the strategy of adopting the zero or negative rate and QE policies of the US or EU, their currency could appreciate sharply, putting huge pressure on the conventional export industries. On the other hand, if they try to avoid this by shifting towards a US-style policy, their domestic real estate markets and other related markets could become enveloped in huge speculative bubble.

Even with a hard money policy, their domestic real estate might attract foreign yield-starved investors, especially if there is a good story; but the prospect of a big decline in the national currency at some future date would hold this in check. And alongside, a reform programme to remove restraints on supply in the domestic real estate market would further reduce the risk of bubble formation. As discussed earlier in this volume, the defiant pursuance of an alternative monetary regime to that followed in Washington and Frankfurt could be accompanied by an explanation from politicians and central bankers responsible (in the small- or medium-sized economy) about the stakes involved and the sacrifices to be made, all for the sake of more enduring prosperity.

And defiance is not all bad news for the citizens of the small country. They may have a historic opportunity to buy foreign asset cheap, with foreign capital inflows fuelled by an irrational frenzy for yield (meaning that the foreigners are over-paying for domestic currency on any rational assessment of future scenarios). Eventually domestic citizens will score a big capital gain on the foreign currency they buy during this period, with the offsetting loss landing on the frenzied yield hunters.

In the great asset price inflation of the present decade, policy-makers in a range of small- or medium-sized countries rejected following the defiant path of hard money. For example, Canada and Australia found their currencies under tremendous upward pressure in the first stage of the US monetary inflation as dollar depreciation and the China monetary boom drove the prices of their key commodity exports towards the sky. The central banks of both Commonwealth countries took the same tack—not allowing interest rates to rise in line with economic expansion fed by commodity export boom so as to contain the strength of their currencies. The result: a boom in residential real estate in the star cities (Sydney, Toronto and Vancouver) far outside the commodity producing regions. A lead narrative featured the flood of newly rich Chinese investors and occupiers of these. And though low, the interest rates had sparkled to a range of income-famished investors in the world outside, including European central banks and other sovereign wealth funds diversifying into these still-positive interest rate monies. Another feature of the monetary policies followed was the build-up of a consumer debt boom, in part taking advantage of the raised value of real estate collateral.

When the commodity boom (and related emerging market boom) cooled and in some cases burst during 2013–14/15, the central banks of these countries promptly lowered interest rates and apparently approved the strategy of even stimulating the already-hot residential real estate and construction sectors further so as to offset the drag from weak commodity prices. The two currencies fell by as much as 25% against the US dollar from their peaks in 2011/12 to their lows in 2015. Another cycle of monetary ease (with the Yellen Fed abandoning all prospective rate rises through the first three quarters of 2016, China drawing up a new mega monetary/credit package, and Japan/Europe intensifying negative interest rate and QE policies) contributed to a further build-up of speculative temperatures in Toronto, Vancouver, and Sydney. This time the authorities responded by opening the tool box of direct controls—including a special high tax rate on foreign purchases of real estate and strengthened prudential controls on domestic institutions lending into this space. There was no evidence of the huge inflow of funds into these currencies during the commodity boom receding, even though those investors encouraged by the IMF to embrace these as new additions of the reserve currency list must have resented by now that advice.

In fact, both countries (Canada and Australia) remained loyal and committed members of the 2% inflation standard. And so did that once hard money country Switzerland. In the 1990s it slowly drifted away from its monetarist past and adopted an inflation-targeting regime, albeit not so laser fixated on 2% as was more broadly the case. The sovereign debt crisis within the European Monetary Union in 2010–12/13 triggered huge demand for the Swiss franc as safe haven, to which the Swiss authorities responded by massive foreign exchange market intervention, a spell of fixing a ceiling to the currency, and ultimately a journey into an emergency negative interest rate regime which persisted for years. The big difference from the Australian and Canadian experiences was the massive foreign exchange market intervention and the adoption of radical monetary-easing measures—perhaps indicative of an even greater potential "overshoot" of the currency which might have occurred if the Swiss had held their hard money ground.

True, the Swiss National Bank prided itself on the vast profits which its portfolio manager made on its investment portfolio—deployed into US equities especially and all the various forms of the carry trade (including into Australian and Canadian currencies). But how would this ever percolate down into wealth for the ordinary Swiss citizen—if indeed the profits turned out to be sustained rather than vanish when the asset price inflation reached its final stage? In fact, most of the SNB's accumulation of foreign currencies occurred during the great unwind of the Swiss franc carry trade which had occurred in the asset price inflation of the first decade of this century. Then the whole world had been chasing speculative profit from borrowing low-interest-rate Swiss francs and yen, encouraged in part by extraordinarily easy monetary conditions in those two countries. When those carry trades snapped in the aftermath of that global asset price inflation (and the snapping was intensified by the eruption of the sovereign debt crisis in Europe), the Swiss National Bank sought to smooth out the rise of its currency to (ensure orderly markets in central bank speak). But that did not justify a huge accumulation of foreign exchange for ever more. Once the potentially disorderly conditions were over, the SNB should have started on a long-time run-down of its foreign exchange holdings not priding itself on how good an investor it was during the asset price inflation of the 2013–17 years.

Under the alternative of the franc having risen to a much higher peak and Swiss investors in the private sector having responded by buying foreign assets which were ostensibly cheap in real terms, they would have had a much bigger cushion against subsequent asset price deflation globally (with the cushion provided by courtesy of losses made by foreigners on their accumulated holdings of Swiss francs); and they would also have had the advantage of consumer goods imported at remarkably cheap prices over an extended period (including the purchase of homes abroad). And the reputation of the franc as a hard money and of Switzerland as defying monetary regimes as imposed by the US and Europe would have gained tremendously—a potentially significant long-run advantage for the Swiss economy.

In general we can say the global 2% inflation standard has not just delivered poor-quality monetary experience to the great powers, but it has extinguished the range of potential fiat money competition and thereby monetary choice available to global investors, to a greater extent than experienced under any previous stage of fiat money disorder. And during the days of warm summer sunshine when asset price inflation is at its peak boom phase with speculative temperatures at scorching highs, who is around to criticize the officials of the 2% inflation regime? They are instead enjoying the adulation of the crowds whose investments are flourishing. That is not to say that all the doubters have become believers. Indeed, the Bitcoin mania in the midst of glowing asset price inflation revealed at its heart a dissatisfaction with fiat money—whether due to ultimate inflation concerns or the view that this had become the ultimate spy. Some may have seen Bitcoin as the redeemer—others were just besotted with greed to cash in from a mad speculative ride, getting off in time before the dive lower. And the realists amongst their number could see all the flaws in the crypto concept including supply conditions, unstable demand, unknown scope for close substitutes to emerge, potential for theft, and more general hacking.

A Postscript on a "State of Inflation Alert"

Back to the world of fiat money as we know it: markets and the prevailing commentaries there sometimes cannot kick the habit of thinking that "they" (the authorities) will respond to significant inflation shock (in the sense of data and events apparently pointing to an increased likelihood of inflation rising well above target over the medium term) by implementing a serious and effective tightening of monetary policy. Take the "inflation alert" which sounded around the global financial marketplace in late 2017 and early 2018.

The alert was grounded on the combination of the Trump/Republican tax cuts and subsequent Federal spending boost (as part of the interim budget deals) which in combination will drive the Federal deficit in 2019 to near 6% of GDP; and this ballooning of red ink coincides with the coming into office of a new Fed chief viewed as likely to have a "good working relationship" with the Treasury secretary (the latter with expressed fondness for a soft dollar), approve the 3% growth target, and (as an ex-private equity baron) have little anxiety about asset price inflation. Alongside all this, the growth cycle upturn seemed to gain new momentum in late 2017 and early 2018 (albeit contrarians warned that this was in fact the peak of the growth cycle). In itself the inflation alert would justify some caution on the greenback, concern about implications for stocks (which historically lose from bouts of high inflation, not least because of increased take for Uncle Sam), and long-maturity fixed-rate bonds.

And indeed from mid-December 2017 to mid-February 2018, the greenback fell by some 5% against the euro and yen, the gold price in dollars rose by around 7%, ten-year US T-bond yields rose by 40 bp; the outlier (compared to what might have been expected under the sounding of inflation alert) were US stocks, which, though on a volatile ride, were around the same level (S&P 500) in late February 2018 as late 2017; but they were well down on their January peak. The fact that the US stock market was broadly resilient to inflation alert albeit not invincible could reveal some ambiguity as to whether in fact inflation is bad for stocks, at least during a phase in monetary inflation when asset price inflation is apparently dominant (rather than goods and services inflation); and everything else the same, a cheapening of the dollar lifts US earnings across a broad range of businesses.

The sounding of US inflation alert fostered, it seems, a new "game in town"; the monthly US CPI report became the focus of much trader activity. Market pundits suggest that the rules of this game would be that if the CPI shocks to the upside (relative to expectations), then the greenback would rise, the gold price in dollars fall, US stocks crumble, and long-term US rates jump, and conversely.

The assumed reactions of the markets to inflation data shock made little overall sense. They implicitly seemed to assume that data shock goes along with an increased likelihood of a serious change in Federal Reserve policy—away from monetary inflation to "orthodoxy". This change would indeed mean a stronger dollar, weaker gold, weaker stocks (at least for some time), and higher long-term rates, amongst other effects. But the big problem for the market pundits: this is just not on offer at all!

There is absolutely no indication that the Powell/Trump/Mnuchin Fed any more than the Yellen Fed would respond to inflation spike by seriously shifting monetary policy towards an underlying tighter condition. Officals speak of "letting the economy run hot for some time" (meaning that an inflation overshoot would be tolerated on the grounds that there had been an undershoot earlier). Maybe the Fed would contemplate making four rather than three miniscule rate rises (for the officially controlled short-term rate)—but so what? Such a miniscule adjustment would most probably still be consistent with monetary inflation becoming stronger not weaker. The stance of monetary policy cannot and should not be measured by the number of miniscule rate adjustments; it is quite possible for one extra step still to go along with monetary policy having become fundamentally more expansionary (as would be the case if inflation expectations and the neutral level of rates in real terms are rising).

In fact the February "CPI day" seemed to prove the pundits wrong. The data was consistent with a ratcheting up of inflation alert, albeit broad and severe winter conditions meant considerable ambiguity. The markets reacted as if there were no grounds for thinking that the Fed was about to get serious about arresting monetary inflation, the greenback fell, the gold price jumped, long-maturity interest rates rose, and stocks rose (some analysts suggested that a downward revision of retail sales data for the previous quarter meant even less prospect of any meaningful Fed tightening any time soon).

There is another big point to make alongside this mirage about Fed "tightening". The term "inflation alert" is itself highly misleading. Monetary inflation has been strong for many years already in this cycle; accordingly asset price inflation has been powerful; in goods and services markets, inflation has been substantial but camouflaged by official statisticians in part and by "disinflationary forces" in part.

If US inflation were measured the same way today as in the 1950s (and in previously economic history), it would now be in a 3–4% p.a. range. So-called hedonic price accounting (adjustment for quality improvements) accounts for the difference, and some statistics experts suspect that the hedonic price adjustment (downwards) has been increasing recently (the past two years), taking account of new ways to measure quality improvements in services. The "disinflationary" forces now driving down prices—rapid globalization, digitalization (including Amazon)—remain strong, and they play an important role in camouflaging monetary inflation in goods and services markets (in essence, no monetary inflation under these circumstances would mean that prices should have been falling somewhat).

In that context (of the already-powerful monetary inflation), what does a state of inflation alert actually mean? Perhaps the best way to think about this is a possible sudden fading of the camouflage (if, e.g. the Amazon effect were to shrink) or alternatively a gain in the momentum of monetary inflation such as to cause a break-out from 2% inflation inertia; and we should also consider intensification of irrational forces in asset markets as justifying monetary inflation alert. One month's data would surely not move significantly the needle as perceived by a rational mind. And wage data are ambiguous—given the late cycle tendency for wage share to rise.

Bibliography

Pollock, A. J. (2017). *What Have the Massive Guarantees of Mortgages by the US Government Achieved*. Housing Finance International Winter 2017.

Salerno, J. T. (2015). *Money Sound and Unsound*. Auburn, Alabama: Mises Institute.

Shiller, R. (2016, July 15). Why Land and Homes Actually Tend to Be Disappointing Investments. *Economic View, the New York Times*.

CHAPTER 10

Negative Interest Rates and the War Against Cash

We have already **seen** that a key idea behind the introduction of the 2% inflation standard was the contention that this would help solve the problem of the zero-rate boundary (meaning that if interest rates fall significantly below zero, then depositors would simply pull their funds out of the banks and hoard cash instead). Specifically, at very low rates of goods and services inflation (or no inflation at all), nominal interest rates might not be able to fall to a low-enough level (given zero boundary) to produce the negative real interest rates essential to economic re-bound in some periods (e.g. in a weak stage of the business cycle or in the context of savings glut). If the regime of the 2% inflation could somehow keep inflation expectations levitated at around 2% throughout, then it would provide a margin for real rates to fall to minus 2% even if nominal rates cannot fall below zero. "Somehow" is of course the salient word here: how to practise "levitation" of expectations.

And this is where the advocates of negative interest rates find their cue. Even if the 2% inflation expectations cannot be sustained, negative real rates could be "engineered" by pushing out the zero-rate boundary, perhaps only by a small amount. Suppose a way could be found for nominal interest rates to fall to say −0.5%; then real rates could fall to negative levels even though inflation expectations during the particular economic climate of the time could not be driven up past 1.5% and so on with other arithmetical examples.

© The Author(s) 2018
B. Brown, *The Case Against 2 Per Cent Inflation*,
https://doi.org/10.1007/978-3-319-89357-0_10

The main barrier to rates falling below zero is the possibility of hoarding banknotes. But storage of these is not costless. And so, in practice rates can fall to slightly negative levels even under a conventional monetary regime. Moreover, banks may decide not to pass negative rates on to customers even if they are receiving less than zero on their reserves at the central bank, because the costs of regaining lost customers could be more than the absorption (by the bank) of the negative income on reserves. Wholesale money deposits by contrast and some large deposits would be subject to negative rates (as quoted by the banks).

Under the global 2% inflation standard, central banks in Europe and Japan have experimented with modestly negative rates as described. In effect reserves at the central bank become subject to a charge (sometimes this is levied just on marginal excess reserves rather than on total reserves, meaning more scope for banks to avoid passing negative rates on to clients).

Are Slightly Negative Rates Worth the Candle?

The question in all this is whether the game is really worth the candle.

After all, in a well-functioning capitalist economy under sound money where prices and wages are flexible both downwards and upwards, the zero-rate boundary does not prevent real interest rates falling to negative levels in real terms (see Chap. 2, p. 21). Expectations of higher prices in the future from a below-normal level now are the mechanism for sub-zero generation. In particular goods and services for which demand is now cyclically weak would fall to a below-normal level from which price recovery would be expected over the subsequent recovery. Businesses and consumers would bring forward their purchases. Perpetual propaganda from central banks led by the Fed about targeting 2% inflation and their potential deployment of a non-conventional tool to this end—negative interest rates—can get in the way of such flexibility by promoting inertia.

Moreover, the grinding down of interest rates on deposits at the central bank to sub-zero, the cutting of the price of deposit services by the banks to below cost, and manipulation down of term risk premium in the bond markets as the hunt for yield assumes panic proportions can all hobble the banking system, for example, holding back perhaps its capacity to fund economic expansion. And in the context of flawed mental processes, inflamed by monetary disorder, who knows the impact of a minus before the sign, however small? Small negative rates on short-maturity government bonds could cause the hunt for yield to reach new pitches of irrationality—as evidenced, for example, in the main carry trades (see Chap. 3, p. 39).

These carry trades all feature potential heavy costs which may not reveal themselves until the end of the present cycle or afterwards. Some of these have been mentioned already. As a further example, we could consider the ballooning of the private equity industry, which has enjoyed a fantastic run on the back of investor demand for the high-yield bonds issued in the course of its highly leveraged takeovers (the businesses acquired typically issue high levels of debt meaning that the net cash paid by the private equity group is small); leverage, high-priced risky bonds, and an ever-rising equity market (meaning in addition a good prospect of disposing of companies at high prices further down the line) have been a powerful cocktail for private equity investors. The narrative becomes that private equity barons have a magical touch in their capability to turn stone into gold—and it is well worth the sacrifice of illiquidity whilst waiting.

The true reality of private equity might well be much uglier as illustrated in a recent survey article (see Daniel et al. 2016):

> *Since the 2008 financial crisis, private equity firms have rapidly expanded their influence, assuming a pervasive, if under the radar, role in daily American life. Sophisticated political manoeuvring – including winning government contracts, shaping public policy and deploying former public officials to press their case – is central to this growth. Yet even as private equity wields such influence in the halls of state capitals and in Washington, it faces little public awareness of its government activities. Private equity firms often don't directly engage with legislators and regulators – the companies they control do. As a result, the firms themselves have merged as relatively anonymous conglomerates that exert power behind the scenes in their dealing with governments. And because private equity's interests are so diverse, the industry interacts with governments not only through lobbying, but also as contractors and partners on public projects.*

NEGATIVE RATES INFLICT DAMAGE ON MONETARY SYSTEM

Alongside the inflammation of irrational processes, we should also consider the damage which the introduction of negative rates, even at tiny negative levels, does to the monetary system.

The view has already been expressed in this volume that a sound money regime depends on a well-pivoted base money for which demand is broad and stable and which pays at all times zero interest (see Chap. 1,

p. 9 and Chap. 4, p. 51). The introduction of negative rates means a departure from the zero-interest payment principle. Perhaps the departure would only be for a short time, but even so it may have an amplified effect on the demand for base money, making this more volatile and unpredictable. Moreover, the whole history of monetary experiments suggests that these are never short, whatever the initial declarations when launched. The experimenters dig in for the long haul.

Moreover the introduction of negative rates conflicts with a key principle of sound money—markets should be free to determine interest rates (no official manipulation). If the latter, why is the central bank taking steps to pilot nominal rates into sub-zero territory? Yes, there could be a permanent tiny fixed charge for holding zero-earning reserves at the central bank (a bit like safekeeping fees for gold under the gold standard), but that should be all, meaning that in principle market-determined money market rates could sometimes get to just below zero, but there would be no long life to that.

It is no accident then that the negative-rate experiment was launched in Europe and Japan at a time when the monetary base had long been removed from the pivot of their monetary systems and the respective central bank (with legislative authority) had abandoned the principle of permanently zero interest on reserves many years previously. Both central banks (the ECB and BoJ) and indeed the Federal Reserve had already exemplified in this cycle the observation that monetary experiments continue far beyond the original timeline. This applies equally to the quantitative easing policies and to the use of non-conventional tools.

Quantitative Easing: An Experiment Without Time Limit

Quantitative easing is an experiment.

According to the original concept, traceable to Milton Friedman and his favorable comment as historian on brief open market operations in early 1932, a strong boost to monetary base via the operation of unspecified black-box mechanisms should prevent a contraction of the broad money supply and even lead to some positive growth (in this aggregate) (see Pethokoukis 2016). Such a bold sustained experiment was not in fact run during the Great Depression; but it was implemented during 1934–36 as the Fed and Treasury in effect monetized heavy inflows of gold (see Brown 2015).

Friedman does not address the exit issue, but presumably he had in mind that once the economic crisis was over, the Fed would withdraw its crisis injections and allow the monetary base to return somehow to its "long-run equilibrium path". It could be that the frictions and downside risks of this exit process would negate the possible advantages, again an issue not addressed (though it certainly became pertinent in 1936 as the Fed started to withdraw excess reserves via a process of raising reserve requirements). In all though, Friedman viewed the process of boosting the monetary base and subsequent withdrawal as a temporary aberration from steady-state monetary piloting in which nominal interest rates, short and long, would be market determined.

In fact, the evidence from the mid-1930s episode (of radical monetary base expansion) already suggested that the "quantitative easing experiment" would not be temporary.

Yes, the Fed in late 1936 and early 1937 raised reserve requirements (in three stages). But the shock of the autumn 1937 stock market crash and the "Roosevelt recession" (May 1937–June 1938) brought a sharp change in course. And then of course, World War II and its aftermath went along with years of vast excess reserves and manipulated (down) long-term interest rates.

Fast forward to the Japan QE experiment of the early 2000s (see previous chapter): this was comparatively short-lived, though in total it lasted four years. Then we come to the QE experiments launched originally by the Bernanke Fed and intensifying through 2011–12. Eight years after its start, there is now a glacially slow pace of slimming the balance sheet but no short- or medium-term date in sight when the monetary base will be back to a normal proportion of the wider monetary aggregates and a normal monetary base expansion path being pursued. In any case monetary base is no longer monetary base in its classical sense (no interest paid) and is effectively depivoted from the monetary system.

The longevity of the experiment is stunning. When Ben Bernanke gave his first press conference in April 2011, he defended QE, its intensification (in the midst of the European sovereign debt crisis and related global economic slowdown), plus the use of other non-conventional tools, as designed to produce the fastest recovery ever from great recession and financial panic. He observed (from historical research) that such expansions are generally slow and painful, quoting the recently published book by Reinhart and Rogoff (2011). That contention has been strongly disputed. For example, Taylor (2013) points to evidence that recovery has usually been robust. Already it was surely evident by 2012/13 that the experiment had failed to produce a strong recovery—indeed it may have handicapped this. Yet the experiment rolled on and on, with its architects taking credit for the "rapid growth of employment" many years beyond the expiry date of the initial QE and before a full review could be possible taking account of how the cycle ended.

One key lesson of this history, which applies as much to Europe and Japan as the US, is that monetary experiments launched on the basis of being short-lived are hardly likely to be so. The monetary bureaucrats in charge and their political masters will find reason to extend and extend and subtly change the purpose from the original failed purpose to a modified subsequent purpose for which they claim success, of course prematurely. For who can confidently pronounce success before knowing the outcomes for at least the whole business cycle and in particular with respect to the extent of mal-investment and other costs of the monetary inflation. And this cautionary lesson applies as much to negative interest rates as to QE.

Negative Interest Rates in Europe and Japan 2014–18

Indeed, one can look at the history of negative interest rates in the present episode of monetary inflation. The ECB introduced negative interest rates in June 2014, with the move apparently being accepted by the Bundesbank as preferable to quantitative easing. In fact, the latter came barely 18 months later, so the euro-zone ended up experimenting with both QE and negative rates; and in 2018 both were still in force, despite the German economy in boom with ample evidence of inflation in asset markets and even the weaker economies growing strongly. And the ECB was promising that both policies would continue at least for a further year (to late 2018).

In Japan the original introduction of negative rates in February 2016 met a storm of unpopularity (amidst a rush for buying safe-boxes) and also sent bank shares into a sharp downturn. All of this most likely convinced the Bank of Japan not to proceed with further rate cuts below zero. Sub-zero rates, however, were still in place two years later despite a booming economy.

Finally the Swiss National Bank moved to negative rates in December 2014, implicitly as a policy tool for weakening the franc; when the ceiling was abandoned for this currency in January 2015, it took negative rates even further into negative territory (centre of a -1.25% to -0.25% band at -0.75%). No surprise that three years later they had not budged despite substantial weakening of the currency, speed-up of the economy, and inflation at near 1%. Some pressure was coming to do so from the US whose Treasury had put the franc on a list of currencies to monitor for exchange rate manipulation but, so far, no action. The manipulation charge was buttressed by the way in which the Swiss negative rate was imposed (on a very small margin of free reserves, meaning that the banks in Switzerland maintained domestic customer deposit rates at zero; in effect the negative rates resembled exchange restrictions on capital inflows).

The power of small negative rates to influence asset markets including currency markets has depended in large part on the power of the narrative about them—amplified by the feature that loss aversion (a type of irrationality; see Chap. 2) seems to be inflamed by the descent of nominal rates below zero, even to a tiny degree. In Europe that has magnified the ability of weak sovereign governments (in terms of credit quality) to sell their debts at highly inflated prices, giving realization to ECB chief Draghi's pledge "to do whatever it takes" to save the European Monetary Union. It remains to be seen if "whatever it takes" includes such a powerful dose of monetary inflation, and the resulting placement of a transfer burden on North European taxpayers eventually causes EMU to collapse under the weight of political reaction in these countries.

ADVOCATES OF NEGATIVE RATES IGNORE ASSET INFLATION

The advocates of negative interest rates do not dwell on the dangers of asset price inflation, and they do not accept that they strengthen the discretionary powers of monetary bureaucrats. And they do not acknowledge that asset price inflation and the impetus which negative rates give to the key irrational forces empowered in that disease are fundamental to how negative rates would provide stimulus. Moreover, asset price inflations cannot just be turned on at will by central banks. There must exist an environment in which speculative narratives can indeed flourish; it may be that there are no groups of plausible stories to chase, especially if investor mind-sets are gloomy.

For example, Kenneth Rogoff in his recent book *The Curse of Cash* (2016) ignores the hazards of the asset price inflation disease and its possible intensification by negative rates. He writes:

> *In brief, although there are a host of issues and objections (including the rules vs. discretion debate), the case for properly designed negative interest rate policy is a strong one. If central banks had the option of setting interest rates to negative levels without limit, they would have far more scope than they do today for*

pushing an economy quickly out of a deflationary spiral and for counteracting the effects of credit contraction after a systemic financial crisis. Lowering interest rates to negative levels would temporarily raise aggregate demand and strongly incentivize banks to lend out excess reserves.

For such efforts to be truly effective, it is necessary to clear the path fully for negative interest rates. First and foremost, this means taking away (or substantially taking away) incentives to hoard cash when interest rates are negative, incentives that presently put a huge check on the effectiveness of policy. It also means preparing all the "plumbing" for negative rates in terms of legal, tax and institutional changes. Again, the present experience of tiptoeing into negative rates cannot be viewed as a decisive test of how they might work after the necessary preparations have been made, because many issues have yet to be dealt with, especially finding a way to deal with a run into cash.

A good place to start in examining Rogoff's contention about a strong case for "negative rate without limit" is to question the concept of deflation spiral and ask where the financial crisis came from. A fall in prices during a recession to a below-normal level from which there is the likelihood of re-bound is not evidence of a deflationary cycle. Yet it seems that Rogoff would apply the tool of negative rates in avoiding this pro-cyclical move of prices, meaning that economic recovery would be handicapped. And as regards financial crisis, is this not the result of money having been out of control, as occurs most dangerously in unsound money regimes?

Yes, Rogoff cites financial crises which occurred under the gold standard (and subsequent severe recessions or depressions); but the originating cause was usually a rickety US banking system, made more unstable by the national bank legislation passed during the Civil War (see Rothbard 2005). In particular, the legislation fostered a pyramiding of the whole banking system on a narrow base of national banks (with state banks holding their reserves for the latter). Further, governments could distort at least temporarily the supply of monetary base away from the path dictated by above-ground gold reserves; such manipulations could be the source of monetary inflation especially in asset markets for some time.

How to Limit Cash Hoarding Under Negative Rates

The main contention of Rogoff here is that negative rates could become a much more powerful tool as an economic stimulant and deflation fighter if they were unrestrained by the existence of cash.

The idea of liberating negative interest rates from the constraints of zero-rate cash goes all the way back to Silvio Gesell's plan concocted in the late nineteenth century and reviewed approvingly by Keynes (see Bossone 2013). Gesell was a successful German merchant in Buenos Aires who was led to the study of monetary problems by the crises of the late 1980s which was especially violent in Argentina. His monetary ideas, refined and re-written through several editions, centred round the hypothesis that the growth of real capital is held back by the money rate of interest. Thus the prime necessity is to reduce the money rate of interest, and this can be done by causing money to incur carrying costs just like other stocks of barren goods. This led him to the famous prescription of "stamped" money with which his name is chiefly associated and which received the blessing of Irving Fisher. Currency notes would only retain their value by being stamped each month, like an insurance card, with stamps purchased at a post office. The actual charge suggested by Gesell was one per mil. per month, equivalent to 5.4% per annum.

There are numerous problems with the Gesell proposal, and these also in part plague other negative-rate plans, especially those where radical possibilities are amplified by schemes to remove the restraint of cash.

In particular, the Gesell proposal means that the money rate of interest would be fixed at a constant highly negative rate through time. But how could this be consistent with any concept of monetary soundness where interest rates are market determined and where the central bank/ authorities are assumed to have no more knowledge than anyone else (sparse) about the so-called neutral or natural rate of interest. On average over time under sound money regimes, one could assume that the invisible hand including much trial and error and some big mistakes will guide market interest rates close to unknown neutral level—the result of immense number of decentralized savings and investment decisions (including borrowing and lending). The likelihood is that under a regime where prices would have some tendency to revert to the mean in the very long run, nominal interest rates on risk-free assets would be substantially positive. Indeed that was the case under the gold standard. Of course, there would be periods when rates were very low, but there would be others when high.

Also, there is the huge issue as to how a fiat money subject to such large negative rates as proposed by Gesell could avoid collapse as present holders sought alternative monies and near money assets (including foreign exchange) not subject to the stamping. Yes, there may be laws of legal tender, but the scope for economizing on this money, if very unattractive, can be the basis for runaway inflation (with prices measured in the legal tender).

NEGATIVE RATES IN WAKE OF FINANCIAL CRISIS

Modern proposals for removing the zero-rate boundary by imposing charges of various forms on cash or restricting the use of cash are mostly put forward in terms of temporary expedients to overcome the aftermath of financial crisis including great recession but not as a permanent status quo (e.g. see Mankiw 2009). Some support for negative rates as a contra-cyclical tool has come from economists who are sceptical of Keynesian pump-priming (e.g. seeing this as becoming a back-door way of boosting public spending to satisfy political clienteles). They would rather reinforce monetary policy (in terms of direct stimulus) than turn to the budget. But both are likely highly sub-optimal compared to the alternative of avoiding financial crises and busts to start with by the pursuance of sound money and relying on market mechanisms on pro-cyclical path of prices to bring about recovery from recessions.

A variation to the Gesell stamping proposal which has some attractions as a means of bringing about negative interest rates on a temporary basis is a suspension of the 1:1 link between currency and deposits linked to a forced conversion of banknotes into new banknotes at a fixed date say several years in the future (see Brown 2015). But this is all highly dirigiste stuff with seriously negative consequences for any early road back to sound money. The government would start the process by announcing that at a fixed date in the future, say five years, hence, 1000 dollars (or francs) in banknotes would be converted into 900 new dollars. Banks would not have to convert (during this period) deposits into banknotes at 1:1 but instead at the market rate for banknotes against deposits (there would be in effect a floating exchange rate, with a terminal rate at conversion day of 1000 old banknotes = 900 dollar deposit). In the interim as regards money transactions (e.g. buying goods and services), there would be a price for cash and a price for settlement by deposit; the former would be higher than the latter by a growing amount over time.

The conversion process would itself involve significant costs (not least security of transport of new and old notes) and also raise serious libertarian concerns. In principle the anonymity of the person exchanging notes could be protected—but who would believe this to be the case? Many holders of banknote hoards would seek to exchange them into foreign currency notes, gold, or other assets ahead of the compulsory exchange, causing considerable chaos and swings in asset market prices.

A more radical alternative proposal of some negative interest rate proponents is to radically reduce the availability of cash in the economy, especially eliminating large-denomination banknotes. If cash is only available in small denominations, then the scope for avoiding negative rates on deposits by cash withdrawal could be reduced, as the storage costs and inconvenience costs of cash as a deposit alternative would be that much greater. Some of the negative interest rate advocates are also warriors against cash—a convenient coincidence—justifying their views by pointing to how cash can facilitate various illegal activities, whether people smuggling, narcotics smuggling, or tax evasion.

The view that the "abolition" or "reduction in use" of cash would serve two purposes—the reduction of illegal activities and giving new scope for negative rates to be used as a contra-cyclical tool—was a central theme of Rogoff's advocacy (see Rogoff 2016). The author concedes there are some "liberty considerations" but largely dismisses these, concluding: "all in all, the case for going to a less-cash society if not quite yet a cashless society seems pretty compelling, with most of the various and sundry objections being easily handled. Facilitating negative interest rate policy is not the main reason for phasing out paper currency, especially large denomination notes. But it is an important collateral benefit".

The facts do not bear out Rogoff's advocacy. A good summary of these can be found in Mitchell 2016. The author points out that there are two reasons why statists don't like cash: first, they prefer a system that would allow them to track and tax every possible penny of our income and purchases; second, Keynesian central bankers would like to force us to spend more money by imposing negative interest rates on our savings. As a practical matter, the author disputes the claim that removal of large-denomination banknotes would deter crime, citing evidence from anti-corruption experts. Moreover, mafia activities which result in victims paying protection in cash would continue, but the victims would be at even greater risk of harm due to being more intricately drawn into the mafia operations as part of the process of transferring revenues.

Negative Rates as Pseudo-Inflation Tax

Rogoff (and other advocates of negative rates) makes no mention of a possible big motive for the introduction of negative rates, especially from the viewpoint of political authorities to which the central bank is ultimately answerable. This is the levying of an inflation tax in circumstances where actual inflation might not emerge—if at all—until far into the future even with radical monetary policies pursued in the present. By moving to negative rates, the government is in effect collecting a pseudo-inflation tax from holders of monetary base and of government debt on which interest rates have been set in line with long-term market rates heavily weighed down by the negative rate environment. The true extent of this negative interest rate tax is the difference between the actual rate (possibly negative) and the rate which would be established in the market if the central bank were not attempting to stimulate inflation (albeit within limits as set out in the inflation-targeting regime).

A further fundamental objection to negative rates and more generally the "war on cash" (in part engaged so as to reinforce the power to drive rates into sub-zero territory) is that money is a consumer good and that the suppliers of this good should be responsive as in any other marketplace to the state of demand. So, if there is a considerable demand for large-denomination banknotes, why would these not be supplied? If one money brand was not responsive in this way, then it would lose business to other brands. That would be the case, for example, under a free banking environment under a gold standard where banks could supply their own brand of banknote (convertible into gold on demand). As one Bundesbanker put it—just because some criminals like driving around in a Mercedes Benz, that is no reason why this vehicle should be banned. And as point of reference, the gold sovereign, which was the principal means of payment in Britain under the gold standard, is worth around US$350 at time or writing (UK£250), whilst the largest-denomination notes in the UK are £50 and in the US$100.

The war on cash literature largely ignores the fact that the competitors to cash have advantages which stem from monopoly or oligopoly power. The credit card companies and more broadly the payment card companies do not gain revenue in the main from directly charging their customers fees to cover expenses (and provide a profit margin)—including payments transfer, anti-fraud monitoring, and enforcement. Instead they collect the revenue directly from the merchant to whom the card is presented in making payments for goods or services. In principle the merchant could pass this fee on to the client by making a surcharge (relative to cash payment); in effect, the merchant would collect the fee for the card company rather than the latter doing this direct. The merchant might also charge for other costs incurred in accepting cards—including potential hustle in claiming redress from the card company against fraud (though there could be some offset here to consider in form of costs saved of storing and moving cash).

In practice though the oligopoly or monopoly power of the card companies means that in many retail, merchants sign agreements with credit card companies according to which they cannot charge customers for the extra cost of processing such transactions (including the fee levied by the credit card company) relative to cash including the fees which are levied. Instead they implicitly collect the fee from the cash customers who are denied a keener price corresponding to the lower cost (to the retailer) of their transactions. No wonder that some of these cash customers decide they may as well use a payment card or credit card in an online transaction rather than making the visit to the store where they would pay cash.

Of course there have been multiple court challenges, especially in the US, to these arrangements. Local and state regulations in the US have played a key role in some cases in reinforcing card power (as against cash), sometimes under the banner of helping low-income households using these (see Hunt 2003). Under competitive conditions, it would surely be the case that the card user would pay for the credit card costs and fees, not the retailer (though the latter may act as collector); and cash users would enjoy keener prices relative to prices that credit card users get under present arrangements.

The absence of large-denomination notes in most monetary regimes means that some individuals find that they are induced even when charged extra to use cards rather than incurring the security risks (including theft) of transferring and holding large volumes of paper money. Security-related costs of transporting or storing cash (whether in the home or at the retail store) are less where large-denomination notes are available. In effect, the war on cash is a bonus for the credit card industry. It is also a bonus to the online retail business. If users of cash could get their due keener price in visiting the physical store compared to the online price which includes a fee to the credit card or payments card company, they would be less inclined to shop online. And we should also consider oligopolistic abuse in the form of the largest online retail firm, for example, Amazon, negotiating a special low fee with the credit card and payments companies. If cash transactions earned the full extent of price reduction which they would enjoy as a means of payment under competitive conditions in spending in brick-and-mortar stores, then there would be less online shopping. It is ironic that governments combine with the credit card companies to prevent the "small guy" using his or her credit card from being penalized relative to cash customers by stores levying charges on card-facilitated purchases (or equivalently giving discount for cash). The small guy loses the opportunity to reduce the costs of purchase through visiting the mall with (some big) notes on hand.

Most important from the viewpoint of sound money theory, war on cash is also a war on monetary base at the pivot of the monetary system. Cash is an important component of the monetary base. The possibility of establishing a sound money regime based on an automatic guidance system for the monetary base in which interest rates are freely determined (not fixed by central bankers or others) depends on demand for the monetary base being broad and stable. Moreover, the monetary base should be a highly distinct asset enjoying demand for uses which are not highly sensitive to small interest rate fluctuations. If successful, the war on cash—and the credit card monopolists should be seen as allies of the aggressors in this war—undermines these conditions, a subject to which we return in Chap. 13. The periodic imposition of negative interest rates would also undermine the pivotal position of the monetary base.

So, the war on cash, as waged in effect by an alliance of Big Government, Big Banks, and Big Tech, is also a war on sound money. From the viewpoint of Big Tech, whether Amazon or say Facebook and Google who thrive on revenues from adverts which are aimed almost entirely at stimulating online spending in various forms, a re-building of cash's payments role—dependent on users of cash getting keener prices than users of cards in line with the underlying economics described here—would be bad news. And in this respect, we should realize that the oligopoly power of the Big Banks as described is a winner of business for these in today's post-digital revolution world. The retail public are drawn to the mega banks whose credit and payment cards are costless as their burden has been shifted to cash customers. In turn these too-big-to-fail banks enjoy access to lender of last resort and other financial assistance functions which mean that they have no natural demand for large holdings of cash or reserves at the central bank. The restoring of a pivotal role for high-powered money (equivalently monetary base) will depend on the breaking up of these mega banks and more broadly a curbing of lender of last-resort assistance (whether to large or small banks) amongst other reforms to be discussed in the final chapter of this volume.

BIBLIOGRAPHY

Bossone, B. (2013). Confessions of a Supply-Side Liberal, Mises July 29,2013: Silvio Gesell's Plan for Negative Nominal Interest Rates.
Brown, B. (2015). *A Global Monetary Plague*. London: Palgrave.
Daniel, J., Josh, W., Ben, P., & Den, H. (2016, August 1). This Is Your Life, Brought to You by Private Equity. *New York Times*.
Hunt, B. (2003). Anti-trust Issues in Payment Networks. *Philadelphia Federal Reserve Quarterly*, Q2.
Mankiw, G. (2009, April 22). Observations on Negative Interest Rates. *Greg Mankiw's Blog*.
Mitchell, D. J. (2016, March 1). *The War Against Cash, Part 3*. Cato Institute.
Pethokoukis, J. (2016, September 6). *On Praise for the Fed's Quantitative Easing Program*. AEI Ideas.
Reinhart, C. M., & Rogoff, K. S. (2011). *This Time Is Different*. Princeton: Princeton University Press.
Rogoff, K. S. (2016). *The Curse of Cash*. Princeton: Princeton University Press.
Rothbard, M. (2005). *A History of Money and Banking in the United States*. Auburn: Ludwig von Mises Institute.
Taylor, J. B. (2013, October 1). *Causes of the Financial Crisis and the Slow Recovery: A 10-year perspective*. Paper Presented at the Joint Conference of the Brookings Institution and the Hoover Institution on "The US Financial System – Five Years after the Crisis" at the Panel "Causes and Effects of the Financial Crisis".

CHAPTER 11

Experiments in Crash Postponement: 1927/29 Versus 2016/18

History does not repeat, it echoes. At the time of writing (early 2018), it seems like there have been strong echoes in an "Indian summer phase" of global asset price inflation through late 2016, in the whole of 2017, and into early 2018, from Wall Street in the late 1920s. That earlier episode culminated in a devastating sequence of financial crashes. The danger of a repeat is widely evident, although the Federal Reserve has taken a crucially different policy step from back then. And in broader context, we should note that in the late 1920s, the world was barely ten years on from the World War I (a point emphasized to the author by Alex J. Pollock and also found in Kindleberger's summing up of the causes of the Great Depression—see Kindleberger 2013).

GREAT RECESSION FOLLOWED BY FIGHT
AGAINST "DEFLATION"

The echoes stem from an essential similarity in monetary circumstance. After the Great Recession of 1920–21, the recently created Federal Reserve (doors opened in 1914) embarked on a course of fighting "deflation dangers" whilst countering incipient cyclical downturns. Fed policymakers were in part responding to contemporary criticism especially as voiced in Congress to the effect that their mismanagement had contributed to the severity of the Great Recession (too slow to halt inflationary policies once war ended and then excess zeal to bring prices down).

© The Author(s) 2018
B. Brown, *The Case Against 2 Per Cent Inflation*,
https://doi.org/10.1007/978-3-319-89357-0_11

The technological revolution unfolding in the 1920s (mass assembly line, electrification, autos, radio, etc.) meant that prices had a natural and benign tendency to fall. The Fed, in resisting this, kept monetary conditions very easy, fostering a powerful asset price inflation which encompassed the market in stocks, real estate, and foreign loans (most of all to Germany). Similarly, in the aftermath of the 2000–02 economic downturn and equity market bust (led by Nasdaq), the Fed turned to "fighting deflation" despite a benign tendency at that time for prices to fall (economic weakness, globalization, a continuing productivity spurt reflecting the IT revolution). The fight against deflation was waged with much greater vigour following the 2007 panic and Great Recession despite a natural rhythm of prices downwards, now due to globalization, digitalization, and economic weakness, rather than any apparent productivity surge (in fact productivity growth was now remarkably low, though this may have masked a situation where under sound money productivity growth would have still been strong—see p. 35).

In 1927 when the US economy floundered in a mild recession, with speculative temperatures moderating across the globe (the Dow Jones index faltering very slightly through late 1926 and the first half of 1927) and in some cases falling sharply (in particular a German stock market crash in May 1927 and the bursting of the Florida land mania in 1926), the Federal Reserve led by Benjamin Strong resolved to give a "shot of whisky" to the stock market (see Pollock 2013). Fresh monetary stimulus, which incidentally helped Strong's friend Montagu Norman at the Bank of England defend Sterling, "succeeded" in breathing new life into global asset price inflation which became growingly apparent through 1928, especially in Wall Street.

Fast forward: since the end of the late 1990s boom, the Fed has been highly focused on "fighting deflation dangers" (breathing inflation at 2% p.a. back into the economy). Accordingly, the Yellen Fed responded to the US growth cycle downturn through 2015 and the first half of 2016 together with a modest setback in the US equity market from mid-2015 to early 2016 by cancelling all its planned mini-rate rises through the first three quarters of 2016. The downturn could be attributed to the energy price slump and related slide in energy sector investment and a pull-back in global trade stemming from a China "growth recession" (featuring real estate market softening and related weakness in construction) and more generally an emerging market slowdown especially in commodity-producing countries accompanied by some decline in global asset market speculative temperatures (a mini-devaluation shock from China in summer 2015 playing a catalytic role).

The US monetary stimulus (accompanied by the ECB and the BoJ extending their radical expansion policies alongside a China state lending boom) culminated in a powerful coordinated global economic upturn and a sharp rise in speculative temperatures across asset markets, evident to all by the second half of 2017. This is where the difference sets in. At the equivalent point in the earlier episode, Fed policy changed direction—but not so with the Yellen Fed and the fellow members of the global central bankers' club.

FRIEDMAN'S CRITIQUE OF THE FED 1928–29 PUT TO THE TEST IN 2017–18

Into the second half of 1928, following Benjamin Strong's death, the Fed embarked on a policy of fighting speculation, even though prices of goods were falling slightly. Herbert Hoover, elected as president in November 28, had been a vocal critic of US monetary policies (including the Benjamin Strong-Montagu Norman "cosy relationship") which nourished a "speculative craze" on Wall Street.

Milton Friedman and Anna Schwartz in their epic monetary history fault the post-Strong Fed (see Friedman 1063), arguing that it would have done better to ignore the speculation and focus instead on sustaining rapid economic growth and fighting the downward tendency in prices. Divisions within the Fed meant that it fell between two stools—lacking the punch to end the speculation which meanwhile reached a new frenzied pitch in first half 1929 but exercising enough restraint to cause the next pause in economic growth (starting in August 29) to develop into something much worse.

Almost 90 years later, the Yellen Fed has put Friedman's contention to the test. It turned back from any serious monetary restraint through 2017 (indeed monetary inflation may well have turned more aggressive, despite tiny adjustments up in official short-term rates) notwithstanding widespread symptoms of asset market froth including corporate leverage (largely via so-called equity buy-backs), a booming credit carry trade, and many forms of momentum trading (some highly leveraged) because inflation was undershooting its target of 2% p.a. largely due to the so-called Amazon effect. The new occupant of the White House was extoling not cursing the rise in the stock market, furnishing indeed a new speculative narrative about the wonders of a big business tax cut.

History will not judge Yellen or Friedman well if indeed this continued monetary stimulus ends in an even more devastating sequence of crashes albeit from a record-high level of speculative temperatures. The true lesson would then be that monetary regimes which seek to stabilize the price level or the inflation rate in face of strong downward rhythm of prices (whether reflecting a spurt in productivity growth or globalization or digitalization) eventually collapse under the weight of crisis.

WHY DID WALL STREET CRASH IN OCTOBER 1929?

Even now, almost 90 years after the event, there is no fully convincing tale of why the Wall Street Crash of October 1929 occurred precisely when it did.

Friedman and Schwartz tell us that the Crash was a delayed reaction to a business cycle peak which in fact the National Bureau of Economic Research now dates as August though not starkly obvious in real time; Temin (1993) cites a weakness in private consumption which had already set in. Writers more focused on day-to-day happenings (see Bierman 1998) emphasize the regulatory defeats for the electric utility companies—stars of the stock market boom—which threatened to contain their monopoly power to charge higher prices; Jude Wanniski (1998) tracks a Congressional Committee vote in favour of the Smoot-Hawley tariff.

Each of these possible triggers lacks total plausibility on their own except through the rear-view mirror. After all there had been a business cycle peak in October 1926; yet after two months of slowdown (as from August to October 1929) to end-1926, there was no crash. Yes, the stock market was flat to slightly softer through late 1926 and early 1927, but that was not the catalyst to any serious slowdown; the recession from October 1926 to November 1927 was one of the mildest of US cyclical history. Benjamin Strong's "coup de whiskey" had been effective at revitalizing the stock market through the second half of 1927 and beyond, why not again in autumn 1929?

Certainly, we can identify dangers in advance of the October 1929 crash, including the build-up of monetary inflation (which during the present episode of monetary inflation from 2011/12 onwards was camouflaged in the goods and services markets by a downward natural rhythm of prices related to such factors as globalization and technological change) and the number 2 economy in the world, Germany, already in recession. (A severe winter followed by a weather-related re-bound in the spring had made the onset of the German recession hard to detect.)

A diagnosis of asset inflation in the mid-/late 1920s would have turned on evidence of an empowerment of irrational forces—much described both at the time of and after the crash (including highly leveraged speculation whether directly on margin or via the new financial vehicles such investment trusts—see Galbraith 1965); and indeed there had been the mania of the Florida bubble (1924–25), albeit in the greater scheme of things it was small—but not too small to indicate the presence of abnormally strong irrationality which though weaker elsewhere was still likely to be present.

But why did the bolt from the blue come when it did albeit amidst a chorus of warnings about a storm ahead at some uncertain point?

There were many naysayers, ridiculing the storm warnings. And indeed, even now across the 90 years since the event, there is a widespread view that the Crash itself does not bear most of the "responsibility" for the Great Depression (1929–33); according to this view the fall of equity prices in autumn 1929 was excessive given the "fundamental situation" of the US and global economy at that time. After all, by April the following year (1930), the bottom fishers in anticipation of economic revival had brought a powerful rally (the Dow Jones index back to almost 300 from a trough of 200 the previous November and the peak of 381 in September). Their optimism about a normal business cycle recovery mechanism asserting itself again this time was to prove false; a sequence of further stock market crashes, linked now to credit crashes, brought Wall Street equities to a fraction of their 1929 low point by the real low of summer 1932 (Dow Jones index at 41.2 on July 8). The pessimists in autumn 1929 could argue that these future credit crashes were alread at least in part "baked into the cake" given the extent of asset inflation in previous years, with only their exact timing uncertain.

The Wall Street Crash of 1929 was in effect the first explosion in a series of explosions (the biggest ran from spring 1931 to autumn 1931 coinciding with the descent of Germany into bankruptcy) through the next 30 months amidst a gathering great depression and the unravelling of the gold exchange standard. This latter had been the first experiment in fiat money stabilization (see Chap. 1). The Crash was symptomatic of concern amongst many investors about the underlying malaise even if many could not articulate their fears in the above terms.

The monetary conditions which produced this sequence can be traced to flaws in the design and implementation of the experiment, including the conduct of the Federal Reserve. The 2% inflation standard—the fourth experiment in fiat money stabilization—has yet to come to an end, but it is quite possible given the extent of irrational force build-up (including highly leveraged momentum trading) that a 1929-style crash will be part of the end phase; unknown but certainly to fear at this stage is whether that end phase will include a spring 1930-style fake re-bound followed by much more serious explosions amidst economic depression. The amount and identity of mal-investment—a big contributor to the extent of depression—only become fully evident in retrospect.

What Is New About Monetary Inflation Under the 2% Regime?

There are some similarities between the monetary inflation which occurred under the gold exchange standard and under the 2% inflation standard. Both involved the Federal Reserve as the monetary hegemon responding by experimentation to a previous severe recession, in large part its own making. The experimentation in the modern era started with the Greenspan Fed responding to the prolonged economic weakness (including recession) of 1990–92; the downturn occurred in the wake of the Federal Reserve drawing back from its policies of monetary inflation as pursued in the years 1985–88. That monetary inflation (1985–88/89) had started with Paul Volcker's participation in the dollar devaluation policy of the second Reagan Administration (as forged by Treasury Secretary James Baker) and continued with Greenspan's first exercise of a "put" in response to the 1987 stock market crash.

In the monetary inflation of the 1990s (1993–2000), Fed policy-making had featured highly discretionary micro-management of short-term interest rates unrestrained by money supply targets and an eventual partial adoption of a 2% inflation target. The bursting of the IT boom and related Nasdaq bubble followed by the 2000–02/03 recession gave new momentum to this new monetary experiment at stabilization (the fourth since the breakdown of the pre-1914 gold standard)—which reached a new crescendo under Greenspan's successor (Ben Bernanke) in the aftermath of the 2007–08/09 Great Panic and Recession.

Both these experiments at fiat money stabilization—the first in the 1920s and the third from the mid-1990s to the present—occurred at times when the natural rhythm of prices was strongly downwards; in the first case (the 1920s), the natural rhythm was powered by rapid technological change (mass assembly line, autos, electrification, radio) and related productivity boom and in the second by rapid globalization (as enabled by the internet revolution) and the increased scope for price transparency brought about by the digitalization revolution (see Chap. 3) (for the historical record, the natural rhythm of prices was also downwards during the third monetary experiment, the Bretton Woods system, as in operation from say 1958 to 1968, given the spurt of productivity growth at that time both in the US and even more so globally—including Europe and Japan; see Brown 2017).

Even so, we should not lose sight of a key difference between the 1920s and now. Goods and services prices undoctored by so-called hedonic price accounting were rising by 3–4% p.a. in most of the period 1996–17 (including the years after the Great Recession of 2007/09); by contrast they were flat or even falling in the earlier period. (On the basis of undoctored prices, real wage rates have been declining substantially in the US under the 2% inflation standard in contrast to their strong rise in the 1920s—corresponding to the distinction between depression-type and boom-type asset price inflation as discussed in Chap. 3.) According to the doctrinarians of the 2% inflation standard, low inflation (with hedonic price adjustment) is the same as stable prices, and there has been no observed tendency towards acceleration. In fact, the years 2016/17 experienced surprising deceleration. The downward rhythm of prices due to the factors mentioned meant that monetary inflation did not reveal itself in the goods and services markets in a form which would cause contemporaries to be concerned about inflation as such. That was the camouflage.

The attempt during both periods (the 1920s, the mid-1990s to the present) by the Federal Reserve to stabilize prices of goods and services (or drive them up by 2% p.a.) despite the natural rhythm of prices being downwards generated powerful asset price inflation. But the reaction to this both amidst the public and policy-makers proved different on the two occasions. In the asset inflation of the mid-1920s onwards, there was no widespread realization amongst the investing public that this phenomenon (asset inflation) was present (albeit that there was a rising chorus of market commentary especially from 1928 about dangerous speculative fever). There was so much economic and geopolitical good news (including as a highpoint the Kellogg-Briand Pact in 1928 where the signatory states including the great European powers and Japan promised not to use war to resolve disputes) that it seemed understandable that the markets would be strong. Yes, there were criticisms of Fed policy and its role in further Wall Street speculation from mid-1927. And these criticisms came from all quarters (politicians, some central bankers).

Fast forward to the asset price inflation since 2011/12, everyone and their dog have known that the Fed was playing a major role in driving asset prices upwards and creating financial market froth (meaning the empowerment of irrational forces). Even so there has been a current of optimism in the marketplace to the effect that prices could become ratified at some point by an emergent economic miracle, and there has been much excitement about current technological change which could go along with this. Another current has been belief in expanding monopoly profits.

Winter 2017/18 Versus Winter 1928/29:
Introduction

The winters of 1929 and 2018 have some similarities and differences which shed light on the underlying inflationary processes. One similarity was a change of guard at the head of the Fed—the death of Benjamin Strong in mid-1928 and the exit of Janet Yellen in early 2018.

Fed Chief Yellen, like Benjamin Strong almost 90 years earlier, as we have seen, had injected a powerful dose of monetary reflation in response to a US equity market pull-back from summer 2015 and early 2016 accompanied by domestic economic slowdown. ("Monetary injection" here is figurative, as there is no way to measure or identify this clearly in a monetary system where monetary base has become totally dislodged as a pivot; the hypothesis here is that the cancellation of three planned rate rises in 2016 at a time of gathering economic expansion amounted to a substantial easing of monetary conditions.)

Strong had acted similarly in response to a minor recession (not known to contemporary economists) in 1926/27 and to a temporary slight softness in the equity market. A co-motive had been the desire to help out his friend Montagu Norman at the Bank of England in holding the pound at its restored gold parity against the dollar without having to raise interest rates which would have been unpalatable in the contemporary UK political climate. Strong proceeded with the interest rate cuts of autumn 1927 despite the earlier objections of German Reichsbank President Schacht who was concerned at the already-heady climate of financial speculation, especially in Germany (see Ahamed 2009). There the equity and real estate markets and the broader loan markets were in various degrees of bubble (albeit that Schacht had engineered a Black Friday on the German bourse earlier in the year by restricting stock market credit), accompanied by massive inflows of foreign loans especially from the US.

Chief Yellen's monetary stimulus of 2016–17 is a direct descendant of the Strong stimulus; but unlike that earlier one, the Yellen stimulus has been extended through a full second year (2017) and probably further, despite obvious evidence of economic and equity market re-bound. The extension was in line with a surprise downtick of inflation, variously attributed to the "Amazon effect" (see Chap. 6) and changed hedonic price accounting practices at the official statistics office.

RATES BACK TO NORMAL DO NOT END ASSET INFLATION: STRONG VERSUS GREENSPAN

Some economists and market-practitioners would dispute whether a one- or two-year interlude of monetary stimulus as measured by small changes in interest rates (either a cut or a failure to rise as expected) can really be the catalyst to a powerful intensification of asset price inflation. For example, BIS economist Philip Turner (see Turner 2017) questions whether the two years of super low interest rates from 2003 to 2004 could really be held responsible for the ensuing financial instability. He cites in particular the 425 bp rise in Fed funds rate from mid-2004 to mid-2006 and its failure to deflate financial market exuberance. But he ignores the catalytic effect of the low rates in spawning irrationality in mental processes— including positive feedback loops and anchoring effects. The strength of the irrational forces unleashed is not effectively combatted in the immediate by a subsequent "normalization of rates".

Greenspan apologists apply Turner's critique (as above) to questioning whether the Fed's glacial tightening and manipulations of 2003–05 really can be blamed for the powerful asset price inflation of 2003–07, especially given the rise of rates to apparently normal levels in steps through late 2004 to early 2006. The answer here is yes (he can be blamed): the speculative fever which has built up during the most intense period of monetary inflation (in this case say 2003–4) is robust for some time (and may even continue to build for a while) against the normalization of rates, reflecting the momentum trading which has formed in several asset markets including credit. It may not be possible to end the fever without speculative over-kill.

WINTER 2017/18 VERSUS WINTER 1928/29: A CONTINUATION

Back to the comparison between winter 2017/18 and autumn 1928, there is a further similarity.

The number 2 economy in the world was in a highly leveraged and potentially dangerous political/financial condition. The Weimar Republic was the counterpart to China in the present episode. Even the most enthusiastic bulls in both cases had a wary eye on the number 2 economy. In the case of the Weimar Republic, though, direct credit exposures internationally were much larger (relative to economic size) on a net basis potentially, given that Germany had been a huge net borrower (to finance a large current account deficit including reparation payments); China by contrast has massive foreign exchange reserves and a huge positive net creditor position internationally. Even so, the global credit exposures to China could be very large given the massive extent of the capital exodus (driven by financial repression and political danger) and the role of foreign capital inflows in financing this.

There were also some big differences.

The November 1928 presidential elections brought Herbert Hoover to the White House (inauguration March 1929). The new president had been a long-time critic of speculation in Wall Street and the role of the Benjamin Strong Fed in stimulating this (especially via its stabilization deal with the Bank of England as mentioned above). And after Strong's death, the effective leadership in the Federal Reserve System was now very concerned about speculation and moved to tighten availability of loans to leveraged purchasers of equity whilst generally tightening monetary policy, even though there was no evidence of goods and services inflation.

It is true that in the late stages of the 2016 election campaign, Donald Trump's side featured ads attacking Yellen for having created a bubble economy and market. But once in the White House, Trump changed his tune completely and took credit for the new surge in the equity markets, claiming that this was due to the success of his deregulatory and tax policies.

And meanwhile in late 2017, the new president had nominated a successor to Janet Yellen (from February 2018) who was widely perceived as a Yellen loyalist as regards the practice and principles of monetary policy; moreover according to media reports, he had been selected on the strong advocacy of the Treasury secretary, renowned by now for his fondness of a weak dollar and advancing budgetary policies which would bring the federal deficit to 6% of GDP in 2019, unparalleled in peacetime at a boom phase of the business cycle. There was every reason to imagine that the new Fed chief was in agreement with the White House policy aims—including the target of 3% plus economic growth, belief that the tax cuts and continuing deregulation (especially in the financial sector) would seriously promote this objective, and the importance of sustaining a continuing equity market boom. All of this had particular political significance with the mid-term elections looming (November 2018). The new

Administration was spinning a new speculative narrative well suited to entice investors in the then hot climate of asset price inflation—the potential for the tax cut and deregulation programme to generate substantially faster growth.

THE SPECULATIVE NARRATIVE ABOUT A MEGA TAX CUT 2018

Reading some of the contemporary media commentaries, one might imagine that the estimated $200 bn p.a. tax cuts between years 2018 and 2025 (after that the cuts shrink on the technical assumption that non-corporate business and personal tax cuts expire) would unleash an economic renaissance in the US as businesses stepped up their capital spending plans and productivity rises in step, alongside a more general upturn in spending related to strong confidence and optimism. There was much talk about US businesses in coming years bringing operations back to the US from once-lower business tax jurisdictions abroad.

There were, however, some big gaps in this story, most of all about how the tax cuts were to be paid for. The failure of markets to reflect this scepticism in late 2017 could be attributed to the distortionary influences of monetary inflation as earlier described in this volume (see Chap. 3).

Presumably everyone and their dog realized that the tax cuts were not manna from heaven. And few could surely bring themselves to believe in a magical Keynesian stimulus especially at this late stage of the business cycle. In so far as the recipients strove to spend the manna, there were various forms in which a bill for this would land somewhere and cause compensating cut-backs. And even without such striving, some bills could be expected in the future. The main forms of the bill, not mutually exclusive, were:

> **first**, a gain of inflation momentum which in effect would levy inflation tax in various forms. These would include a rise in the real rate of capital gains tax, a growing shortfall in depreciation allowances (based on historic cost rather than replacement cost), an erosion in real terms of nominal exemptions in the personal tax code, a capital levy (real loss) on holdings of monetary base and of government bonds (this latter is in the form of a capital levy whose effect on spending by those affected might be different from other forms of tax); and extensive manipulation of interest rates below the neutral level (a form of financial repression).

second, a rise in real interest rates as the increase in spending stimulated by the tax cuts meant that other domestic spending had to be squeezed to make room;

third an increase in taxation likely to start a few years from now and including a rise in the rate of dividend tax and capital gains tax (alternative forms of taxation on profits to the corporate tax).

Realizing these likely scenarios, investors may well not reward businesses which boldly step up their capital spending even though the post-tax equity risk premium had risen (in consequence of the tax cuts). Instead, one might witness them continuing to prefer strategies of boosting cash pay-outs whether via dividends or equity buy-backs whilst maintaining or boosting already historically high levels of indebtedness (especially outstanding corporate bonds) to take advantage of the exceptionally low interest costs (reflecting the spread compression induced by hunger for yield and more generally the downward manipulation of rates by the central banks). Leverage ratios, though, do not seem high during a period of extremely frothy equity markets, when debt and equity totals are measured at market value. Overall macro-economic debt ratios, such as the ratio of total non-financial corporate sector debt to GDP, can nonetheless flash a warning (as is the case in early 2018 in the US, especially if we take out the huge cash surpluses in Big Tech).

In particular, stronger inflation could threaten the high valuation of equities which gains from the perception of a perpetual sweet spot ("low inflation", high profits, and solid growth). Corporate decision-makers, realizing the mood of the shareholders, would act accordingly. Of course there are those non-corporate business owners set to enjoy big tax cuts, but they too may be similarly reticent, preferring a build-up of financial assets rather than ploughing into real investments.

It was possible to imagine an "unstable equilibrium" for some time where businesses build-up or distribute more cash—and the savings from this balance the increased size of the federal deficit. Interest rates would remain low and inflation not accelerated. Even so, there could be widespread unease about the eventual higher inflation or higher interest rate scenario should this "attentism" wilt or the government itself become more tolerant of inflation as a means of reining back its real indebtedness.

And rational sceptical investors should have focused on the incidence of the eventual tax increases.

It is possible that this would bear heavily on labour income and consumption (including entitlements) rather than dividends and capital gains. The result could be lower consumption and higher investment than otherwise at a lower level of interest rates—but the road leading to that new path would be very rocky, both politically and economically.

Cuts in business profit tax vastly (and disproportionately) benefit the monopolists and oligopolists. Businesses at the margins of a competitive field are not typically making large profits. The reward to monopoly power (rents) may actually make the economy less dynamic as it enhances the present status quo.

Apologists for the big business tax cut could cite the 100% expensing of capital spending.

But this factor is likely to be unimportant in the greater scheme of things. Take a $1 million piece of equipment which would previously have been depreciated over five years and is now depreciated over one year. And so instead of $200,000 annual depreciation, meaning a reduction in the tax bill of US$42,000 p.a. for five years, there is now a tax saving of US$210,000 all in year 1 with nothing thereafter. At a five-year interest rate of 3%, for example, the effective tax benefit of the depreciation acceleration is just above US$20,000 in present value terms, say 2% of the overall investment. Will that bring about a capital spending boom? Hardly!

Inflation Alert, February 2018: Fake or Genuine?

Some of these concerns about a possible outbreak of goods and services inflation in the US, with the inertia barrier of 2% becoming pierce, surfaced in the US equity market early in 2018. These might have been prompted by the sheer amount of red ink in the widespread budget forecasts, the strength of the present growth cycle upturn, data releases, and statements by senior officials (especially at Davos by the Treasury secretary in favour of dollar devaluation).

It was arguably an easier job potentially to diagnose monetary ease or monetary inflation in the 1920s than in the late 2010s. In the earlier episode, monetary base was still at the pivot of the US monetary system, albeit much less so than under the pre-1914 gold standard; and as we have seen (see p.   ), there was considerable ambiguity about the underlying demand for monetary base and how this had been influenced by the emergence of the Federal Reserve, the changed reserve requirements, and the widespread confidence that bank crises were now impossible. The easing of 1927 (e.g. or earlier in 1922) can be seen directly in the monetary base interventions. Even so there was room for disagreement as to whether monetary conditions were getting easier or tightening, given the change to the system as wrought by the end of the pre-war gold standard and the advent of the Federal Reserve.

It is likely that this caused the demand for high-powered money to be lower than what extrapolating past tendencies would suggest (which offers one reason why Milton Friedman/Anna Schwartz could claim that the Fed during these years was on a high tide of good performance rather than on an inflation wave). The latter conclusion may have been more evident if those authors had considered the possibility that the demand for monetary base had taken a step downwards compared to the situation under the pre-1914 gold standard.

In the present period where monetary base had become totally depivoted, there has been no ready-made focal point for measuring the impulse of monetary policy. Nonetheless it is plausible that rolling back all planned rate rises for three quarters of 2016 and then implementing only three tiny rate rises in 2017 despite all the evidence of strong growth cycle upturn and equity market/broader asset market strength could well be indicative of monetary inflation, especially as the dollar was tending to weaken despite negative interest rate policies and intensified QE in Europe and Japan during this period.

Milton Friedman's Counterfactual Experiment 1928/29 Now Factual 2017/18

We can view the situation of end-2017 and summer 1928 in the prism of Friedman's observation about the late 1920s: to quote (Friedman 1963):

> *The continuing bull market brought the objective of promoting business activity into conflict with the desire to restrain stock market speculation. The conflict was resolved in 1928 and 1929 by adoption of a monetary policy not restrictive enough to halt the bull market yet too restrictive to foster business expansion. The outcome was in no small measure a result of the internal struggle for power within the System which followed the death of Benjamin Strong in October 1928. How to restrict speculation became the chief bone of contention; the banks, led by New York, urged quantitative measures of higher discount rates and*

open market sales; the Federal ^{Reserve} *Board urged qualitative measures of direct pressure on banks making security loans. A stalemate persisted throughout most of the crucial year 1929. This not only prevented decisive action one way or the other in that year but also left a barrage of divided counsel and internal conflict for the years of trial that followed. – The cyclical expansion from 1927 to 1929 is one of the very few in our record during which prices were a shade lower at the three months cantered on the peak than at the three months cantered on the initial trough.*

In effect Friedman and Schwartz are not blaming the Fed for creating asset market inflation (and as we have seen, this concept should include the empowerment of irrational forces across asset markets including the giant carry trades) by its policies through 1927 and earlier; but they are admitting that there could have been some degree of US stock market "froth" in 1928 onwards (into 1929) (in any case, Friedman and Schwartz do not explicitly refer to the concept of asset price inflation). They fault the Fed for having fallen between two stools—not having tightened sharply and quickly enough in 1928 to end the asset price inflation at that point (they do not use the specific term) or not having decided to ignore the froth and instead focused policy on economic stimulation and resisting "price deflation". In their opinion, both outcomes would have been superior to what course was actually followed; but of the two preferred, they opt definitely for ignoring the asset price inflation and resisting "deflation" instead. Indeed Friedman/Schwartz hypothesize that the eventual severity of the recession which started in August 1929 was in large part due to the fateful decision of the Fed to attack Wall Street speculation at such a late date.

There are surely grounds for questioning whether by mid-1928 a powerful Fed tightening to hasten the end of the inflating stage of the asset price inflation disease (with the speculative temperatures rising) and bring on the deflation phase would have culminated in a better outcome than the feebler attack (on the speculative froth in the US equity market) which was undertaken. The asset price inflation was not a one-year wonder as the above passage suggests but a disease which stretched back to the mid-1920s with huge (but as yet unknown) mal-investment already in place yet still to be recognized. A late fierce attack on the disease in the second half of 1928 would not have undone all the damage already embedded but yet to become apparent though it might have prevented even more mal-investment for a few months more.

Moreover, the attack would have been on monetary inflation in general of which asset inflation is one "twin" (together with goods inflation, in this case camouflaged by rapidly rising productivity growth); and so it would have induced a fall in goods and services prices, perhaps catching up with the cumulative natural downward rhythm, but that would still not be symptomatic of monetary deflation. And the asset price inflation disease went far beyond the stock market, including an array of asset markets (including real estate and crucially the lending boom into Germany). Indeed those other markets were already experiencing falls in speculative temperature well before the stock market crash. Maybe it would have been better for the Fed to have gone somewhat slower on monetary tightening at such a late stage.

But that is a far cry from judging as Friedman and Schwartz did that an aggressively expansionary policy through the second half of 1928 and into 1929 would have produced the best results of all. They reach that conclusion on the basis of 1923–27 having been a high tide for the Federal Reserve and in complete negation or denial of the view here that there had been any serious monetary disorder during that period. Thus for these authors, the extent of froth and its accompaniment to be dealt with in early or mid- or even late 1928 was quite modest compared to what features in Austrian School-type accounts of the same period. They would not recognize the huge mal-investment in the Weimar Republic as part of the monetary problem. They do not explicitly recognize the phenomenon of asset price inflation and are not inclined to apply the Austrian business cycle theory given the difficulties of testing this empirically.

Suppose there had been no tightening of Federal Reserve policy through late 1928 and the first half of 1929 and instead it had doggedly eased policy (as Chief Yellen did almost 90 years later) despite all the evidence of froth so as to fight falling prices. Then yes, the rise of the stock market through late 1927, 1928, and 1929 would have most likely been more powerful—though that is not certain. The inflationary nature of Fed policy might have become obvious to all, with a corresponding raised awareness of likely eventual bust (and indeed in the run-up to the 1929 crash, there was widespread commentary about the dangers of speculation; certainly those may have been one factor in the surprise slowdown of the economy in late summer 1929). It is plausible that the ascent of the market could have been sharper and the fall sooner (indeterminate whether from a higher peak or not but likely so). Maybe instead the economic upturn could have been extended—and the key here would have been the construction boom and real estate markets which in fact peaked in 1928. Yet if the peak came fundamentally in response to revelation of over-supply (and immigration had slowed sharply following controls imposed in the mid-1920s), then an extension of monetary ease might not have made much difference.

A key question: what would an extension and accentuation of monetary inflation through 1928–29 have done to the foreign lending boom into Germany? In reality, this cooled down and even went in reversal (net flow reversal) through 1929 in response to climbing US rates. The pull-back of foreign funds (and reduced rate of inflow) played a catalytic role in the German recession which had started in 1928 (but was disguised through the first half of 1929 by first a severe winter and then a weather-related re-bound in the spring). The German downturn coincided with a new round of negotiations (as scheduled in the Dawes Plan of 1924) to determine a final long-run resolution of the reparations question. The national socialists and nationalists combined in a populist rage against any "sell-out" by the SPD-led coalition government in Berlin (see Brown 2012, 2017). The combination of rage against reparations and business cycle downturn was a deadly cocktail on the German political scene as became growing obvious through a series of local and regional polls, culminating in the shock election result of September 1930 (in which the Nazis emerged as the second largest party). If somehow an extended monetary ease in the US had given a new lease of life to the lending boom and the German economy, perhaps that Nazi triumph would have been avoided. By the time an eventual crash and recession developed, say two years later, the reparations settlement of 1929 would have been far in the background and the Nazis possibly in a less strong position (than in 1920) to gain from the adverse economic conditions.

This is all conjecture only. Such speculation belongs to the historical counterfactual. And there are many alternative narratives. It is possible that a postponement of the Wall Street Crash by a year or more plus a better German economic outcome in 1929–30 sustained by continuing capital inflows would not have lowered the support for the Nazis below danger level, though it would likely have been substantially less than the historical record. But who knows—the Young Plan was in fact a good deal for Germany in which reparations had been cut far from the Dawes Plan and with considerable flexibility (for deferring payments). President Hoover was well inclined towards strengthening the US-German relationship and as a renowned internationalist who after the First World War had led the American Relief Administration providing food to Central Europe could potentially build trust there; in any case after a year of two of seeing how the Young Plan was applied in practice, the populist rage against it stoked up by the Nazis might well have subsided. When the crash and recession eventually struck it might have been less severe overall than what occurred if indeed by then the pro-Weimar coalition in Germany could have sustained its majority and the road to the political and thereby economic abyss in the then second largest economy have been blocked. All such speculation belongs to the Cleopatra chapter of counterfactual history.

All told, a broad hypothesis might be that at a late stage of the asset price inflation disease (part of an overall monetary inflation which might still be camouflaged in goods and services markets), whether or not the central bank belatedly tightens policy in an attack on speculation might not carry great significance for the outcome, given the strong endogenous forces already at work to bring on the final stage of asset price inflation and the accompanying recession. Time will tell whether that is the case with the Yellen/Powell Fed experience of 2017/18. Will the eventual crash be larger from a higher top and to a lower bottom than otherwise with an economic downturn which is similarly even more serious, or are the eventual metrics of recession and financial distress not much different? That is the experiment we are now witnessing.

Bibliography

Ahamed, L. (2009). *Lords of Finance: The Bankers Who Broke the World*. London: Heinemann.
Bierman, H. (1998). *The Causes of the 1929 Stock Market Crash*. Santa Barbara: Praeger Publishers Incorp.
Brown, B. (2012). *Monetary Chaos in Europe*. Basingtoke: Routledge.
Brown, B. (2017). *The Flight of International Capital*. Routledge Library Editions (Financial Markets) Volume 9, 2017 (original edition, 1987).
Brown, B. (2018). Goods Inflation, Asset Inflation, and the Greatest Peacetime Inflation in the US. *Atlantic Economic Journal*, 45(4), 429–442 December 2017.
Friedman, M. (1963). *A Monetary History of the United States*. Princeton, NJ: Princeton University Press.
Galbraith, J. K. (1965). *The Great Crash, 1929*. Boston: Houghton.
Kindleberger, C. (2013). *The World in Depression 1929–39*. Berkeley: University of California Press.

Pollock, A. (2013, September 11). *The Fed Is as Poor at Knowing the Future as Everybody Else*. Statement Before the Committee on Financial Services, Subcommittee on Monetary Policy and Trade.
Temin, P. (1993). Transmission of the Great Depression. *Journal of Economic Perspectives, 7*(2), 87–102.
Turner, P. (2017, November). *Did Central Banks Cause the Last Financial Crisis? Will They Cause the Next*. LSE Financial Markets Group Paper Series, Special Paper 249.
Wanniski, J. (1998). *The Way the World Works*. Washington, DC: Gateway Editions.

CHAPTER 12

Wealth Creation and Destruction Under the 2% Regime

Wealth management under the 2% inflation standard has been deeply challenging.

How should the investor navigate the asset price inflations which have been a dominant feature of this regime? The strengthening of irrational forces, the booming carry trades, and the likely eventual end stages of crash and recession provide both opportunity and peril. In the long run, economic prosperity suffers from the great economic and financial convulsions induced by monetary inflation, but that hypothesis does not go hand in hand with a prescription for investment strategy in the meantime or even in the long run.

A fundamental question to be asked: should the normal rules or guidelines for investing be suspended or modified to take account of the potential large distortions created by the vast monetary disequilibrium which forms under this regime. After all, these norms (dominated by efficient risk diversification and a high bar to active management) are based on the over-riding assumptions of market efficiency and rational expectations—yet the hypothesized influence of monetary distortions as described here on markets is to empower irrational forces. Given our very limited knowledge of the mental processes driving these irrational forces and our severe inability to forecast their rise and fall is clever timing possible (trying to be a little ahead of asset price inflation as it moves through its various stages and from one asset class to another)? Doubts are magnified by the historical evidence of significant differences between the various episodes of monetary inflation and the distinctive attributes of each even though there are also common themes. Would we in fact fare better just playing along with the normal rules of portfolio management, albeit that the assumptions behind them are not valid in this case?

Asset Price Inflation Diagnosis as an Investment Tool

It could be that diagnostic powers regarding asset price inflation even of the most skilled analyst are so weak that investors would do best to assume the market follows a random walk. The study of asset price inflation may well yield results of macro-economic and policy-making significance, but it may not be useful to the investor. Yes, there may be some common elements in all the great asset price inflations (each accompanied by the other twin of monetary inflation, goods inflation, though sometimes camouflaged) from the Great Dutch Monetary Inflation onwards (in the 1630s); but the distinctive characteristics of each may be so large and variable as to over-ride any reliable inference for asset management.

That is not the conclusion here, but many practical investors and investment advisors take that view implicitly or explicitly. The opposite conclusion is that skilful diagnosis of asset price inflation can improve the likelihood of superior investment performance; the diagnosis would include probabilities of asset price inflation gaining new strength before it moves into its late dangerous stage alongside probabilistic forecasts of speculative temperature rises and falls across an array of asset classes; views on the carry trade (in credit, currency, illiquidity, and maturities)—the path to the peak of the boom and the subsequent bust—would also be part of the process. Even so, such diagnosis excludes the wild monetary inflations beyond the normal experience of the monetary history laboratory.

Not playing along with the conventional rules of investment management can be a lonely stressed affair especially during a late boom phase of an asset price inflation episode in which prices across a range of asset classes may be making new records and the particular individual under-performing many of his or her peers. At just such a time, the popular media will be full of demonstrations that those who followed passive buy-and-hold strategies did better than almost all those pursuing active management strategies based on any form of expertise, including monetary diagnosis. And here is the individual expert under-performing who thought he or she could do better.

The monetary expert, based on his or her diagnosis of asset price inflation and the wider economic and financial context, might assess there is a 50% plus likelihood of a 50% dip (from present levels) in equity prices and widespread related distress across other asset classes over the next three years. He could fully justify an under-weight and perhaps short position in some risk assets, even if that 50% does not materialize in full and if the sequencing between asset classes (in particular, equity, real estate, and credit) is different from that in the original central scenario. For example, the violent fall in credit market temperature might occur after the similar fall in equity markets, with a lag of a year or more, rather than the other way round. But tell that to her peers or even to herself in moments of doubt!

And there are the more sophisticated grounds for self-doubt. If I am so concerned about the irrational processes under way and the likely bad ending, why are many others not equally reticent to hold or buy inflated assets at this point in time, meaning there would be no over-valuation to start with? The monetary expert, in hypothesizing an opportunity of profit based on diagnostic power, must believe that this is in short supply or at least that there are not many people applying it for various reasons. One reason could be that many of similar opinion (about asset inflation) believe that they can diagnose the boom phase of asset price inflation and conclude that this still has some time to run. The expert could perceive that the rational assessment is distorted by desperation for yield across a widespan of the investor universe and speculate that the mispricing can persist for a long time yet and get larger. Many of those now dancing with the music may trust their skills to get out before the music stops, even though in aggregate (for all such experts) this is implausible.

Some of the experts are working for investment institutions and may themselves have a list of key investment clients. Such people inevitably consider the business costs and benefits of selling their essentially unproven and unprovable diagnostic powers with respect to asset price inflation. Should their clients in consequence miss out on significant months or even years of rapid capital growth, the advisor may well lose his or her following and with that fees and reputation. And so many might make oblique statements about now being a dangerous time and warn about asset price inflation but advise that in the meantime dancing with the music is surely the best way forward. The spectre of becoming renowned as the Don Quixote fighting the danger of asset inflation which never turns to deflation and even worse might give way to a period of economic miracle is too much to bear. Let's put off tough decisions based on the monetary diagnosis to a later date perhaps in one year's time and hope that the worst does not happen within that time. Then that same decision gets rolled over when the one-year horizon is reached.

Inevitably the aim of the individual applying supposed diagnostic skills with respect to monetary inflation and asset price inflation in particular to outsmart the market will mean under-performance of peers for some time unless he hits the jackpot and chooses just the right day to exit and go short! And the aim certainly does not mean being out of the market and even short all the time. Skill in diagnosis should allow the individual to ride the tide for some considerable time. Short positions in aggregate asset classes are certainly one means to the end of cumulative high returns to be obtained from diagnosis, all subject to realization of the particular high transaction costs of such strategies and also emotional resilience to tolerate barbs when making losses about how "shorting is the widow's trade" and such! Moreover, there is a minimum bar of irrationality and related distortion which must exist before the normal positive risk premiums which are built into expected returns for equities under efficient market conditions are likely turned to negative from the rationalist's viewpoint. Abnormally low but still-positive risk premiums do not justify aggressive short positions. Finally, having been so defiant that this is an asset price inflation episode likely to have a hard landing, the individual should be boldly ready to increase short positions in a situation which seems likely to be such a hard landing, though there can be no certainty of this in real time, and he may be whiplashed by a wave of bottom-fishers.

The Monetary Expert with a Diary Can Diversify Skills

Is it an impossible task to profit from skilful diagnosis of asset price inflations?

As in all such issues, we can find individuals who did well, despite losses in advance of the main opportunity. But was their performance due to luck or skill? That is impossible usually to prove from aggregate data. Only a logbook of day-to-day thinking and actions would answer the question definitively. And of course, even if the individual did not profit because in the end asset price inflation faded away in the midst of an economic miracle, in real-time taking account of underlying probabilities, her strategy may well have been formidable and correct. But luck was against her. A brave individual can tell that to herself but not to her clients!

The monetary expert might seek to diversify the random element in portfolio outcomes by applying skill across a range of asset classes and across time rather than making just one big bold "bet". For example, the expert might recommend backing a strong directional view in the currency markets or credit markets, which could accompany a short position, for example, in one part of the equity or real estate (equity markets). And the expert may be comfortable in applying various technical measures of market sentiment so as to time entries or exits into these strategic positions.

Take the situation in early 2018, most likely well into a late phase of asset price inflation as described in Chap. 11 (which made key comparisons with the late 1920s). This diagnosis was widely appreciated and commented upon, albeit that there were also many dissenters. Even so, a look at the forecasts and advice from the well-known equity brokerage houses on Wall Street and globally carried uniform forecasts of further stock price gains coupled with strategy recommendations to remain very positively committed to equity risk. Yes these analysts admitted in most cases that a bear market is always possible but also unlikely; they hedged their advice to some extent with remarks such as the S&P 500 index typically experiencing a downward correction every year of about 10% within a still rising trend, but that would likely be from a higher price than today, and the year-end price would be substantially higher than now.

Some analysts and journalists trumpeted the fact that over the past 38 years (1980–2017), the S&P has typically gained 10% p.a. That is better than it sounds given that 1980 marked the market depths of the Volcker monetary squeeze about to get under way and the great back-to-back recession of 1980–82, whilst 2017 was well into one of (if not the biggest) asset price inflations in history. The case against the pessimists (or rather strategists who would hope to gain from being out of the market or short ahead of asset price inflation reaching its final stage) is that most years the market rises (72% of the years since 1950, 79% since 1980). The long-term historical odds of stocks rising next year are about two to three times greater than stocks falling. Historical statistics demonstrate US equities in particular are fundamentally biased upwards over time.

All this is true, but times are not equal, and historical trends are not unassailable truths about the future (in contrast to statements such as the sun will rise and fall each day). During periods of likely late asset price inflation as diagnosed skilfully, the "probabilistic outcome" is not a sure guide to action even though confidence in the estimates (of probability) might be "reasonably high". An issue in any estimation of probability is the problem of small sample size. Episodes of asset price inflation perhaps every ten years do not provide much information about who has skills in diagnosis and who does not—given the impossibility of ruling out a large margin of luck. Under the 2% inflation standard, asset price inflations have been more frequent, but even so the dilemma of determining whether an individual has diagnostic power (about asset price inflation) and whether this can indeed improve investment decision-making remains largely indeterminate on the basis of any statistical test. And this has bearing on the confidence of the person making the diagnosis in his own judgement.

So, should the investor with a keen understanding of asset price inflations past and present put that understanding in a box which is not allowed to influence his or her practical decision-making? That action is not justified by the conclusion that there is no statistical test to prove the benefit of such diagnostics. In that situation of uncertainty, the rational conclusion would be that these diagnostics may be useful and applicable but there can be no guarantee of that. It could be rational to apply the diagnostics but not in a way which suggested total confidence in them. And indeed, at the level of the market as a whole, such lack of confidence and overall doubt about diagnostic skill explain why the irrational forces which build up under monetary inflation in asset markets can continue to have substantial influence on prices despite their recognition in principle by a wide span of actors (and observers).

Ingredients of Asset Price Inflation Diagnosis

There are several key ingredients to the process of asset price inflation diagnosis—meaning the effort to assess what stage we are in (of the disease) and its prognosis (what happens next and further ahead). The first is staging; the second is recognizing the dynamics of monetary inflation of which asset price inflation is one key component (the other is goods inflation which can remain camouflaged during extended periods by such factors as globalization, digitalization, business cycle downturn); the third is discovering and assessing the speculative narratives; and the fourth and final is application of findings from the laboratory of history concerning previous asset price inflations.

Staging involves the recognition that asset price inflation goes through phases—early, mid, late, and end as already described in this volume. In a mid-phase, speculative temperatures may already fall sharply in one or more asset markets, whilst continuing to rise elsewhere. The prolongation of asset price inflation depends here on the successful implementation of a "Greenspan put"; if unsuccessful, the late and end stage may both arrive very quickly. By contrast, if successful, there can be a new empowerment of irrational forces which carry the disease forward as much as for several years. Success depends in large part on the speculative narratives still having the power to captivate under the prevailing distorted monetary conditions. That is not inevitably the case. Revulsion may have set in where scepticism rules (that was the case, e.g. in October 1929, when strong monetary injections could not re-fuel asset price inflation).

Clearly recognizing the monetary dynamics means understanding what lies behind the wider monetary inflation process of which asset price inflation is part. The twin of asset price inflation, goods and services inflation, is always somewhere around, albeit sometimes well camouflaged. A study of history and of the present situation may alert the person making the diagnosis to the implications of a sudden change of behaviour by one monetary twin for the other. For example, a sudden flare-up of goods and services inflation may go along with a grown likelihood of asset inflation moving into its next phase. More generally, the analyst tries to assess why the central bank is pursuing the particular version of unsound money and what will determine the extent of cumulative disequilibrium. Are there political or other factors which may bring the process to a halt? What will be the consequences for the inflation process—both in asset markets and goods/services markets?

Discovering and assessing the speculative narratives is important to understanding both the dispersion of temperature across asset markets and the likelihood of sudden reversals. The analyst should seek to dissect the speculative narratives—finding the weak components which in normal rational mode investors would form the pieces of a countervailing narrative; that would be the basis of the healthy scepticism which gets smothered under asset price inflation. Yet by discovering that alternative narrative, the analyst can get an idea about potential losses and overall mal-investment when this particular asset price inflation episode reaches its end.

The use of the history laboratory is crucial to the diagnosis process but not in the sense of expecting identical outcomes. The present may be an echo chamber of the past but not a repeat performance. In any case there are no identical starting points or intermediate stages. We should be guided by Balzac's guiance that the author be able to individualize types whilst typifying individuals—likewise for the diagnosis of asset price inflations and indeed of all economic phenomena (including, more broadly, the business cycle).

Diagnosis of the Asset Price Inflation from 2011/12

Let's illustrate these points about diagnosis through the present monetary inflation starting in the aftermath of the Great Recession. The monetary dynamics were determined by an aggressive and radical implementation of policies so as to achieve the aim of 2% inflation. The availability and plausibility of speculative narratives was enhanced by the underlying robustness of the global economy. Since the mid-1990s, we have witnessed a period of rapid technological change much of it in areas which directly impinged the daily lives of individuals and seemed to add new sparkle (the internet, social media, telecommunications, etc.). And outside these areas, there was much excitement easily understandable about the shale oil and gas revolution, the electric car, and much else. Rapid globalization meant the sky was the new limit in many narratives. And thus when the mid-stage crises came in some asset classes (commodities, emerging market economies, China, oil and gas bust), it was quite possible to jump-start the new or old narratives with help from monetary injections.

The asset price inflation of the mid-1930s (1934–7) serves as a counter example (see Brown 2016). There were indeed many warnings during the early years of the present asset inflation that it would end with a 1937-style crash—the sudden decline of the US stock market near the beginning of the Roosevelt recession of 1937/38—following a powerful expansion of the monetary base through 1934–36. But there were important differences from that experience.

There was no collection of powerful speculative narratives at that time (although technological progress was evident, most of all perhaps with respect to television and air transport). The harrowing nature of the series of crashes from 1929 to 1932 and the unimaginable depths of depression had left their mark on the possibility of credulity amongst investors for speculative narratives, even given promising new technologies and their exploitation. Global military conflict, including a possible world war, was within the realm of mainstream scenario building (albeit near the edge at this stage). Finally, the then Federal Reserve chiefs were not radicals pursuing a brave new monetary experiment; massive balance sheet expansion had happened in part by accident in response to huge inflows of gold.

As soon as there was evidence of hot speculation and even a whiff of goods and services inflation (as in early 1936), the Fed was shifting in the direction of monetary restraint. That was quite different from the situation in the present cycle when monetary radicals were in command and there was a powerful downward rhythm of prices camouflaging inflation in goods and services markets. (In 1935–36 there was an upward rhythm of prices, in part related to a recovery of these from depression lows. This contributed to some over-diagnosis of inflation risks by monetary policy-makers.) Yes, there have been serious and growing geopolitical concerns during the present asset price inflation but surely of a lower dimension than those in the mid-1930s.

The present monetary inflation did reach a mid-stage characterized by some pull-back in speculative temperatures in 2014–15. One focus was energy markets (the revelation of over-investment in high-cost exploration which had occurred on the basis of the oil price remaining for ever at sky-high levels, but now the price had collapsed; a related factor was the fantastic increase in US shale oil and gas production, itself promoted by extremely easy credit market conditions for the producers here despite the high risks and poor prospective profits); more broadly the pull-back included commodities and emerging market economies especially China and even spread to a mild downturn in US equities; alongside there was a growth cycle downturn in the US (in part related to a temporary sharp decline in energy sector investment) and in several other advanced economies. The mini-devaluation by China in summer 2015 seemed like a wake-up call to investors sucked into asset markets at high prices by the current speculative narratives. It was possible to imagine that this would be the end phase of this asset price inflation, with a full recession developing through 2016.

Arguing against that conclusion was the strength of the monetary response and the still powerful narratives related to digitalization and globalization. Yes, in spring 1937, the Fed had pulled back from raising rates and intervened in the bond markets to prevent long-term rates rising, but it did not undo its hikes in reserve requirements; by contrast in 2016, the ECB and Bank of Japan variously accelerated their programmes of quantitative easing and journeyed further into negative rates, whilst the Federal Reserve had not even started the journey towards normalizing the monetary base. And in China, the world's number 2 economy, radical fiscal expansion immediately monetized (and disguised as lending to state enterprises) got under way.

And so 2016 did not mark the start of another Roosevelt recession. Rather, the Yellen Put "succeeded", and there was the start of a new robust economic upturn and intensification of monetary inflation, still effectively camouflaged in goods and services markets. Indeed in 2017 reported goods and services inflation in the US and Europe was remarkably tame—attributed in part to an "Amazon effect" and changed estimation procedures at national statistical offices to take account of quality improvements (see previous chapter). The investors who positioned themselves on that outcome did very well. Those who got the diagnosis badly wrong suffered.

The already-enticing narratives regarding Silicon Valley and the digitalization revolution became even more powerful. Investors saw through their rose-coloured spectacles a future where the FAANGs would collect exponentially growing monopoly revenues, whether from advertising or retail platform access or both. A new round of revolutionary cost reductions in the production of shale oil and gas averted the worst feared outcomes in that space and indeed went along with a re-bound of speculative temperatures there (in both related credit and equity markets). And as regards monetary policy, a strengthening of the inflation camouflage via digitalization (the Amazon) effect removed any pressing argument for central banks to rein back monetary inflation. Indeed, given the complete dislocation of monetary base from the pivot of the monetary system, there was no reliable way of gauging how much stronger monetary inflation dynamics had become. Who would put much or any credence in the circulating econometric evidence, even though these had become the gospel of the 2% inflation standard at least amongst central bank officials? The inertia of expectations around 2% which had built under this regime was untested—how would it ultimately break, violently or gradually?

Is It Time to Cut Back Equity Exposure?

Was it time yet to severely cut back exposure to equity risk—or more broadly carry trade involvement—and even to go short in equities? According to the conventional view, reducing equity exposure to below normal and even more aggressively going short are expensive strategies; the normal expected rates of return on a well-diversified equity portfolio are so high relative to returns on fixed-rate safe investments (the difference is the so-called equity risk premium) that these strategies carry significant loss, unless the individual is prepared to stake a strong view that the market is far out of line from normal pricing based on rational assessment of future prospects. How strongly held could such a view be in early 2018?

A glance at the speculative narratives powering prices higher could certainly provide grounds for doubt. For example, in the highly speculative market for FAANGs and similar (Facebook, Apple, Amazon, Netflix, Google), there was the assumption of present or future virtual monopoly profits growing at high rates for the indefinite future. And yet the climate for these companies was changing—with the growing likelihood of an eventual regulatory or wider tax assault on the power of Facebook and Google (Alphabet) in particular. Many in the marketplace thought the assault would more likely start in Europe than the US and the focus would be on abusive use of private data (a possible solution involved users of these platforms retaining ownership of their data) and various competition eliminating practices. Others were sceptical about any such assault, cautious that regulation favors the established mega-firms. Even without regulatory or anti-trust action, there exist grounds to question the speculative narrative of forever-growing revenues at double-digit pace, especially regarding advertising whose effectiveness was in doubt and which depended on unchecked "data mining".

Moreover, who knew how technological change could bring new competitive challenge? For example, the technology media speculated about block chain becoming harnessed to individual's use of the internet in ways which would allow him to retain ownership of his data rather than this remaining a gold mine for Big Tech (in particular via attracting advertising revenues). Finally, there was much anecdotal evidence of momentum-type trading in these stocks with positive capital gains enticing greater inflows of funds especially from Asian investors.

Amazon did not yet possess overall monopoly power and may never do so across the retail sector, but anti-trust experts raised the possibility that this existed in sub-sectors and with respect to blocking new entrants in some fields and abusing small existing competitors in others. A huge feature of the Amazon story is a large messianic following which believes in spectacularly high profits in the future, albeit never today. Any enterprise field which the "messiah" would enter—whether health insurance, transport, food retailing, and much more—will turn to gold, albeit not immediately. (Sceptics, by contrast, could be fearful of any steps—such as cooperation on new forms of health-care provision—that would ferment an alliance between Big Tech, Big Banks, and Big Government; see Chap. 10.)

Yes, a company enjoying access to equity capital priced on the basis of certain belief in a future El Dorado could deliver fantastic services to its clients that others could not match, and gains in market share could be tremendous. But how long would this last? Investors seemed unconcerned about the derisory low present earnings as a percentage of market capitalization, accepting the narrative that Amazon was re-investing its revenues wisely. Even so it is only depreciation (capital consumption) that nets from gross earnings, not total investment; the underlying reality is that depreciation (capital consumption) made up a massive proportion of current revenues. Perhaps the belief was that once Amazon had established its monopoly positions, there would be a long period when investment spending could fall back.

Looking beyond the FAANGs, there were broader concerns regarding the present market chasing of narratives of permanently high profit rates. The grown monopoly power which lay behind these is open to challenge. And in any case, the profit rates themselves could have reflected an array of financial arbitrage operations and abnormally low interest costs (together with increased leverage) which might well prove unsustainable. And there were grounds for suspecting that the popular speculative narrative of late 2017 about how the Republican corporate tax cuts would permanently buoy post-tax profits in the US and so justify higher valuations had had exaggerated influence under the global inflationary monetary conditions which persisted.

Yes, an unfunded corporate tax cut would buoy post-tax earnings from corporate assets in the US—and this could increase demand for equity assets both from US investors and from global investors (likewise there would be some decrease in demand for foreign equities where tax rates had remained unchanged). But the durability of these shifts could be questioned. A shift of political power in Washington could bring substantial increases in dividend and capital gains taxes within a few years—and the latter could increase in real terms without explicit hikes in nominal rates if inflation eventually accelerated. And foreign tax rates could fall.

In any case corporate tax cuts were not manna from heaven. In so far as their recipients spent the bonus, there would be upward pressure on interest rates and an increased potential for inflation (were the Federal Reserve to lean against the pressure). Eventually inflation tax in its various forms might match a considerable part of the tax cut, and a sizeable amount of this would fall on the owners of equity capital (e.g. increased real effective capital gains tax rates, insufficient depreciation deductions in real terms).

So most likely the corporate tax cut narrative was exaggerated in the market's enthusiasm. But was the overall thrust of inflationary monetary policy likely to continue? The answer (from the viewpoint of end-2017) was yes.

President Trump had nominated Jerome Powell as Fed chief to succeed Janet Yellen early the following year, seemingly on the basis that the Treasury secretary got on well with him and they could work closely together. Powell had presumably convinced his job interviewers that he really id believe that the Administration's tax cuts and de-regulation policies raised substantially the potential growth rate of the US economy. Did not that make it likely that any setback in economic growth (and the White House was promising 3% plus now in the long run on the basis of tax cuts) especially ahead of a difficult challenge looming in mid-term elections would lead to an intensification of monetary stimulus (perhaps in the form of not raising short-term rates in line with jump of inflation expectations)?

And as regards the policy of leading foreign central banks, lingering beliefs in the market-place that the Bundesbank would seriously challenge ECB policies of non-ending monetary inflation had virtually faded away. At the ECB meeting in December 2017, there was not even a whiff of opposition from the Bundesbank against Chief Draghi rolling over massive monetary printing for at least a further nine months and negative rates continuing alongside. In Japan PM Abe had won a super majority in another snap election, crushing a divided opposition, and his BoJ chief seemed to have every intention of continuing the fight to achieve 2% inflation, by ever-more radical monetary means if necessary. In China, yes, there was chatter about some tightening of fiscal/monetary/credit policies now that the communist party summit was over and President Xi was confirmed with strengthened dictatorial powers (including no term limit), but all that was not a foregone conclusion. Perhaps the path of raised inflation (albeit still camouflaged to some extent in goods and services markets) would be chosen meanwhile rather than tough medicine.

Yet though the investor could conclude that inflationary intent remained strong, that was not enough to necessarily sustain asset price inflation in its present hot phase. Emerging market economies which in aggregate account for 60% of GDP at so-called PPP exchange rates and at the epicentre of the global credit carry trade could suddenly slow down, with risk factors including high lieverage in the corporate sector and massive real estate speculation. More generally, huge momentum plays, whether in FAANGs or more broadly in the credit, term risk, and liquidity premium carry trades, could blow up. These all depended on strong gains continuing—but even under a scenario of continued global economic growth and easy money, that was not guaranteed by any means. And there was much comment on irrational investor strategies to buoy returns to date but which could blow up (e.g. the writing and collecting of put premiums or more generally the selling of volatility, i.e. receiving insurance premiums to guarantee others against a rise of volatility). And who could tell that the sudden rise of goods and services inflation in any of the major economies could set off a serious decline in government bond markets globally which would threaten to bring asset price inflation into its end phase?

In the credit or liquidity carry trades, event risk always loomed as a factor of potential disturbance. A large debtor could become distressed and send shock waves through the global markets. A Chinese debtor was an obvious candidate given the widespread appreciation of how over-leveraged the Chinese economy had become (much of the lending historically related to real estate but more recently to a boom in foreign asset acquisition); and though much of the lending was internal through the state banks to state entities, there was also a large potential private sector element and also involvement of foreign lenders (into Chinese paper). In broad terms a serious degradation in the credit rating of sovereign China could shake the global credit markets and wider asset markets. There was also plenty to worry about with respect to other emerging market credits in the context of the Yellen Put (2016–17) having ignited a new carry trade boom into these. Some mentioned India as a potential "grey swan".

In the US there were a wide range of potential weak credits—US commercial real estate companies with large shopping mall exposure, private equity-owned firms with leveraged debt outstanding, non-US banks large loan exposure to hot real estate markets, and highly leveraged corporate debt around the world. And many years of hunting for yield had left a wide range of investors with huge overexposure (relative to any normal basis) to credit products. The US corporate sector had become ever-more leveraged (in terms of debt to GDP but not debt to market value of equity so long as this was sky-high in price) as the financial engineers had sought to boost profitability by retiring equity and selling high-priced bonds. The wider margins were part of a good story for equities, but the soft underbelly included rising leverage in fundamental terms, though disguised at froth equity market levels; any sudden fall in business valuations once froth has dispersed would now fall especially heavily on equity owners (given much higher than normal debt-equity ratios). Any attempt of investor hunter for yields to rein back holdings of credit products to normal levels could set off a crisis of illiquidity in key credit markets.

But why should any of this happen in the first few months of 2018? Surely there was still time to enjoy the heat of global asset price inflation from the long side? No doubt that was the comfortable thinking of a wide span of investors in late 2017. A keen appreciation of asset price inflation and its present dangers (of entering a final stage), including similarities with 1929 as described in the last chapter, could easily have led the thoughtful analyst into advocating well below-normal exposure to risk—and even to go short in some cases.

A big one-week tremor in global equity markets led by Wall Street at the start of February 2018 brought a familiar question back into prominence for many investors. Was now the times to get off the speculative train, even though equity prices had fallen 5–10% below their recent dizzy highs? If some investors had believed that they could safely exit the train at the moment of their choosing, the almost-instant large losses of February 2 and February 5 had illustrated an old lesson—that their chosen moment would likely coincide with that of a stampede, and then they would be tempted to remain on the train for a better opportunity in the future; but the next tremor, even bigger, might come first!

The signs in late January 2018 that goods and services inflation as reported may be on the point of accelerating were at least superficial cause to worry that any resumed speculative train journey could be much shorter than previously imagined as a booming economy would encounter a jolt from a flare-up in inflation expectations. The tremor of early February, if it cooled meanwhile the economic boom (e.g. households could become more cautious as well as businesses, especially where highly leveraged), could mean a resumed journey ahead with the red lights of inflation alert now further down the line; but the cool-down meanwhile would inject new hazards into the journey, including pangs of disappointment about earnings and increased likelihood of adverse credit events. In any case the signs were only tentative and could be rebutted by subsequent evidence.

The bursting of the bubble in risk-parity strategies in the early February 2018 equity market tremor went along with higher estimates of market volatility. The risk-parity investors had essentially been piling up assets of low perceived volatility and increasing their overall volatility by leverage. They had also taken the view that volatility was over-priced in the market (notably for VIX), and so they had amassed short positions in volatility (VIX) against some of their own long equity or equivalent exposure. When equity markets gapped down in early February 2018 most likely because of sudden concern about the deteriorating inflation outlook and perceptions of volatility jumped, the risk-parity investors found themselves in crisis mode. They joined other investors near the exits of the speculative train who had long counted on getting out when the time came, realizing that the asset price inflation at some stage would move on to its dangerous last phase. But at the exits, they find a stampede, and many decide to postpone the end of their journey. The risk-parity investors in many cases did not have that luxury (to delay) given the extent of their leverage outstanding.

Even once the turbulence had settled, the new norm would be one where put and call options on the same equity position would become more expensive (a key input into option pricing formulae is so-called equity volatility). As students of finance 101 learn, a risky corporate bond is in effect a holding of equity in the given firm without any leverage against which large in-the-money call options have been written (see end Chap. 3). If market estimates of volatility are revised up, then the holder of risky bonds requires a larger premium from the equity holders for granting them similar call options—that means a higher coupon for bond issuance (in other words, the coupon cost of corporate debt relative to safe debt increases). That could have profound effect on the booming credit carry trade and ultimately on the evolution of the business cycle (accelerating the downturn).

And who knew whether trauma from the tremor could impact willingness to embrace non-critically FAANG wonders?

Early 2018 Case Study

We have already seen above that the diagnosis of asset price inflation should be sensitive to the possibility that the central bank will respond to any significant pull-back of speculative temperatures by exercising a "Greenspan put" or equivalent—meaning that it abandons plans for monetary tightening or "normalization" meanwhile. These put do not always work. If the speculative narratives have simultaneously faded and there are new grounds for overall pessimism, the sometimes magic of the put might not apply.

How could investors assess in early spring 2018 the likelihood of a looming Greenspan put (in fact a Powell put), given that the US equity markets had broadly pulled back by around 10% from their early-year highs, with selling bouts triggered first by inflation fears (early February) and then by Big Tech and trade war concerns (late March)? The short answer was a low likelihood; a small correction in equities which had not obviously spread to credit in a context or raised inflation alert would surely not trigger a put.

The danger of inflation had increased in market perception since late 2017 given the passing into law of huge unfunded tax cuts (heavily concentrated on business profits) and new spending allocations made in the early 2018 budget resolutions—altogether meaning the federal deficit could reach 6% of GDP in 2019 (the economy still projected to be in the boom phase of the economic cycle). And this was alongside the appointment by President Trump of a Yellen loyalist, Powell, an ex-private equity baron (an industry which thrives on asset inflation) and likely Trump loyalist who would head the Fed and then likely to pursue the 3% growth target and be averse to stock market pull-backs given that the president had made so much of high stock prices in his speeches. He assumed office at the start of February.

Actual economic data on wages, prices and overall demand had gone along with a background story during January of rising inflation pressure in the US, albeit as usual there was much fog leads. At the Davos economic forum, the US Treasury secretary had spoken fondly about a weak dollar. Then on the first Friday of February (Jobs Friday), the latest employment report (for January) seemed to reveal a jump in "wage inflation". Some commentators though were justifiably sceptical. The increase in hourly wage rates seemed to stem from a decline in hours worked (in fact indicating cyclical slowdown); and in the late phase of an economic expansion it is typical for the wage share to rise even under non-inflationary conditions.

It is not strange that the lead narrative in the marketplace about the US monetary situation should shift suddenly at a time when there exists such considerable flux amidst much uncertainty. And that is precisely what occurred in the first two weeks of February 2018—matched by a highly volatile ride for equity markets.

US monetary policy, which had veered towards attempting added stimulus (notwithstanding three tiny official rate rises) during the last two years of Janet Yellen's reign (first the Yellen Put of 2016 then responding to the increased camouflage of goods inflation by Amazon and the latest in hedonic price accounting by going even slower on miniscule rate rises through 2017), seemed set to become even more expansionary, otherwise described as "inflationary".

The neutral level of interest rates had very likely jumped during in the growth cycle upturn since spring 2016—and four rather than three miniscule Fed rate rises during 2018 would not mean that the gap of official rates below neutral would narrow meaningfully. Yes, the return of inflation vigilantes in the long-term interest rate markets could become an irritant to the monetary inflationists; but these characters had most likely become extinct (and even if some still existed, they were not rushing to become Don Quixotes to be massacred in the next exercise of vast rate manipulative power of the Fed and other central banks).

So, was all now clear ahead for the equity market bulls? If the Trump-Mnuchin-Powell Fed was on the course of ever-more powerful monetary inflation, at least until the November mid-terms, why not continue to enjoy the party, notwithstanding the corrections of February and March 2018? The proverbial punchbowl is not about to be withdrawn.

There were some grounds for caution, nonetheless:

First, a weakening greenback could inflame perceptions of inflation. Perhaps that could re-ignite anxieties about the eventual negative implications for shareholder wealth. And who knows—the sinking dollar could progress into a full-scale crisis of the greenback (an implausible scenario from the viewpoint of Summer 2018, given the soft money policies followed by the ECB and the BoJ, and given heightened existential risks in the euro as a populist government took office in Rome!).

Second, just because the Fed is stepping on the monetary accelerator (as would be the case when miniscule rate rises are falling behind the rise in neutral level) does not mean that all is clear for asset price inflation ahead. History provides only a small sample size, and there is no example of asset markets plunging when the central bank is "stepping on the gas"; but our ability to appraise pressure on the gas pedal is limited, and there can be a sudden pushback (as, e.g. if the neutral level of interest rates suddenly falls).

For example, the business cycle may suddenly move into a new weaker stage (and along with that, the neutral level of rates would suddenly fall). Indeed some pessimistic commentators in early spring 2018 were pointing to continued slowdown in monetary and bank lending growth and a pullback in coincident indicators (including the so-called nowcasts, e.g. the Atlanta Fed GDP estimates in real time). Negative asset market shock (credit event, re-rating of profit outlook, speculative narrative telling suddenly exposed as emperor's new clothes fable, etc.) is possible especially after many years of scorching high temperatures. In late March 2018, a sudden (in the event transitory) decline of the FAANGs, for example, was triggered by "Facebook shock" (revelations of private data misuse) and negative comments from President Trump and from prominent senators—including Sanders and Rubio—about Amazon's interference with a level "playing field". Households and businesses may suddenly pull back and become cautious. Market dynamics can suddenly produce short circuit (momentum fails); and we have already mentioned above looming danger in credit markets related to volatility bubble bust. Or the Chinese economy could suddenly surprise on the downside after their New Year holidays.

Yes the monetary policy-makers in the world of fiat money exert huge influence on the timing of the business cycle as it passes through various phases. But they are not omnipotent regarding the determination of this cycle.

A Postscript on Keynes and Buffett

A "common sense" folklore has formed through the decades warning investors and would-be speculators about taking on wagers against market irrationality.

Let's start with the Keynes quip that "markets can remain solvent longer than you can remain solvent" (see Leithner 2017). The English economist is renowned to have made this comment around the time when a bad bet in the currency markets (speculating that the Reichsmark would collapse in line with his pessimism on Germany's capacity to pay the reparation bills as expressed in his polemics (most famously Keynes 2008); in fact the currency rose sharply in spring 1920 on optimism that the German economic and political situation was improving) would have bankrupted him if it had not been for the financial assistance from a friend.

In fact highly leveraged bets in a highly charged currency market where everything is in flux were the true irrationality at that time; all the various hypotheses circulating about the future of the mark and the post-war economies of Europe (including the Weimar Republic) had some plausibility. Market overall assessments were not obviously irrational.

When it later came to irrationality in asset markets as fuelled by Federal Reserve-led monetary inflation, Keynes was always on the side of playing along with the irrational forces not against them (though it is dubious whether he even suspected irrationality, given his revealed monetary analysis). In particular, he was heavily invested in US equities just as two great booms were about to crash (summer 1929 and spring 1937) and suffered large loss in consequence. Again in both cases, he was speculating on the basis of his own economic ideas proving to be correct—he approved of the Fed's policies in the 1926–28 years on the basis that these were essential to stabilizing sterling and carried no evident inflation risk (the concept of asset inflation is never acknowledged by Keynes), later he was a big supporter of Roosevelt's New Deal policies including their radical monetary components.

We could replace Keynes' quip with a general statement that there are strategies which can be formulated and seem to improve the "investment opportunity set" for episodes of asset price inflation where monetary conditions have empowered irrational forces. The strategy builders envisage an eventual end phase of speculative temperature fall and recession. But given the huge uncertainties involved especially related to timing, risk should be carefully monitored. The strategies should not expose the investor to anything approaching bankruptcy danger if the asset price inflation continues longer and more ferociously than expected.

Fast forward from Keynes' warnings about taking on the forces of irrationality to Warren Buffett's eschewing of investment strategies based on macro-economic themes including the path of monetary chaos. Buffett admits certainly that sometimes monetary chaos has wrecked his plans. This happened spectacularly in 1969 when equity markets crashed as the Federal Reserve belatedly and briefly instituted tight money policies to combat the powerful rise of observed inflation in goods and services markets; asset price inflation had been virulent during the years 1963–68 albeit with a pull-back of speculative temperatures during the 1965 "credit squeeze". That had been the environment in which Buffett's individual investment philosophy proved phenomenally successful with his clients outperforming the broad market indices several times over without taking big leveraged bets. When the losses occurred, Buffet returned funds to his clients, making a very graceful apology.

Buffett never returned to pure portfolio investment activity, concentrating henceforth on effectively direct investment in businesses and building a mighty conglomerate. A guiding philosophy was to find businesses which enjoyed some degree of monopoly power (surrounded by the so-called moat). Some of his critics have viewed financial strength and proverbial connections in the corridors of power were the basis for huge bets that paid handsomely in the aftermaths of panics, whether macro or micro (see Snider 2015). The homely advice handed out to his followers to shun the professional investment managers (especially the hedge funds) and to avoid gold as an investment have looked good at times—particularly when stocks were sky-high as in the hot phases of asset price inflation or when gold was in the doldrums as during rare periods of Fed hard money policies or when economic boom was under way.

In broad terms Buffett is sceptical about anyone's ability to make profit from assumed monetary-induced irrationality in markets (taking account also of the difficulty in timing a "re-entry" to the stock market having once exited), and he certainly does not claim that he has any such skill. But that position of humility coupled with great success for his shareholders and previously fund clients does not build a strong case against wealth managers seeking to use diagnosesa of asset inflation as a tool for better performance. And his anti-gold rhetoric (about barren relics which do not share in the income of prosperity) would for many years not have served his listeners well. The bottom line is that financial genius does not depend on an understanding of monetary inflation (at whatever level, whether intuitive or otherwise). But such understanding surely does not undermine genius and may well lead to even better outcomes (both for the genius and those he or she advises); and the non-financial genius has no reason to act blind to monetary inflation including asset inflation; knowledge and understanding in this area should help her make better decisions than otherwise but with no guarantee of superior outcomes.

BIBLIOGRAPHY

Brown, B. (2016). *A Global Monetary Plague*. Basingstoke: Palgrave.
Leithner, C. (2017, February 26). *John Maynard Keynes as Investor-Speculator: A More Balanced Assessment* (Leithner Letter No. 205–208).
Keynes, J. M. (2008). *The Economic Consequences of the Peace*. Bel Air: BiblioLife, 1919.
Snider, J. (2015, July 10). The Crony Pretense Behind Warren Buffett's Banking Buys. *Real Clar Markets*.

CHAPTER 13

From the Fifth Monetary Chaos to Twenty-First-Century Gold

Predicting the exact path of asset price inflation towards and beyond its final phase is an enterprise thwart with much uncertainty. The same predicament applies to speculating about the end of a monetary regime, in this case the 2% inflation standard. The two issues are of course interdependent. The late phase of the present asset price inflation may bring such a deep crisis and recession that forces emerge which bring the present monetary regime to an end. Alternatively, there may be no such build-up of anti-regime forces. That may await a further episode of monetary inflation which evolves into a phase of powerful goods market inflation as low inflation inertia breaks and the econometrics on which the policy-makers base their rate manipulations is revealed as deeply flawed; the 2% inflation standard collapses—its failure evident to all. A new period of monetary chaos would then ensue. Eventually wild inflation could be the catalyst to forces gathering which would empower a new monetary regime—the fifth since the collapse of the pre-1914 gold standard—designed to bring order out of chaos.

WHEN MONETARY INFLATION BRINGS REGIME CHANGE

A high rate of goods inflation was the catalyst to the launch of the monetarist regime in Germany and Switzerland in the early/mid-1970s and briefly in the US at the start of the 1980s. It was also arguably crucial to the birth of the gold exchange standard in the mid-1920s. (This came in the wake of high or hyper-inflations in France and Germany.) Much further back in history, high inflation during the Greenback period was the essential condition for political forces gathering sufficient power to take the US on to the gold standard (see Mitchell 2009).

In all these cases, high inflation (and certainly hyper-inflation) proved to be broadly unpopular, even though there may have been a few gainers. Asset price inflations without high goods inflation even when ending in a big bust do not bring a crescendo of forces such as to achieve a shift in monetary regime. Though they may well bring the existing regime to an end, they would not suffice to empower or anoint a new regime.

Accordingly, the Wall Street 1929 crash and the Great Depression snuffed out the gold exchange standard. There followed many years of monetary chaos made worse by world war. The designers of the next regime, the Bretton Woods system, were influenced by the prevailing folklore especially amongst leading monetary officials about what had gone wrong in the disintegration phase of the gold exchange standard (destabilizing capital flows in particular as according to the widely influential diagnosis of Nurkse (1944)—a view subsequently disputed; see Bordo and James 2001). They were insensitive to or unaware of the more fundamental criticisms of the gold exchange standard related to the build-up of asset price inflation.

Subsequently when the high inflation which emerged under the Bretton Woods system caused that regime to collapse, Germany and Switzerland were immediately ready to install a new monetary regime—monetarism. The Great Inflation from the early and mid-1960s to the Great Crash and Recession of 1973–75 had featured powerful asset inflation and goods inflation, albeit of varying intensity in absolute terms and relative to each other through the whole episode (see Brown 2017).

By contrast the panic of 2008 and the ensuring Great Recession proved not in themselves to be regime-breakers—the 2% inflation standard survived, and the experiments under its banner became even more radical. That was in large part because the politicians and the central bankers were able to blame the bankers and others for what happened, whilst absolving the monetary regime.

In any case, unlike the gold exchange standard or Bretton Woods system, the 2% global inflation standard does not turn on close international monetary cooperation. Yes, there are the continuing G-7 and G-20 meetings of finance ministers and central bankers. These are empty, however, of real content. The "natural condition" of the 2% inflation standard is intermittent and even semi-permanent currency warfare. Each central bank (under political direction) picks and chooses when to step up its efforts to achieve the 2% target knowing full well the implications of such variations in the "intensity" of monetary policy for the behaviour of its currency.

Neither major political party in the US has been ready to launch an attack on the 2% inflation regime. The Democrats and their president were uniformly and strongly behind the status quo—and backed a radical implementation of policies designed to fortify the 2% inflation standard in the wake of the panic and Great Recession. Yes, some of their number insisted that the regime include a powerful army of regulators, but there was no question about the regime aim (2% inflation within the so-called dual mandate).

The triumph of the Republicans in the Congressional elections of 2014 on top of their regaining the House in 2010 fuelled some expectation of monetary reform. But a big hurdle in the way was the fact that the Republican advocates of reform had no plan for regime change. Their chief economic consultant, Stanford Professor John B. Taylor, who had been the senior international official in the first Administration of George W Bush, was intellectually committed to the 2% inflation standard. His well-known "Taylor rule" for guiding Fed interest rate fixing grew out of a vision where benign central bankers could divine the neutral rate of interest and estimate correctly the coefficients of an economic forecasting model founded on neo-Keynesian teachings (including the Phillips curve); armed in this way, they could supposedly achieve the aim of 2% inflation.

Professor Taylor claimed that monetary policy-making based on his "rule" would do better than discretionary policy-making; but he had absolutely no problem with the 2% inflation target. Yes, he has been critical of the Greenspan and Bernanke Fed for fanning "bubbles"—but the fault lay with flawed discretion and lack of consistent respect for econometric-based guide rules, of which his is the best!

Republican Monetary Policies

The Republicans did not search for any alternative to the 2% inflation regime—and to be fair, there was no leading highly recognizable exponent of such a case (unlike Milton Friedman for monetarism) or any other country example to point to as was the case when the Bretton Woods system collapsed. The reformers did embrace greatly enhanced congressional oversight, and if organized effectively, this might be the springboard in time to meaningful monetary reform. Congressmen who served on the monitoring committee, sitting continuously with full immediate access to transcripts of meetings and power to call for exhaustive testimony from policy-makers (well beyond the ineffective pantomime of the present semi-annual Fed chief testimonies) and to invite outside experts, might have found their way to a better regime. Still there was no obvious and ready-made alternative regime on offer. Meanwhile the sparkle of asset price inflation during its phase of rising temperatures and a long albeit modest business cycle expansion reduced the apparent urgency of any action from the viewpoint of political expediency.

Even so, the "Republican sweep" in the November 2016 election, which brought Donald Trump to the White House and re-asserted Congressional majorities (still a thin margin in the Senate), did catapult the subject of monetary reform once more into a live zone, not least given that the new president had attacked Janet Yellen for bubble monetary policies during the campaign. Yes, there was still the hurdle that the Republicans lacked a super majority in the Senate, so any Fed reform legislation could be filibustered there unless they were to work towards building support "across the aisle" which seemed highly implausible. Long gone were the days when "sound money" found its main nucleus of support within a conservative wing of the Democratic Party (and indeed as recently as the elections of 1976, it had been Jimmy Carter giving speeches against Republican monetary policy, followed by the action of nominating Paul Volcker to be Fed chief in 1978, understanding full well that this would bring an anti-inflation shock therapy). Yes, the Republican senators in driving forward Fed reform did say at one point that they had Bernie Sanders (on the left of the Democratic Party) as an ally, especially on the issue of audits, but no joint action ever materialized.

Without Congressional action, there was scope for the power of presidential nomination to usher in reform (very quickly many chairs became vacant on the FOMC, including the vice-chair, and chair Yellen herself was due to retire at the end of January 2018). But without any guiding concept of reform, the new president and his selected search committee appointed new members who were stalwarts of the 2% regime and enthusiastic about the Administration's programme most especially related to tax cuts and bank deregulation. This combination of credentials would also suggest that the eligible candidates were likely to formulate monetary policy in a way which would be helpful towards avoiding setbacks in the approaching mid-term Congressional elections.

The few remaining sound money enthusiasts amongst the Republicans in Congress, notwithstanding the tone of the new president's Fed appointments, could have sought to impose restraints—barraging Fed officials and unwelcome nominees with pertinent and charged questions and insisting on Administration action on monetary reform as a condition of their cooperation on other issues dear to it. It seemed in 2017 that the scramble for a big business tax cut extinguished US monetary reform as a component of the Republican programme. Representative Kevin Brady, who had sponsored several monetary reform bills in recent years, had now become chair of the powerful Ways and Means Committee (responsible for taxation).

When, eventually, President Trump nominated an ex-private equity titan and long-time Yellen loyalist to succeed Janet Yellen as Fed chair, there was no audible murmur of disgruntlement from the Republicans. At the final vote in the Senate, only four Republican senators voted against Powell's nomination—including former Trump presidential rivals Ted Cruz, Rand Paul, and Marco Rubio. Sound money advocates had reason to be in despair. Would a new chief whose fortune stemmed from private equity which flourishes in the context of the cheap leverage and frothy equity markets—characteristics indeed of asset inflation—who had backed (albeit apparently with less than full Bernanke-ite zeal at the start) for many years as Fed governor a radical policy of monetary inflation and had zealously attacked any proposal for auditing his institution, really now change his spots? And yes, many commentators professed that he genuinely believed in the prosperity-bringing potential of the Republican tax cuts—belief that doubtless endeared him to the appointments committee; but was he wearing rose-coloured spectacles when he prognosticated in late March 2018 that one (or possibly two) further tiny rate rise before Election Day in 2018 would be consistent with non-inflationary monetary policy?

The Concept of Sound Money Regime

The purpose in this chapter is to explore a possible sound money regime to follow the global 2% inflation regime—most likely after another episode of monetary chaos (the fifth since the collapse of the gold standard). How could this new regime appeal to those for whom sound money is a leading objective? What is the combination of possible political, economic, and market circumstances which could make this objective practical politics? Along the way, there is an attempt to assess the meltdown risks of high inflation or hyper-inflation emerging at any point.

Sound money does not mean stable prices in the short or long run. Rather the guiding features (of sound money) are market determination of short- and long-term interest rates free of any official manipulation; the quality of money and "consumer satisfaction" with it are the lead objectives of the money "suppliers"; persistent moves of money prices (of goods and services) in one direction should not be expected over the long run, there should be some tendency for prices to revert to the mean but in no precise or assured manner; money must not be a tool of the sovereign usable towards funding expenditures (without legislating tax rises or floating loans on the free market at non-manipulated rates) and bailing out cronies including the banks.

In the long span of history, the nearest approximation to such a regime has been where the monetary base corresponds to above-ground gold supplies and its growth determined by the amount of newly mined gold. No doubt there were improvements possible in the pre-1914 gold standard, for example, competition in the issuance of banknotes. Repeated danger came from banking instability, especially in the US, usually a consequence of regulations severely distorting competitive forces and encouraging perverse risk-taking which only became apparent at moments of tension; also there was the threat of suspension in times of war or domestic revolution.

A lead question is whether a return to such a regime is even technically possible, leaving to one side the issue of whether the political forces necessary to its triumph could ever be mustered. Any move back to gold would most likely occur at a nation-state level rather than several large nations acting together. There is an intriguing possibility though that a group of small nations could lead the way in restoring gold monies—to be discussed later in this chapter. A key scenario to consider is the US effecting a monetary regime change in favour of gold, even though this is highly implausible from the viewpoint of the present (at time of writing).

Anti-Gold Myths

Before mapping out such a possibility, it is important first to dispose of some widely spread anti-gold myths. Larry White does this very effectively (2017). He starts with some preliminaries. A "gold standard" is a monetary system in which gold is the basic money—so many grains of gold define the unit of account (e.g. the dollar), and gold coins or bullion serve as the medium of redemption for paper currency and deposits. In a classical gold standard, there is no interference with the functioning of the market production and arbitrage mechanisms that equilibrate the stock of monetary gold with the demand to hold monetary gold. The US was part of an international classical gold standard between 1879 and 1913.

According to White, many mainstream economists today instinctively oppose the idea of the self-regulating gold standard because they have been trained as social engineers. They are experts, and an automatically self-governing gold standard does not make use of their expertise. Yet the actual track record of the classical gold standard was superior in major respects to that of the modern fiat money alternative. The near-zero secular inflation rate was not an accident. It was the systemic result of the slow growth of the monetary growth stock. White cites data according to which the annual gold mining output between 1829 and 1929 ran between 1.07% and 3.79% of the existing stock, with the one exception of the 1849–59 decade (6.39% growth under the impact of Californian and Australian discoveries).

White faults the critics.

First, some average out their data to include the period of the gold exchange standard in the interwar period, and some even include the war years when the US dollar in fact remained convertible into gold. But post-1914 there was never again a full gold standard. And in any case, the tight monetary conditions for which the Fed has been blamed in the years 1931–33 were not the result of a gold constraint; the Fed had plenty of gold.

Second, some critics have viewed fiat money through rose-coloured spectacles. They have argued in defence of expert monetary guidance that even the classical gold standard was second best to an ideally managed fiat money where experts call the shots. Yet expert-guided monetary policy fails in well-known ways to improve on a market-guided monetary system. Experts persist in using erroneous models. Policy-makers set experts to design policies that are not to meet the public's goals. The public understands that the central bank has no pre-commitments, and so chronically sub-optimal outcomes can result even where the central bank has full information and makes most benign interventions.

AGAINST FISCHER'S ADVOCACY OF DISCRETIONARY POLICY-MAKING

White quotes Stanley Fischer as a leading economist who prefers discretionary policy-making to anything smacking of a rule-based monetary order, most of all as in the case of the classical gold standard (see Fischer

2017). Fischer asks why monetary policy decisions should be made by a committee rather than by a rule. His reply:

> "The answer is that opinions – even on monetary policy – differ among the experts". Consequently we "prefer committees in which decisions are made based on discussion among the experts" who try to persuade one another.

Fischer takes it for granted that a consensus among experts is the best guide to monetary policy-making we can have:

> emphasis on a single rule as the basis for monetary policy implies that the truth has been found, despite the record over time of major shifts in monetary policy – from the gold standard, to the Bretton Woods fixed but changeable exchange rate rule, to Keynesian approaches, to monetary targeting, to the modern frameworks of inflation targeting and the Fed's dual mandate and more.

Accordingly, Fischer suggests that historical shifts in monetary policy fashion warn us against adopting a non-discretionary regime because they indicate that no "true" regime has been found. White retorts:

> *That governments during the First World War chose to abandon the gold standard (in order to print money to finance their war efforts) and that they subsequently failed to do what was necessary to return to a sustainable gold parity (devalue or deflate) does not imply that the mechanisms of the gold standard – rather than government policies that overrode them- must have failed. Observed changes in regime and policies do not imply that each new policy was an improvement over its predecessor – unless we take it for granted that all changes were all wise adaptations to exogenously changing circumstances. Unless that is, we assume that the experts guiding monetary policies have never yet failed us.*

A Return to Gold in Twenty-First-Century Mode, Not Pre-1914

What practical arrangements would be necessary to return to a gold standard today such as existed prior to 1914?

The task is truly daunting, not least because no one can have any precise idea of the price of gold at which there would be starting monetary equilibrium—where monetary base (entirely in gold form) across the initial "gold bloc" was equal to demand at an average level of money market rates which were neither restrictive nor inflationary. Moreover, getting these gold stocks in place (as monetary reserves) across the various member countries could involve large cumulative transfers, and this could cause considerable tensions (interest rate gaps between nations, distrust). Related to all this uncertainty would be the amount of gold likely to flow into monetary base from alternative uses as today's private holders of gold across the world might decide to lighten up, given that there is no longer appreciation potential against the lead gold currencies (except in the event of breakup).

Given present official holdings of gold, the member countries of a new gold standard could practically include the US (holdings as of end-2016 8000 tonnes), Germany (3800 tonnes), Italy (2500 tonnes), France (2500 tonnes), Switzerland (800 tonnes). China is a possible member if some wilder unofficial estimates of official gold holdings were correct. Countries with only small gold reserves (relative to economic size) could not be feasible starting members (though possibly if holdings of foreign exchange reserves are large, a commitment to build up gold reserves over a period of years would be credible).

If the US were unilaterally to take the opening move back to gold at a price moderately above early 2018 market levels (say $1500 per ounce), with the Treasury moving its gold into the Federal Reserve in exchange for government bonds in its portfolio, that would amount to around $360 bn, just below one-third of the normal monetary base (on a trend line from just before the start of quantitative easing). Under a revamped gold standard, however, it may well be that the demand for monetary base is much higher than under the present regime, given the attraction of gold compared to fiat notes and also given the permanent suspension of lender of last-resort function and too big to fail (see Chap. 10, pp. 162–3 for more detail; essentially, if no lender of last resort, then bank would find themselves having to hold much larger amounts of high-powered money so as to meet sudden large fluctuations in net withdrawals, whether as cash or for transfer to other financial institutions).

On the other hand, some presently private-held gold by US residents would flow into this aggregate in addition to official holdings. A gold-dollar standard as outlined would mean that some present holders of the yellow metal would switch into dollar bills and bonds to earn interest, so long as they expect the link to hold; this switching would mainly occur out of gold now held in the form of bars rather than jewellery, and we should remember that jewellery is around half the above-ground stock of gold;

private investment in bars or equivalent and official holdings are each around one-fifth; estimates of above-ground gold supplies are as high as 140,000 tonnes, where 1 tonne equals 1000 kg, and the January 2018 dollar price per kilo is around $43,000; this amounts to $6–7 trillion, compared to US GDP of under $20 trillion. And there could be inflows of gold from the rest of the world into the new gold-backed dollar which would boost the total of gold reserves in the US (see Pringle 2012).

Overall in choosing the official price for gold, US officials would want to avoid setting off a powerful shrinkage of the US monetary base due to an underlying situation where the demand for gold outside the US was powering large exports (of the yellow metal). Similarly, they would not welcome a situation where the automatic mechanisms involving gold resulted in the supply of monetary base in the US getting a boost beyond what made sense from the viewpoint of stable monetary conditions. Nothing would be for certain, but an official price moderately above today's market level might be the best solution; the proportion of the monetary base in the US which would be metallic, and shifts in this proportion over time, could be quite volatile. With the total monetary base at 6–10% of GDP, and the Treasury financing gold operations (such as to underpin the gold parity of the dollar—see below), that would surely be manageable.

A main purpose of adding gold into the monetary base as a fully convertible asset (dollars exchangeable into US gold coin at a fixed price and gold bullion exchangeable into gold coin at the mint for a flat small fee) would be to add to the breadth, depth, and stability of demand for monetary base, also making it less elastic with respect to small changes in interest rates, given especially the importance of the jewellery component. (High elasticity means that prices could rise far without generating substantial resistance from monetary forces; instead there would just be a small rise of rates. By contrast, with modest inelasticity, there would be a bigger rise of money market rates, together with a subdued reaction of long-term rates; under a sound money regime, these largely ignore swings in short-term rates—see Chap. 4, p. 49).

This is all crucial towards re-putting monetary base at the pivot of the monetary system (see Chap. 10). Steps alongside towards re-fortifying the pivot would be re-introducing large-denomination US dollar banknotes, anti-trust and related action to curb the power of the credit card and payment card monopolists or oligopolies to wage war against cash (in particular by suppressing or outlawing fees for card use), curbing too-big-to-fail protections, restricting deposit insurance and lend of last-resort aid—all so as to underpin bank demand for high-powered money.

But even despite all this, there is no path visible back to totally automatic rules as under the pre-1914 gold standard. That path would require that the Fed relinquish control over the total supply of high-powered money, and indeed all high-powered money would be gold or gold-backed. In the context of only one country on gold, the US, and huge uncertainties about the evolution of demand for gold under such circumstances, that step is not remotely feasible, at least until very much further down the road. And in the interim, there would be no prospect of reviving a multi-lateral gold exchange standard, where countries outside the US effectively pegged their currencies to the dollar, whilst having no effective internal convertibility for their currencies into gold, and where all fluctuations in their reserves occurred in the dollar component. Some countries may decide to go down that route on a unilateral basis.

Yes, several large countries could at some stage follow the US example. Germany is a possible candidate, but not whilst in European Monetary Union. EMU could not survive a gold money regime given the extent of sovereign debt and bank weakness, no longer papered over by a money printing press. And across the union as a whole, gold reserves would be insufficient. Hypothetically France and Germany could form a new much slimmer monetary union based on gold.

The ultimate return of Germany to gold would not mean the resurrection of the gold exchange standard or a full gold standard. The US would in effect be fixing a supply path for monetary base (as defined for the US) of which gold would be a vital component. Germany, say, adopting gold money would have direct impact on the US monetary situation, most particularly by establishing (indirectly via the "gold points") a narrow band of possible fluctuation between the German and US currencies. But the US would enjoy the benefits of monetary hegemony. A bout of speculative capital flows, perhaps triggered by perceived fragility of the gold bloc (in this case Germany and the US), would be much larger relative to the German than the US holdings of gold, and so the burden of temporary interest rate adjustments to contain gold loss would be a much bigger issue for Germany than for the US. That is why a twenty-first-century gold standard may not extend beyond the US. If indeed smaller foreign countries "return to gold", it may be only those with very large gold reserves (relative to economic size). A wide range of countries may well opt for pegging their exchange rates unilaterally to the new gold-backed US dollar but building up meanwhile the share of their foreign exchange reserves in gold.

A Return to Gold by One or a Group of Small Rich Economies

It is possible to imagine a "return to gold" which is led not by the US but by small rich countries with a highly developed financial centre, highly solvent banking sector, and highly rated government debt, and with domestic labour and product/service markets where prices are potentially highly flexible in both directions (important to offset swings in the gold exchange rate). These would return to gold on their own but also be aware that others are likely to be acting similarly, and so they are part of a group, albeit with no central control authority. Switzerland, Holland, Canada, Luxembourg, Hong Kong, Taiwan are examples. (We could even imagine a seceding rich province from a present larger political jurisdiction could solve the monetary problem at birth by opting for gold.) The gold bloc described would be in effect a way in which the small countries described could escape the dilemma of joining large fiat monetary unions where they have no effective say in the outcomes and the monetary quality is decidedly sub-par. The gold money alternative allows the small country to reap many of the advantages of a large money (liquidity, low transaction costs, access to broad loan and bond markets (these are not available for a small-country fiat money) without substantial exchange risk, stable global purchasing power, international demand, and acceptability) without the disadvantages.

The given small country could plan to amass gold reserves over many years but announce the programme at the start (of its "return to gold"). The small country's exchange rate vs the dollar and other currencies would effectively move one to one with the gold price (in terms of those same currencies). But a new element of importance in the demand for gold would be the behaviour of the demand for money in the given small country (or group of small countries); that might well help to stabilize the overall global demand for gold, making this a superior monetary base for a global gold money (used throughout the world but not the national money except in the given small country). The gold price itself might become less volatile overall when stabilized in this way (in terms of global purchasing power) though it would become more subject to the country-specific influences (of the country where gold had become money). One advantage for the small country which elects to become the global gold pivot in this way is that its money would assume an international importance (bringing business to the related financial centre) that far transcends its economic size.

Private Gold Money

In a world where gold money is pivoted nationally as described—whether for the small countries as described or for say the US—it would take two forms both internally and globally. First there would be national gold money (whether francs or dollars) circulating throughout the globe, convertible into sovereign gold coin (national banknotes or deposits at the issuing central bank would enjoy the conversion possibility on demand). Second there would be gold money not in national form (no government role in its supply, whether minting, coinage, or otherwise) convertible into gold as specified by the private issuers.

Banks anywhere could issue deposits in non-national gold money. These would be re-payable on demand in gold bullion (or some specified gold coin not determined by government). Borrowings could also be denominated in gold. Those involved in "manufacturing" these monetary claims and liabilities could hedge their corresponding positions in national gold money markets (US or Switzerland or other small countries as described) albeit subject to the risk that the given country could exit the gold standard at some point (no doubt financial markets could price options or futures which would cover this risk related to the rate of exchange between the gold money and gold). These parallel non-national gold monies would likely have a much bigger role where the national gold monies (with government involvement) are issued by small countries rather than the US.

Quasi-Gold Roles with Over-Rides

How could the US monetary authority (the Fed or alternative) be reined into following rules regarding the supply of high-powered money under a twenty-first-century gold standard as outlined earlier in this chapter? The answer: to adopt quasi-gold rules but almost inevitably with over-rides possible which meet certain criteria. Note, by contrast, that small countries returning to gold would not operate independent monetary base control; monetary base in a small country cannot in isolation be the pivot of a stable money order and indeed under a full gold standard of the pre-1914 type would fluctuate (in percentage terms) much more than for large countries under the influence of gold flows. Instead, in the small country, short-term rates would be determined by the gold position—whether these were in short supply or in glut relative to normal cautionary amounts to hold so as to honour the gold convertibility pledge; monetary base would be determined endogenously. (Purchases and sales of gold would add and subtract accordingly from the monetary base.)

Back to the example of the US again on gold, the monetary authority might deem that the annual increase in monetary base should be between 0% p.a. and 1.5% p.a. A period of much more rapid than trend productivity growth reflected in unit labour cost falls should go along with some small boost to monetary base over a multi-year period—as could occur in the situation of especially rapid globalization or particular technological change such as digitalization where prices come under sustained downward pressure. But these boosts would not be designed to stop or reverse the price decreases within a short period of time (rather they would correspond to the fillip to gold mining which occurs under the classic gold standard when costs of production fall in nominal terms). The emergence of sustained high money market rates at a time when long-term interest rates were persistently below those could indicate that a structural shortage of monetary base had developed (perhaps due to a jump in demand for high-powered money), and this could justify a temporary supply boost.

It is unimaginable that the US could adopt a monetary regime based at least partly on gold as described without ultimately the approval of Congress. And the White House would be an active partner through the nomination of monetary and other officials in line with implementing the new regime and willing to work towards the passage of the required legislation to complete the process. The legislators and the White House would have to make the case that the past monetary regime and any interim situation had been responsible for the bad outcomes experienced—including possibly financial crash, great recession, and high inflation.

The politicians and monetary officials involved in the transformation would have been successful in raising much anger against the old regime and its co-travellers, whether oligopolistic too-big-to-fail bankers or the central bankers levying inflation tax on the small and the weak. They would have to be skilful at assembling lawmakers who could devise a code of monetary rules which whilst flexible could not be ignored or wilfully sidestepped. Yes, the judiciary (and the Supreme Court) included would have a role in enforcement, all subject to the knowledge that ultimately there are strong political trends in judicial opinion making.

We know from monetary history that one political actor weighing against a regime built on automatic rules (traceable in origin to how the gold standard worked) is the apparent loss of discretionary power to "stimulate" economies out of recession. And there are the big issues of how government operates without any access to a money printing press and how the banks can be safe when the lender of last resort and the principle of too big to fail fade away.

Those behind a new regime as described should make the following case.

The big monetary stimuli have occurred in the aftermath of great recessions and panics which themselves resulted from earlier episodes of unsound money. Sound money by going along with less severe (if any) episodes of monetary inflation including asset price inflation should mean a smoother ride and greater economic prosperity. The reduced or eliminated scope for stimulus is a gain overall, not a cost. And the dwarfing of too big to fail and lender of last resort should mean that competitive forces bring about a tier of highly capitalized medium-sized banks holding large amounts of monetary base. These would win most customer deposit business; and alongside there would be riskier banks where depositors and other lenders were fully aware of risks of temporary payment and other types of suspension (in return for which higher yields were available). Emergency plans for equity-debt swaps would be part of a package of transparency which financial institutions made available towards winning customer trust.

No to Inflation Taxation

How would government manage without access to "the money printing press"?

In answering this question, we must give that popular phrase meaning in today's monetary context where monetary base has been dislodged from the pivot of the system.

The original notion of "taxation by inflation" came under monetary regimes where all money took the form of gold coin, its content effectively vouched by the governing authority. Without public knowledge, the governing authority would trim coins which came into its possession (either through tax payments or imports/new mining) and re-issue or make new issues of coins with less than the promised gold content. It would pay for goods and labour with these coins initially at the established level of prices, meaning that the surplus in issuance now possible (because of the debasement) gave it command over greater economic resources for some time. Progressively though the increased amount of coins in circulation would cause prices to rise in line with the increased supply. And then the tax collecting potential would fade.

Incidentally it would fade much faster if the public became aware of what was happening, and prices rose in anticipation of the increased money at large. The tax levy in effect takes the form of individuals at first accepting the debased coins as if they were the real item without upping their prices. If there is full awareness of what is happening, then there is still some scope for government revenue-making; this would come from the increased demand for debased coins as circulating medium in line with higher prices (and to make good the withdrawal of the old circulating medium in so far as individuals hoarded the old coins realizing their superiority to the new ones). Hence in the case of Gresham's law applying (bad money drives out good) as is the case where all know what is happening and the rate of exchange between the old and new money is fixed at 1:1, the government still makes revenue from the debasement.

Such power of taxation by inflation does not exist under a well-functioning gold standard. Under a modern fiat currency regime, it exists through the monetary authority lifting the path for the expansion of the monetary base (the rate of money printing, including deposits with the central bank) and using this to purchase goods services and labour. The effect of the monetary base expansion in the classical case (where this is all non-interest bearing) on prices depends on the nature of monetary demand.

If demand for monetary base is elastic with respect to small changes in interest rates, then the initial impact (of an increase in its supply) would be to depress money interest rates such as to trigger a re-distribution of public holdings away from bills on which interest income falls to currency and sight deposits backed by large holdings of cash. In turn these low rates could set off an inflationary process, in part via currency depreciation and in part through the generation of excess demand in various goods and services markets. Again, as in the gold debasement case, if there is transparency about the boost to monetary base growth, the price rises would come sooner, and the gains in revenue which the government could make at a particular steeped-up pace of monetary base would be smaller. Even if there were near-full transparency, the government would enjoy some temporary boost to its command over resources due to erosion in the real value of monetary base outstanding. An increase in demand for money along with the higher prices would give scope for the authorities to gain purchasing power—though this would be held in check possibly by a fall in the demand for real money balances as the public sought to cut down on the amount of their exposure to possible inflation tax in the future.

Once we introduce government bonds and bills alongside non-indexed taxation regimes, the scope for the government to profit from inflation comes from a somewhat different combination of sources. The process starts with expansion of monetary base. If this results in unanticipated inflation, then windfall loss is suffered by present holders of fixed-rate government bonds and fiat money meaning the creation of more space (not equal) potentially for new issuance before credit limits reached. These windfall losses for individuals do not correspond 1:1 to gains in revenue for the government. In an environment of excess demand created by monetary inflation, the fact that some individuals are squeezed by real unanticipated loss creates more space for other individuals (whose portfolios were less exposed to inflation loss) to obtain goods and services.

The revenue for government comes from the scope to issue new paper (bonds or fiat money) as individuals re-build their real holdings of these as inflation erosion takes its toll (albeit that the level of demand for these is likely to fall in light of the inflation danger). Another element of inflation revenue for the government (not itemized as such) comes from manipulating interest rates to well below any plausible estimate of neutral rate and well below anticipated future inflation. All of this can happen with reported inflation staying down at a low level, albeit with the potential to suddenly spring higher at some unknown point in the future (at which case there is a greater real windfall loss).

In fact, if money printing does not drive up the reported rate of consumer price inflation, as in the well-known situation of recent years where there has been strong camouflage of monetary inflation in goods and services markets, there may still be considerable scope for the government to obtain a boost in inflation tax revenues. The potential comes in part from the power of interest rate manipulation including sometimes the introduction of negative interest rates. If there were honest accounting in the public finances, the interest cost of the government debt would be estimated at the non-manipulated interest rate; and then there would be a credit for inflation tax in the form of the spread by which the manipulated interest rate is below the hypothetical non-manipulated rate. In practice this does not happen, and even if a zealous accountant were to try to complete this assessment, the problem is lack of knowledge about where interest rates would be without the manipulation.

Alongside this collection of inflation tax via manipulated interest rates by the government, equity owners in effect become inflation tax collectors from holders of debt paper issued by their businesses. The profit from such financial engineering may well dwarf that from potential new long-gestation capital investment, whose eventual pay-off anyhow is diluted by a possible crash and recession in the final stage of asset inflation. Rising leverage to take advantage of inflation tax collection (which also includes the compression of spreads on risky bonds induced by hunger for yield) has been an important component of the corporate profits boom in the present cycle, albeit that the main speculative narrative put much greater weight on the magic of monopoly power as bolstered by the "winner take all" feature of the digitalization age (see Chap. 6).

In recent years, the Fed's commitment to the 2% inflation standard, buttressed by radical experimentation in interest rate manipulation, has created a famine of interest income from which Uncle Sam has been a main gainer. Just look at the dwindling interest bill on government debt. As the federal deficit to GDP ratio now climbs to a new peacetime record for the US economy in a late boom phase of its business cycle, this partly hidden and widely under-estimated form of inflation tax alongside its older forms loom large as potential expedients to tackle crumbling public finances.

The monetary officials who administer today's 2% inflation regime deny that they are tax collection agents. They claim that the interest income famine stems from natural misfortune (dwindling investment opportunity, excess savings) and that 2% inflation really isn't that bad given the difficulties of measuring quality improvements. A powerful downward rhythm of prices attributable to globalization and digitalization has allowed them to pursue monetary inflation and levy inflation tax in the new form of interest rate manipulation—all whilst complaining that "inflation is too low" and winning friends enriched by asset price inflation. Some officials (and their political masters) have also been enthusiastic about the apparent scope for engineering a further fall in unemployment via monetary policy so long as inflation is below target. They either reject the pessimism of sound money advocates that any such trial engineering will end up in tears from an eventual asset (and credit) market bubble-and-bust sequence and that in any case the monetary uncertainty holds back investment and productivity growth; or they don't care given the short-run gains in popularity brought by rising asset prices.

A stellar effort by economists to unmask central bank tax collectors would be a real contribution to capitalism and freedom. They should start with a history of past collections and progress to the identification of new forms. When they arrive at the Republican tax cut, serious economists should reject any notion in the sales propaganda that the architects have succeeded in bringing manna from heaven.

In so far as the immediate beneficiaries of the cuts increase their claim on resources, they generate forces (both public and private) which restrain competing demand. A rise in market interest rates could be part of the process. Inflation tax collections are another part. And some equity owners might contain their enthusiasm by realizing that hikes in the effective rates of dividend and capital gains taxes could lie ahead even without a Democrat sweep election. Viewed over many years, the tax on business income would shift accordingly from upstream (where corporation tax collection occurs) to downstream. That is hardly a radical lightening of burden.

In general the inflation tax which derives from money printing is a levy on holders of money (and bonds) which restrains their demand for goods and services (making more resource space available for government commandeering or alternatives). This levy should be distinguished from the inflation revenue flowing to government. This corresponds to the creation of extra scope for government to acquire goods and services, essentially through issuance of banknotes and other forms of monetary base or through an increase in the possible issuance of government debt without exceeding credit limits. This scope arises as holders of money (and bonds) who have suffered erosion by inflation try to make good their holdings (though perhaps to a lower level than was usual in the past given now present inflation fears).

Where there is unanticipated inflation not recognized by all at the same time, the levy is dissipated and does not just flow to government but to other individuals who are better positioned. Where the inflation tax derives from interest rate manipulation, then the government obtains a direct take from a suppression of its interest rate bill. The inflation tax in both forms does not come mechanically under the 2% inflation regime from the expansion of monetary base as in the earlier regimes described, given that this is no longer a highly distinct asset for which there is a broad demand itself tightly related to income and wealth.

Another form of levy under the 2% inflation regime comes from "bracket creep". Modern tax regimes often include fixed nominal bands above which higher rates of tax kick in; and similarly, there are nominal ceilings to the amount of deductions possible against tax. No indexation of these means an effective rise of real tax rates without any new legislation. Capital gains tax is levied generally on nominal gains. Inflation means a given tax rate on nominal gains corresponds to a higher rate on the real gain adjusted for inflation; and this surcharge increases with the rate of inflation. Depreciation allowances on business capital are determined on the basis of historic cost. If replacement cost is rising far above historic cost, then the effective rate of tax on corporate profits can rise sharply if indeed the business has to sustain its capital stock in real terms.

The potential for a big leap in inflation tax (and revenues) comes from the eventual breaking of inertia under the 2% inflation standard and the outbreak of much higher inflation. That sudden break-out is the strongest potential force—both political and economic—which will galvanize the political system to confronting unsound money of which the global 2% inflation standard is the current manifestation.

BIBLIOGRAPHY

Bordo, M., & James, H. (2001, October). *Haberler Versus Nurkse: The Case for Floating Exchange Rates as an Alternative to Bretton Woods*. University of St. Gallen, Department of Economics Working Paper, 2001–8.

Brown, B. (2017). Goods Inflation, Asset Inflation, and the Greatest Peacetime Inflation in the US. *Atlantic Economic Journal, 45*(4), 429–442.

Fischer, S. (2017, May 5). *Monetary Rules*. Speech to Hoover Institution.

Mitchell, W. C. (2009). *A History of the Greenbacks*. Bel Air, California: Bibliolife.

Nurkse, R. (1944). *International Monetary Experience; Lessons of the Interwar Period*. Geneva: League of Nations.

Pringle, R. (2012). *The Money Trap*. Basingstoke, UK: Palgrave.

White, L. (2017, June 13). *Experts and the Gold Standard*. Alt-M: Ideas for an Alternative Monetary Future, Cato Institute.

Index

A
Abe, Shinzo, 96, 106–110, 197
Anti-gold myths, 212–213
Asian savings surplus narrative, 40, 50
Asset price deflation crisis, 8
Asset price inflation, 7, 12, 21–24, 29–44, 46, 48, 50, 51, 57, 59, 63, 65–67, 69, 76, 78–80, 82, 84, 86–88, 90, 91, 98, 99, 101–103, 111–114, 122, 125, 131, 133, 141, 143–146, 155, 166, 171, 173, 175, 179, 180, 182, 186–194, 197–200, 202–204, 208, 210, 221, 224
  definition of, 28–29
Audit the Fed, 65–68

B
Bad bets, 80–86, 203
  income famine investors, speculative narratives, 80
Bernanke, Ben, 5, 6, 17, 19–20, 44–49, 62–67, 70, 105, 106, 109, 111–113, 153, 170, 209

Big Tech
  in present asset price inflation, 8, 79
  promoted by asset inflation, 23
  in war on cash, 85, 160, 162
Boom-type asset inflation, 35, 36, 38, 39, 43, 171
  characteristics, 32–34
Bretton Woods system
  end of, 3
  its brief effective life, 4, 171, 208
Buffett, Warren, 203–205
  diagnosis of asset inflation,
  lessons for, 204
Bundesbank, 13, 44, 98, 117–120, 123, 124, 126–129, 154, 197
  its failure to halt Europe's journey to 2 per cent inflation standard, 121–122
Bunning, Senator, 63
  opposition to Ben Bernanke, 62, 63
Bush, George W., 17, 19, 63, 64, 100, 209

C

Camouflaged inflation, 37, 69, 86–90, 96, 98–100, 194, 197, 201, 223
   the role of digitalization and technological change, in 1920s boom, 170

Carry trades
   credit, 33, 36, 41, 42, 103, 167, 198, 200
   currency, 33, 39, 41, 103, 141
   liquidity, 33, 34, 39, 197, 198
   term, 33

Cash hoarding, 149, 156
   problem for negative interest rates, 156–158

Coalition for sound money, 68–72

Congress (US)
   its acquiescence in 2 per cent inflation standard, 56–57
   price and/or inflation targets, 16, 17, 59, 62, 65

Contemporary arguments against 2% inflation standard, 23–24

Crash of 1929
   causes, 57
   a counterfactual history of, 181
   similarity with 2018, 172

D

Deflation, the fight against, 19, 101, 102, 165–167

Depression type asset inflations, 21, 29, 34–42, 44, 80, 171

Diagnosis of asset inflation
   ingredients of, 190–191
   as investment tool, 190–191
   from 2011/12, 203–205

Digitalization
   monetary inflationist, enabling of, 78–80
   its role in the great monetary inflation of 2011 onwards, 168

Draghi-Merkel pact, 126–128

Dual mandate, of Federal Reserve, 60, 64, 214

Dutch monetary inflation of 1630s
   East India Company shares, 28, 86
   real estate, 28
   tulip bulbs, 86

Dysfunctional long-term interest rate markets
   role in housing market asset inflation, 135

E

Emminger era, 118

Equity market analysis
   under asset inflation, 36, 178

Ersatz gold, 4, 6, 47, 54

European Central Bank (ECB)
   embraced 2 per cent inflation standard, 124–126
   German Chancellor and Bundesbank President, defy its 2 per cent inflation target, 120, 128, 129

European Monetary Union (EMU), 98, 103, 115–124, 127, 129, 130, 142, 155, 217
   founders and no sound money vision, 115–119

F

FAANGs (Facebook, Amazon, Apple, Netflix, and Google), 194–197, 200, 202
   the bubble in and asset inflation, 110

Facebook, 162, 195
   affected by monetary inflation, 79–84

INDEX   229

Federal Reserve Act, 55, 57, 60, 68
   revisions in the mid-1970s, 117
Feldstein, Martin, 88, 89
   technological change influences inflation, view of, 89
Fischer, Stanley, 5, 6, 14–17, 213–214
   discretionary policy-making, advocacy of, 15, 213–214
   a founder of the 2% standard, 14–17
FOMC meeting, July 1996, 5, 55, 57
Friedman, Milton, 6, 15, 28, 38, 45, 46, 78, 91, 99, 152, 153, 168, 173, 178–182, 209
   critique of Fed Policy (1928–1929), 180

G
German abdication of hard money power, 128
Global 2 per cent inflation standard
   euro-zone joins, 125, 154
   Japan joins, 20, 96, 107–108
   US journey to, 20
Globalization, 5–7, 21, 31, 35, 37, 43, 59, 69, 75, 77, 78, 86, 108, 122, 125, 126, 131–132, 134, 146, 166, 168, 170, 190, 192, 193, 220, 224
   role in camouflaging goods inflation, 190, 201
Gold exchange standard, 1, 3, 17, 57, 58, 169, 170, 207, 208, 213, 217
   end of, 208
Gold money, exist in private form, 219
Gold standard
   return to 21st century, 214–217
   small countries, lead the return, 218
Google, 80–83, 162, 195
Great Recession, US (1920–1921), 58

Greenspan, Alan, 5, 12, 17–21, 43, 44, 50, 56, 61–63, 65, 101, 129, 170, 178–182, 200, 209
   apologists for his monetary inflation, 173
   role in launching 2 per cent inflation standard, 209
   Strong put of 1927, 91

H
Hard money, 5, 69, 71, 97, 109, 115–130, 133, 141–143, 204
High house prices, a plague, 132–133
Housing market, 8, 136, 140
   asset inflation in, 134–135
Hunt for yield, 29, 34–37, 40, 47, 150, 198
   fuels speculative narratives, 29, 35

I
Income famine, 34, 35, 37, 39, 50, 111, 224
Inflation shock, 8–10, 104, 105, 144
   late 1980s, 11–13
Inflation tax
   negative rates a form of, 160–163
   no to, 221–226
Interest on reserves, 44, 47, 52, 105, 152
   inconsistence with sound money principle, 44
Investment spending, 51, 196
   weak under depression-type asset inflation, 40
Irrational behaviour
   in financial markets, 7, 30
   role of monetary conditions in causing, 92, 102, 203
Issing, Otmar, 117–119, 122, 123

J

Japan
  asset price inflation, end phase of, 111–114
  camouflaged inflation post-Plaza, 98–100
  depression and rapid recovery (1990–1997), 100
  economic miracle, 96–97
  journey to 2 per cent inflation, 96–97
  monetarist experiment, edge of, 97–98
  quantitative easing, first episode of (2000), 101
  radical monetary experimentation, carry trade (1998–2007), 101–103
  2 per cent inflation Megillah, 109–110

K

Kahneman, Daniel, 28, 34, 47
Keynes, Maynard, 2, 17, 157
  insolvency and irrationality, bad advice on, 203–205

L

Leverage, 29, 35–37, 70, 71, 76, 136, 137, 140, 151, 167, 196, 198, 199, 211, 224
  falling leverage ratios, illusion, 176
Long-term interest rate market, 3, 9, 19, 20, 30, 40, 49, 50, 55, 59–61, 105, 108, 132, 136, 153, 201, 212, 220
  dysfunction under 2 per cent regime, 41, 43, 107
Louvre Accord, 12, 129

M

Manipulation of interest rates, 23, 36, 43, 175, 224, 225
Merkel, Angela, 126, 127, 130
  Maastricht monetary constitution, a dead letter, 122–124
Monetarism, 4–6, 12, 45, 47, 52, 62, 117, 118, 128, 208, 209
  as practiced by Bundesbank, 13, 117, 118
Monetarist experiment
  end of, 5
  Germany, 4, 5
  Switzerland, 4
  in US, 4, 98
Monetary normalization, 30, 38, 41, 52, 99, 200
  radical experimentation under 2 per cent, 51, 52
Monetary policy anaesthesia, 52
Money supply targets, 4, 61, 98, 170
  abandoned by Greenspan, 61–64
Monopoly rents, 35, 81–83
  speculative narrative, post-2011 asset inflation (Big Tech), 81, 194

N

Natural rhythm of prices, 21, 22, 31, 32, 37, 52, 57, 59, 76, 78, 79, 86, 90, 102, 126, 166, 168, 170, 171
Negative interest rates
  advocates of ignore asset inflation, 16, 66, 155–156
  experience with in Europe and Japan, 48, 72, 92, 133, 142, 154–155, 178
  as source of damage to monetary system, 126, 150–152

Negative sum game, Big Tech
 adverts, 82
Neo Keynesians, role in 2% standard,
 67, 133, 209
Neutral rate of interest, 22, 32, 33,
 51, 64, 79, 91, 146, 157, 201,
 202, 209
 affected by digitalization revolution,
 86–90
New Zealand, launch of inflation
 targets, 13–14

P
Plaza Accord, 5, 12, 98–100, 129
Price-earning ratios, boom-type *vs.*
 depression type asset inflation, 37
Private equity boom, 76, 126
 promoted by monetary inflation, 102
Prospect theory, asset inflation, 34

Q
Quantitative easing (QE)
 an experiment without time limit,
 152–154
 Friedman thoughts, 152
 the hidden agenda, 126

R
Real estate taxation, 138–140
 concept of neutrality, 139
Re-entry problem, normal signalling,
 bond markets, 50–52
Republicans
 failed efforts at monetary reform, 65
 failed opposition to Bernanke
 and Obama Federal Reserve,
 64–65
Republican tax cut (2017), 109

S
Secular stagnation, 40, 48
Shiller, Robert, 28, 132
Shirakawa, Masaaki,
 100, 107
 resistance to US led monetary
 inflation (2008–2012),
 107–108
Small country currency dilemma,
 140–144
Sound money
 characteristics of, 31
 concept of, 14
 definition of, 21
Speculative narratives
 justify bad bets, 80–86
 role in asset inflation, 7, 35, 175,
 191–193, 196
Stages of asset price inflation,
 29–30
Stages of fiat money disorder
 fifth, 9–10
 first, 1–3
 fourth, 5–8
 second, 3–4
 third, 4–5
Strong, Benjamin, 2, 46, 57, 66,
 166–168, 172–175, 178
 Congressional pressure for a price
 rule, resistance to, 57
 fuel asset inflation, 59
Subsidy on leverage, housing market,
 136–137
Summary of, case against 2 per cent
 inflation, 20–23

T
Twins of asset inflation and
 goods inflation, 31–32,
 180, 191

U

US journey towards
the 2 per cent
standard, 20

V

Volcker, Paul (Fed),
4, 11, 12, 62, 68, 71,
98, 128, 129, 170,
189, 210
abandonment of monetarism, 5

W

War on cash, 85, 160–162
Weimar Republic, 119, 173, 174, 203
asset price under, 180

Y

Yellen, Janet, 5, 18–19, 41, 61, 63–65,
68–70, 88, 90, 91, 133, 142,
145, 166–168, 172, 174, 180,
182, 193, 196, 198, 200, 201,
210, 211

The manufacturer's authorised representative in the EU is Springer Nature Customer Service Centre GmbH, Europaplatz 3, 69115 Heidelberg, Germany. If you have any concerns regarding our products, please contact ProductSafety@springernature.com

Printed and bound by CPI Group (UK) Ltd, Croydon, CR0 4YY

23/03/2026

02076672-0005